Jas. Q. Moore

CHARLES H. SPURGEON, THE WORLD'S GREATEST DIVINE.
Taken when about 35 years of age.

LIFE

OF

CHARLES HADDON SPURGEON

THE WORLD'S GREAT PREACHER.

BY

RUSSELL H. CONWELL,

AUTHOR OF

⠄VES OF EX-PRESIDENT GARFIELD, HON. JAMES G. BLAINE, BAYARD
TAYLOR, ACRES OF DIAMONDS, ETC., ETC.

We love Christ better than sect and truth better than party."—Spurgeon.

ILLUSTRATED.

EDGEWOOD PUBLISHING COMPANY.

1892.

PUBLISHER'S PREFACE.

In publishing the life of the late CHARLES HADDON SPURGEON, the publishers feel a peculiar pleasure and believe themselves especially fortunate in having secured the Rev. Russell H. Conwell, the founder and pastor at The Temple, of Philadelphia, to prepare the work. There are many reasons why the popular preacher, who might justly be called the Spurgeon of America, should in this way pay a loving tribute to the memory of his great English ecclesiastical brother, and why such a book must have an absorbing interest for all readers. Foremost among these might be considered his personal acquaintance with the great divine of gigantic efforts and wonderful achievements, and the deep study he has ever given to his popular brother preacher's life and the measure of its successes.

As a fellow-preacher of the Gospel, he knew better than any layman how to interpret the hidden springs of success to count the cost of Herculean efforts made, and better understand the great man's life-work in all its thousands of minute details which he, as an intimate personal friend had the opportunity to observe.

Like Spurgeon, he has the power to earn and raise large sums of money, but he devotes every dollar beyond a reasonable living expense to the cause he has so much at heart. His remarkable line of work, also, in many ways corresponds with that of Spurgeon.

5091

The similarity in the work of the English Spurgeon and the American Conwell has often been commented upon by press and people. Spurgeon made, and Conwell is making, a complete sacrifice of talents, time and health to the one aim in life—the salvation of souls. Each commenced life a poor boy, and had an early life fraught with discouragements and temptations.

The author's grand work for the Grace Baptist Church of Philadelphia, has justly distinguished him as the greatest preacher of his denomination in this country. He was a student at Yale College, and graduated in the Law Department of Albany University and was admitted to the New York bar in 1865. His health not permitting the practice of law, he began as traveling correspondent of the *Boston Traveller* and the *New York Tribune*, during which time his constant companion and warmest friend was Bayard Taylor, with whom he traveled all over the world, and obtained distinction as a journalist.

In addition to the pastorate of a church which has one of the most remarkable houses of worship in the world, open every hour of every day and night in the year, and is never untenanted, Dr. Conwell is the head of Temple College, connected with the church fostered by him, which is for the free education of working-men and women in the classic collegiate branches, with fourteen professors, a preparatory department that sends pupils to Yale, Harvard and Amherst, and giving itself degrees equal to those of Princeton. He is the head of the Samaritan Hospital, also an outgrowth of his personal effort and example, which is doing incalculable good in Philadelphia.

In addition to his church work, Dr. Conwell lectures all over the United States, to large and delighted audiences.

He is also a prolific author. The most important of his works are a "Life of Garfield," which he wrote at the home of the martyred President, in Mentor; "Why and How the Chinese Immigrate," the material for which he gathered in the Chinese Empire; "Life of Hon. James G. Blaine," "Life of Bayard Taylor," and "Acres of Diamonds," each of which has been appreciatively read by thousands of readers in this and other countries.

Russell H. Conwell has what his associate pastor has been pleased to call "sanctified common-sense," coupled with an excellent education and training in writing for the people. He writes in an easy, flowing style. We think it will be readily recognized that with his exceptional abilities as an author, his wonderful popularity as a lecturer, and his great work as a minister of the Gospel, he is preeminently qualified to write the true romance of the life of CHARLES HADDON SPURGEON.

THE PUBLISHERS.

THE TEMPLE, BROAD AND BERKS STS., PHILADELPHIA.

The First Meeting-House and the Present Temple of the Grace Baptist Church, of Philadelphia.   Russell H. Conwell, Founder and Pastor.

RUS ELL H. CONWELL, D. D., L.L. D.,

Pastor Grace Baptist Church, Philadelphia.

TABLE OF CONTENTS.

TABLE OF CONTENTS.

LIST OF ILLUSTRATIONS.

Mrs. C. H. Spurgeon.

CHAPTER I.

CHILDHOOD'S HOME.

Spurgeon, speaking himself, of one of the romantic incidents in his remarkable life, said "to me it was a wonderful thing and I no more understood at that time how it came to pass, than I understand to-day, why the Lord should be so gracious to me."

The whole history of this remarkable man, through all the various scenes of his eventful experiences, certainly presents one of the most miraculous records to be found in modern or ancient times, and yet his manner has been so quiet and his mode of life so modest that many of our most intelligent readers are wholly unconscious of the fascinating character of his interesting story.

Many writers, whose wisdom in other respects seem to be unquestionable, declare that the day of miracles has passed ; but taking another view of the same thought, we can but come to the deliberate conclusion that the day of miracles is by no means passed, but that they are of daily occurrence and that they fail to make the startling impression they formerly did, because of their great frequency.

But the life of Spurgeon contains so much that is

strange, unusual, wonderful, and even truly miraculous, that it will require most careful statement and most conservative reasoning to convince the reader that the record is literally true.

To separate such a story from the superstitions which are naturally thrown about it by the ignorant, and from the criticisms which are thrown over it by the fastidious scholastics is a most difficult undertaking. It makes one tremble to look into the conflicting mass of material, with the purpose of arranging the events so as to make a continued and reasonable history.

His early life has not been written as a consecutive story, except in the most condensed form : and then many of those who have undertaken to set forth his history have omitted or glossed over the most startling things connected with his experiences.

To tell the truth fearlessly, to meet the criticisms of those who are ready to accuse the writer of superstition, and to make the world see that the most romantic things are in real life and that miracles are not confined to the days long since buried in tradition, requires some little hardihood and a Spurgeon's determination to "tell the truth and shame the devil."

Any life has in its very inception a miracle far beyond the scrutiny of the most microscopic philosophy and in its unaccountability baffles even the most searching imagination. A human life is in itself a divine miracle, filling the thoughtful student with awe, and compelling him to bow in reverence before that mysterious power which though inscrutable, must nevertheless be distinctly recognized.

Spurgeon's life is a continued series of remarkable events, even when considered in the most prosaic manner.

His parentage, his birthplace, his country, his relation to his time, his marvelous success under most adverse circumstances combine a variety of causes and consequences beyond the logical arrangement of the most analytical mind. Every life has its romance, every life its mysterious impulses, every life its strange events, every life its unaccountable results. But here is a life which is romantic beyond precedent in the walks of life where we find it. The greatest preacher of the world, made so by causes unusual and strange, is lifted to his lofty position by miraculous events for which there is no reasonable accounting in accordance with anything that is called the law of nature.

In any biography we need to take into account the effect of hereditary traits, of the moulding character of scenery, association, and climate; but these in the life of Spurgeon do not account for all the mysterious results which we find in the work of his life. There are strange turning points in his history, the causes of which are beyond our understanding, and which he himself often declared "real miracles beyond hope of explanation."

His life is a romance, which if, instead of being

real, was produced in a work of fiction, would be regarded as an altogether improbable story.

Mr. Spurgeon and his friends have always felt that it would be dangerous to attempt to assert the unexplainable side of his success or present it fully to the public, lest it should bring hindering detraction, criticism, and unbelief in connection with his great work of preaching the gospel. Yet in the old days such manifestations of the miraculous unknown were regarded as confirmations of the gospel, and paraded as the best evidence of the fact that the speaker was endowed by the unusual power of God. Why then should they not be presented now? For "God still moves in a mysterious way, His wonders to perform." Looking at his life from the point of view which we now occupy since his death, and looking back upon the crowded audiences, the masses of people in the public squares, the ragged throngs on the quays; upon the Orphanage, College, Hospitals, Schools, and Chapels, the world-wide benevolences, the missionary enterprises, the thousands of public and private ministrations, Mr. Spurgeon seems like a giant of intellect and superhuman in his industry.

But we will begin with his life at his humble home and trace it through the varying scenes where it was touched with the modifying circumstances of his surroundings, and thus be better able, step by step, to ascend to the position which he held when he died. No man can comprehend Spurgeon without

BIRTHPLACE OF C. H. SPURGEON.

taking that method in examining his life. It is a record which is as inspiring as it is wonderful, which is as lovely as it is marvelous. Not that we believe Mr. Spurgeon to be a saint, or an angel from heaven sent unto earth by a definite and special dispensation, for he had his human faults and committed his errors as other men have done. His mistakes and short-comings rather serve to make more prominent and distinct the remarkable achievements of his career. He seems more like one of the minor prophets,— human yet often inspired.

How it makes one ache to be able to present the story clearly, concisely, and yet comprehensively for the instruction of thousands who have heard of Mr. Spurgeon, but who know but little about the facts of his inner life. Could his story be told with the pen of a Macaulay, or with the talented friendship of a Boswell, it would necessarily take its place in the standard literature of the English-speaking people. But whether told with eloquent terms and vivid descriptions, or in rude and blundering phraseology, it certainly ought to be told, and the more often it is related and the greater the variety of ways in which it is presented the better for the generations that are to be.

Charles Haddon Spurgeon was born at Kelvedon, county of Essex, June 19th, 1834. His father at that time was engaged in business at Kelvedon, the pursuit of which does not seem to have been very lucrative. His parents were in humble circumstances, his mother during these years frequently in ill health. His father and his grandfather were both successful preachers of the Gospel, but both of them received an early education in practical business through the first part of their lives. His father did not enter the ministry until his life was nearly half finished. But his father was poor, and his grandfather had a comfortable living and sufficient property to keep him altogether above want.

And in the story of the life of Charles H. Spurgeon we need to understand quite fully the circumstances in connection with the history of his parents, their traits, customs, and home, that we may ascertain the influence these things had upon the young boy's nature. But it cannot truthfully be said that Charles came from a family of great men. For though his ancestry for several generations were known among their neighbors as pious persons of excellent character, yet they were never regarded by their contemporaries as possessing any remarkable genius or special claim for the niche in which the world places its great individuals. All the more the wonder is it that he should accomplish what he did accomplish and all the more prominent become the singular events which led to this remarkable promotion.

Charles was especially "his grandfather's boy." For, as early as he could recollect, he was sent from the home of his parents to that of his grandfather and grandmother, at Stambourne in Essex, near the borders of Suffolk, and there, through the most formative years of his childhood, was trained by these most excellent people. His grandfather was a most instructive preacher, who for fifty-four years occupied the same pastorate and lived in the same house.

What a misfortune it often is for a child to be trained by his grandparents! For some reason they are usually more indulgent, more lax in every kind of discipline, and see in their grandchild a prodigy when no one else dreams of such a thing. His grandparents were not an exception to this general rule, but he had a most excellent aunt, living also at his grandfather's house, named " Aunt Ann," to whose care he was largely committed, and who seems to have been a most talented woman, both in moral character and in the wisdom of her daily common sense.

His grandfather's house was considered a mansion for that day. It was very large and situated in most lovely natural surroundings. His grandfather was a staid, scholarly gentleman, rather quaint but scrupulously neat in his attire; courteous in his demeanor, kindly in all his intercourse with his equals or inferiors; a noble specimen of the old English country gentleman. It is said that he wore the old-fashioned breeches, buckled shoes, and silk stockings; adhering with rigid formality to the attire of the generation before him. He was born at Halstead in Essex, September 29th, 1776. He followed business occupations until he was twenty-six years of age, when he determined to enter the ministry. Taking then two years of study at an Academy, he entered upon the work of preaching to a very weak, poor, and small congregation, at Clare in Suffolk. That church grew to be a healthy, spreading, and prosperous pastorate in the four years he remained there. He belonged to the Independent or Congregational Church connection, and is said to have never preached in any places outside of Clare and Stambourne; yet he was widely known as a genuine Christian and a faithful friend, and the sight of his frilled shirt, long vest, and dress cravat always brought caps from the heads of the reverent rustics. He loved children and delighted in the company of young people, having his pockets filled with confections for the one and his mouth filled with words of cheer for the other.

Mrs. Spurgeon, the grandfather's helpmeet, was a fine, industrious woman, who made it her conscientious duty to be a sincere and persevering helpmeet to her husband. She was quiet in her manners and retiring in her disposition, yet found her way into the most useful works of charity, and often occupied positions of honor on the boards and committees of benevolent enterprises. She was one of those lovely old ladies who win the affection of every one, who seem to be able to go through this world accomplishing a great deal in silence and without friction.

She and her daughter "Aunt Ann" cared for the

PLAYING AT THE FIRESIDE.

great house, with its large hallway, its cozy bed-rooms, its long sitting-room, library and dairy and enormous dark closets, with a neatness that was surprising and with a regularity that was like clock work.

It was in this old manse, standing adjacent to the one-story meeting-house, that Charles spent the early and most important years of his boyhood.

Although its external appearance is somewhat imposing and was evidently a well-lighted and com-fortable home when it was constructed; many portions of it, at the time Charles went there to live, were like a prison, owing to the fact that the windows had been walled up to avoid the taxes which the govern-ment placed upon windows. Mr. Spurgeon has often during his life referred to the absurd custom which they had in his boyhood days of taxing the sunlight and assessing an individual in proportion to the number of windows which he enjoyed in his home. So this old house had a great many rooms in it which were perpetually dark, into which the boy only peered with fright, and which to his boyhood's imagination were probably peopled with hobgoblins, ghosts, spirits, and an occasional fairy. In the hall of the house, which seems to have led from the wide front doors all the way through to the back yard, there was a large fireplace, about which Charles often played through his years of childhood. Over the fireplace in the wide hallway there was a large, old-fashioned painting of David contending with Goliath which was far more indelibly painted upon the mind of the boy than it was upon the fading canvas.

It was at this fireplace that he sat many a night poring over some simple story written in the dullest manner, trusting to the flickering light from the hearth rather than to the tallow candle and its accompanying labor with the snuffers.

Dear old fireplace! Who that hath enjoyed the luxury of lying flat upon the floor and gazing into its brilliant embers can cease to call down blessings on its sweet associations. Inspiring old hearth! Around which the faces of loved ones gathered in youth, and about which they never will cease to gather while memory retains its control. Lovely hearth of an affectionate household! What paintings artists have seen in its rising flames, what armies young conquerors have seen in conflict in the battle of its crackling fagots, what sweet and inexpressible lines of pathos the poets have seen written in the coals or heard sung in the hum of its rising gases. Dear, old-fashioned fireplace! Who was the vandal that banished such a boon, such a scene of comfort, such a source of inspiration from the civilized world?

Charles never forgot the lessons inculcated by that inspired teacher, the brilliant fireplace. Again and again in his speeches, addresses, sermons, and editorials, sparks from that old fireplace appear with vivid distinctness and reveal, unconsciously to the writer, the source of his beautiful thoughts.

It was on that hearth-stone that he made the little sleighs, struggled with toy wagons, rude and rough and uncouth and laughable ; but which, to his childish mind, were marvels of mechanical achievement. It was there that he cut patterns in that rough brown paper which was preserved for that purpose by his economical grandmother from the wrappings brought from the store. It was there that he drew with charcoal strange caricatures of the individuals he had met. It was there that he listened to the folk lore of the neighborhood, from which was always carefully and conscientiously culled anything which was injurious in its influence upon a childish mind. There he saw his grandfather and grandmother night after night through the rolling years, sitting with the great Bible opened on their laps and poring over its pages with a fascination never found in any other volume. It was there that he learned to revere the taste and affectionate kindness of his dear "Aunt Ann," who was continually approaching the hearth to brush up the ashes or arrange the fire.

Then there was the large sitting-room, into which guests were ushered on state occasions. The magnificent apartment, to his youthful eyes, where persons were greeted with such forms as to make him feel in the presence of the Queen.

There also was the dining-room, with its old, well-worn table, its chairs which had come down through more than one generation, the little cupboard in which was so neatly sorted all those wonderful treasures of tarts and cakes and sweet-meats so enticing to the taste of every boy. Doughnuts and cakes made specially for him by the dear old grandmother and often moulded into rough images of hares or elephants. How often he clambered upon the chair and sometimes upon books placed in the chair, that he might be able to gaze in upon those stately dishes which were only brought forth on occasions of unusual festivity. Next to the upper shelf were kept the bright snuffers, and how proudly he set down that day in the red-letter calendar of his life, when he was able, for the first time, to reach to that shelf and take down the snuffers.

Then there was the bed-chamber with its high-posted bed for the elder people and its low, square trundle bed for the boy.

There in the upper story of the old manse was that dark room into which once the brilliant light of day was allowed to come, but upon which the horrid tax-master had drawn his permanent curtain. In it were deposited a large number of old theological musty volumes never of interest to any save to those who wrote them. Yet among this rubbish of useless, dusty books the boy did find, so early that he could not remember when, the *Pilgrim's Progress*, with its grotesque illustrations of Pilgrim's journey on his way to heaven. There also he found a story of the martyrs and especially the history of Bishop Bonner, whose cruelty sent so many to the stake, and whose own end gave the childish reader great satisfaction because of its poetic justice. It was only on an exceedingly bright day, when the inner door allowed some reflected light to enter from another room, that the boy would venture into its dusty precincts.

But no closet, no dark room, no apartment whatever of the great homestead was intentionally shut out from the investigation of the boy by his indulgent grandparents. Nothing was too good for him. No house too large. No closet too secret, to be closed from his prying mind.

What an influence this dear old home, with its quaint, queer associations had upon the character or disposition of the boy, of course no philosopher can say. It is easy to surmisingly attribute a flash of genius to some particular circumstance, event, or scene in the history of a great man, but it is utterly impossible to connect with certainty the cause and effect in such relations.

Charles' own mother attributed to the associations exterior to the old manse more credit for the moulding influences which affected his early years than she did to anything within, except the teaching and kindness of the grandparents and aunt. But all of these associations must have been parts of the mental and moral discipline which Providence used to make the man.

Stambourne was not a village, but a mere collection in more or less close proximity of little farms, and indulged only in a blacksmith shop and a small store in a dwelling-house, for its professional and business life. The roads crossed near the old meeting-house, and the yards of the dwellings were inclosed with hedges, and often sweetly shaded with ancient limes and strangely-trimmed yews.

The school-house where Charles began to receive his education is said to have been a part of a dwelling-house, held in a room with a rickety floor, having one window sadly out of plumb, where the plaster was falling from the walls, and where the rain seems to have come in during unusual thunder-storms.

In none of these early years in school or at home did he exhibit those precocious qualities which are often erroneously attributed to the opening years of great men. Some writers have claimed that Charles showed those startling evidences of genius in the first years of his school life. But one of the teachers has left upon record the statement, shown in her reports, that he was rather dull, slow but persistent, doing thoroughly whatever he had in hand.

He was a very awkward boy, short, thick, with a very heavy head of hair, eyes not especially brilliant, nose short, and mouth large. No one esteemed him to be a handsome child, and it is said that both in form and feature he greatly changed during the days of his boyhood.

His school study was characterized by nothing of especial interest to others, except the fact that he showed an unusual inclination to make close and comprehensive inquiries concerning any subject presented, either in books or in conversational discussion.

He always desired to know " the why and the where-fore," and not being especially brilliant, it was some-times quite difficult to make him comprehend the length and breadth of the answer for which his questions called. But he was a good-natured, kind-hearted, open-handed boy, always willing to divide with his schoolmates any sweets with which he had been favored, ever alert to assist any school-boy who was behind in his lessons, seeking eagerly to run upon errands for the teacher, and, withal, remarkably truthful.

The statement which some seemingly cautious biographers have made concerning his unusual pre-cociousness in childhood appear to have been founded upon his after life or upon local tradi-tions. It seems to be very clear, however, that in truth he gave no special promise in his early school-days of the greatness which afterward crowned his life.

Stambourne is situated at the very headwaters of the Colne River, and the spring which furnishes the source of that river is situated not far from the old parsonage where Charles spent his youthful days. As a boy he often waded in the brook, which played such fantastic tricks about his feet, and laughingly chattered to the mosses, ferns, and evergreens which laced the banks. There he eagerly sought the shin-ing pebbles, which his imagination often magnified into diamonds and inestimable gems, or watched along its banks for the lizard and dwarf-fish for which he had a strong passion. That brook and two others which united with it a short distance below the manse, were to him an inspiration lasting to the very latest day of his life. There were books in these running brooks which he alone could read. There were voices in these falling waters which he alone could understand. There was a benign influence in their shadows which prophesied to him the future. There was a refreshing in their coolness which was peculiarly gratifying to a child of his imaginative temperament. He loved the sparkling waters. Again and again has he used them as illustrative of gospel truth, and the glittering brooks of Stambourne rippled, sang, and flashed through much that he said, and through vastly more that he thought. The far-spreading trees which bowed over the banks, with benedictions of holy peace, the weeds, and brush, and undergrowth, with the rocks and stones on which he often stood, all these, glorified by sacred memory, were inseparably connected with the living waters of the river of Life. They seemed to lose none of their charms for him through the varied experience of a working life.

That his mother was right in attributing so much to the influence of the rural scenery surrounding Charles' young days is apparent to the student of his writings as well as to his personal friends, because of the unmistakable suggestions of waving fields of grain, of fruit-laden arbors, of blooming trellises, of outstretching trees, of hills and dales, of pastures, of verdantly arched highways, of mist-covered meadows, of clear sunshine, of simple, homely talk, of frank, pleasant manners, of hardy toil, of broad common sense, which continually shone forth in his conversation and in his public addresses.

The country boy is the favored boy. Alas, for the child of the city. Alas, for him whose early years are spent in the city's prison of brick and mortar, stone sidewalks, harsh pavements, smoky skies, ceaseless din, unnatural cries, tainted atmosphere, and heated rooms. If the early associations of childhood do make or unmake genius, then it is interesting to note that the majority of the great men and women of all the civilized ages have passed the early years in rural surroundings, in country homes, or amid scenes like that of the " *Cotter's Saturday Night.*" Whatever else may be attributed to the influence of natural scenery and rural life, it may be safely assumed that the strong physique which carried Spurgeon through so many years of the most arduous labor, was due, at least in part, to the fresh air, and out-door exercises, simple garb, and rustic manners of that farming hamlet of Stambourne, in Essex.

His childhood does not show any peculiar traits in connection with his boyish sports. Like any other boy he greatly enjoyed his rocking-horse, which stood in the hall in the old parsonage, and to which he often referred in after years when speaking to children. Like every other English boy he was

greatly excited by all out-door sports, and was wonderfully fascinated with the fox chase. Once a year
he was permitted to stand by the roadside and see
the fox-hunters pass. That was a day long to be
remembered, and was of greater interest to him
then than some of those transactions were to him
afterward, which shook the foundations of the
nations. He was a homely, natural boy.

His grandfather seems to have had the same difficulty in keeping the boy quiet at seasons of devotion which other grandfathers have had with other
boys, and especially arduous the task on those Puri-
tanical Sabbath days when it seemed to be so sacrilegious for a child to indulge in any worldly
amusement. It appears that Charles was often
placed in the room with his grandfather, while the
women of the household were absent or were engaged in some special labor, in order that he might
be kept from mischief. Those were hours of hard-
ship fully as painful to him as they have been to
many other boys.

In after years he often facetiously referred to the
Evangelical Magazine, which was always put into
his hands by his grandfather, with the hope that the
two pictures, one of the celebrated minister and one
of some mission station, might serve to keep him in
peaceful meditation. His grandmother or his aunt
very frequently informed him with great solemnity
that if at such times he did not keep very quiet, he
might so disturb his grandfather that the old gentle-

man would be unable to preach, and consequently famishing souls would die for the need of gospel food. Those were solemn hours in the history of the child, when sitting there with his grandfather in the shadowy room in silence so chillingly wierd, and fearing to speak or move his little foot lest his grandfather and God should see him and be displeased. Yet about this feeling there seems to be no singular feature such as would in any way account for the after extraordinary results of his religious life.

Some of the social events, however, connected with his home at Stambourne must have made a very deep impression upon his thoughts and consequently upon his character. His dear old grandmother one Sabbath morning remarked to her husband that she did not feel able to attend services, and so would remain at home and read her Bible there, while he was preaching the gospel in the Chapel. She seated herself in that old arm-chair not far from that dear old fireplace and spreading the Bible out upon her lap, adjusted her spectacles and began its devoted perusal. They left her sitting there and went across the yard into the old church. But when they returned after the service, walking into the house without premonition of harm, they found the sweet old Christian woman with her head bowed upon her breast, her spectacles lying across the Bible and her finger pointing to the words " the hand of God hath touched me." She was dead! Her spirit had ascended to her long-expected home.

Mr. Spurgeon has frequently, too, referred to his boyish experiences in three places which were ever especially dear to his memory. One being the Sunday-school room, in which he says "his Sabbath-school companions frequently kicked up the dust and sometimes kicked the teachers." It was there that he learned Watt's Catechism, and heard the homely stories related as illustrations of Bible truth in a manner peculiar to the humble people of that day, but wonderfully expressive and correct in their exegesis.

Another place was the old tombstone in the churchyard near his home, which was placed over the grave like a reversed box, bottom upward. It was made of marble and one side was loose, so that he could easily remove it and, crawling into the box over the grave, replace the slab at the side, thus hiding himself securely beyond discovery. Often he lay there in hiding and thought on many childish air castles; and sometimes remained there past his dinner hour, even when he had distinctly heard the call. He says that he often lay there facetiously holding his breath while the household searched the churchyard, and while some of them, frequently standing directly above his head, searched vainly for the truant. Another place dear to his child-ish heart was the horsing-block, which also was constructed in the form of a box, although made of wood, and much larger than the tombstone. One side of this horsing-block, used also as a hitching-post, was partially open, and into it the farmers pressed the falling leaves which were swept up from the neatly-kept highway. Those lime-tree leaves were crisp, dry, and warm, and made a most comfortable nest into which the boy crawled clandestinely.

There, secure from observation, warmly ensconced in a luxurious bed, richer to the boy than the couches of palaces are to the man, he would lie and repeat his lessons, which Mrs. Burleigh, the day-school teacher, had assigned him, or sang over and over a verse of Scripture which he was expected to repeat at the next Sunday's prayers.

But he was like a wild bird in that retreat, and on the approach of any footstep, became quickly silent, and even became an unwilling or willing listener to neighborhood gossip, carried on by persons seated on the horsing-block, or leaning against it, while they stopped for conversation.

CHAPTER II.

EARLY EDUCATION.

The study of any successful man's biography, whatever his profession, business or trade, is helpful to every other man in any other station. For the same great causes which carry a man to success in one part of our civilization are necessary to the accomplishment of great purposes in any other position. The fact that Mr. Spurgeon was a preacher, need not make his life any less useful in the most practical sense, to the farmer, the mechanic, the merchant or the lawyer. There is, however, one discouraging feature in using the life of Mr. Spurgeon for the purposes of imitation, in the fact to which reference has already been made, viz.: that some of the events which led to his promotion are beyond explanation, and remain in the realm of the miraculous. No study nor reasoning, no contemplation of facts seems to clear up the wonderful mystery.

Let us nevertheless devote a short time to the study of the natural causes and influences which may not be considered mysterious and which will be very helpful to every reader who desires to make the most possible of his life,

42

Many of the most trustworthy biographers ascribe a large share of all human success to the influence of early education ; others make equally prominent the inheritance of hereditary traits carrying with them the force of genius.

Some writers upon Mr. Spurgeon's career, like that most excellent Christian, Rev. James J. Ellis, ascribed much to his family and ancestry. This is quite natural to an Englishman, trained under a hereditary monarchy.

The evangelist George C. Needham and also Mr. Stevenson, Mr. Spurgeon's most excellent biographers, lay considerable stress upon his inherited mental characteristics. But to an American, taught by American literature and with a life-long association with a leveling democracy, these kindly efforts to give great credit to the long line of good men which preceded him appear to be rather strange and often quite absurd. Some men are born great, but families are not. To be a great man's son gives no patent on human greatness. More often we find that the great man was the son of a poor man, and often a descendent of the igno-rant or of the very commonplace. Families like the Peels in England and the Adams of America are exceedingly rare, and as a usual thing there is no hope of genius nor is great intellectual force expected in the second generation of any great man.

It is said that Mr. Spurgeon's ancestors were among the religious reformers of Holland, who

under the fearful scourge of the Duke of Alva,
suffered such privation as to induce them to fly from
their native land and find domicile in England. That
they were good men and noble Christians among
those who thus left their native land in the time of
its trial there is no question, and no one can doubt
but that the ancestors of Mr. Spurgeon are all they
are represented to be, and specially noteworthy is
the fact that two hundred and more years ago they
were imprisoned for daring to worship God according to the dictates of their own conscience. But no
one seems to claim for them any special genius, and
in fact had they possessed it, or the marvelous acute-
ness which is sometimes hinted at, the forefathers
would have remained in Holland and fought out the
battle of Christian freedom there.

They were evidently plain people of the peasent
classes who saw no opportunity of being useful to
their native country and consequently acted wisely
when they sought a new home in a free land. Certainly the Spurgeon families of Essex and Sussex
which in these after days have been locally very influential and especially noble in their Christian
character, have not taken great interest in the history
of their ancestors, and appear to know but little concerning their achievments.

Through the three or four generations with whom
the reading public is now somewhat familiar, the
Spurgeon families have been characterized for their
plain common sense, sturdy industry, and stubborn

JAMES SPURGEON.

adherance to certain Christian doctrines, and to have led a quiet, homely life.

Neither his grandfather James Spurgeon at Stambourne, nor his father John Spurgeon of Colchester and London, were ever especially distinguished for their educational attainments. They were scholars of the old Congregational school, who read carefully a few standard books, who thought deeply, but whose reading was not extensive.

While it is true that almost any man with the most ordinary powers may be able to preach a classical sermon and adorn it with quotations from Cicero, Demosthenes, Augustine, and Luther, and while it is also true that it requires both genius and most extensive learning to speak simply and clearly in plain English, yet his father and his grandfather exhibited those qualities as a result of a peculiar inherited character, rather than that of extensive education. They were not copyists. They were distinguished for their odd originality. They were often humorous and witty, presenting truth occasionally in a grotesque dress which could never be forgotten, and which more often accomplished the ends for which they spoke than the most polished essay could have done.

There are blunders which are victories, and there are truly great orators whose language is ungramatical and unrhetorical.

The Spurgeon family has remained quite closely identified with the country villages in which its earliest English ancestry took up its abode. They have not been a migratory people, have sought no ambitious station, but have been specially remarkable for clean Christianity, and the English disposition to be solid, earnest, and Godly. Yet in this they are not to be distinguished above a thousand other families like them who have resided and still reside in the country towns of dear old England.

It seems therefore quite unreasonable to say that the attainments and victories of Charles were due to any unusual prominence in the life or nature of his family inheritance. He illustrates the great lesson which England is now speedily learning, that statesmanship or piety are not to be sought especially in descent, but rather in the individuals whom Providence raises up for the furtherence of its great designs. Mr. Spurgeon himself has said: "The boast of pedigree is common but silly." Families as families, have no right to the landed domain, to palaces, to the castles, to the offices, or to the throne.

These positions must soon be filled only by persons of especial fitness and unusual mental activity, who depend for their influence not upon their descent, but upon their personal ability.

Of course none but an extreme hobbyist could leave out of account, the force of ancestral examples, such as were presented in the life of grandfather James Spurgeon. And specially influential upon his disposition must have been the influence of Charles' grandmother, his Aunt Ann, and of his own sweet spirited Christian mother.

His father is said to have remarked, that as the parent of seventeen children, "I have frequently worn a shabby coat when I might have possessed a good one, had I cared less for my children's education." But the touching sacrifices made by his father seemed to have been excelled by the self-abnegation and devotion of his noble mother.

Mrs. Jackson, a sister of Charles, wrote of their father eight years before he died, saying : "in previous biographies very little is recorded of this venerable man of God, who has now attained the ripe age of four-score years. He has always been an embodiment of homeliness, and from the earliest recollections of his children, he imparted a charm to the home life of his family. His sons and daughters were never so happy as when he gathered them around him for recreation, instruction, and devotion. They hailed his return from business and from religious services with delight, for they knew he would not fail to delight them by relating in his own captivating manner the incidents which had come under his observation during the day. Thus 'pleasant evenings' were wisely provided at home, and the temptations which characterize and endanger 'modern society' were avoided. Those early days of happy family life are remembered with devout gratitude."

But a well-known incident related by Charles' father, opens a window into the domestic inner life of

4

the family, through which we catch glimpses of a region presided over by one of God's most saintly characters. In conversation with Dr. Ford, con erning the domestic life of Charles' early years, John Spurgeon said: "I had been from home a good deal, trying to build up weak congregations, and felt that I was neglecting the religious training of my own children while I toiled for the good of others. I returned home with these feelings. I opened the door, and was surprised to find none of the children about the hall. Going quietly up the stairs, I heard my wife's voice. She was engaged in prayer with the children. I heard her pray for them, one by one, by name. She came to Charles and specially prayed for him, for he was of a high spirit and daring temper.. I listened until she had ended her prayer, and I felt and said, 'Lord, I will go on with Thy work; the children will be cared for.'"

But reserving for the next chapter observations connected with Charles' early moral and religious education, let us examine somewhat closely the methods by which he obtained such wide, and varied, and useful information. It has often been said that Spurgeon never had a college educaiton. While that is technically true, it is far from true in reality. He had a college education. Yea, he had a university education. He was one of the learned men most prominent in these closing years of the nineteenth century. But the fact that a person in Spurgeon's circumstances could secure such extensive information and obtain that neccessary discipline of mind to compete with the rushing forces of civilization in this age of the world, without actually attending the college or the university is a very important fact. It is not unreasonable to infer that he would have failed as a great preacher and organizer, if he had taken a course in the college or university.

The stubborn fact that he did reach the highest possible position in his profession, without a college training, must be squarely met by all advocates of modern systems of public instruction. It makes clear to the student that our methods of instruction and our systems of school discipline are at least, not a necessity for the attainment of the highest education.

Something is rotten in the states of Denmark, England, and the United States, when it is possible for boys and girls without money, without fame, without special hereditary influence, to reach the noblest positions in the world's activities, without the aid of the great endowed, institutions which receive such continued encomiums. That schools and colleges, universities and scientific institutions are of great value goes without the saying. But that they might be of much more value than they are is also certain. For they should combine if possible in their course of instruction the same influences and discipline which comes to a poor boy working his own way upward through thousands of difficulties and under the most discouraging circumstances.

Lincoln would not have been the saviour of his nation and Spurgeon would not have been the Elijah of his age had they received the usual college education. Such a course would have changed the circumstances and put them in an entirely different relation to the events which moulded them into the characters the world so much needed.

Here, then, is the fact. It is a stubborn thing. It demands the very careful and persistent attention of our great educators. While a college diploma ought to be always a badge of greatness, and ever accompany the history of the most effective intellects, yet it is a startling fact that for some reason it is not practically the certain badge of honor which it should be.

Why should Charles' own younger brother, James, with his more extended opportunities and his especially thorough college training hold so humble a place in the world's estimation, while Charles, securing his education by entirely different methods, is a household word to the farthest reach of the civilized world? The question does arise whether it would not have been far better for even James, if he had entered at once on his life work when he was sixteen years of age and trusted to different methods for the helpful instruction he would need in his profession. We cannot answer this, but we say that the consideration of a life like that of Charles H. Spurgeon will some day revolutionize all our methods of instruction and make them far less weirdly theo-

retrical. It will bring us all down to matters more practical, more in accordance with common sense and with our daily common needs. Be it known now that a poor boy even in aristocratic England may secure a college education without attending Cambridge or Oxford. An untitled rustic may acquire all that discipline of mind and stability of character which the best institutions of the world can give, and secure them even amid the homeliest surroundings or in the most distant country village.

Charles H. Spurgeon's figure will ever stand in the minds of tens of thousands of young men in rustic life, combined with a most eloquent gesture, pointing forward to the highest positions in the world, and speaking with distinct tone, saying," there is hope for the humblest man," Nothing the college gives is impossible to the industrious, to the honest, although he may have no opportunity to sit under the training of gifted minds in the halls of the distinguished centres of learning. His name will ever be the sign of hope and an encouraging inspiration showing the way to magnificent possibilities from the humblest home in the most sparsely settled rural districts.

Universities are not to be despised, but on the contrary to be faithfully encouraged. But, thank God! Charles H. Spurgeon did not go to college. The world needed one such an example to break the crust of a depressing school artistocracy.

His mental training, of course, began at his grandfather's house in Stambourne and we are told that his letters were taught him by his Aunt Ann. She loved to relate in after years many little anecdotes illustrative of his " great mind " as a boy. But an examination of them does not show any special precociousness. They are like all those incidents which are so carefully preserved by mothers, grand-mothers, and indulgent aunts about their first-born son, first grandson, or favorite nephew.

His grandfather also occasionally assisted in teaching him to read. But the impress of his grandfather's noble character seems to have been the most important branch of his early learning.

> " Example draws where precept fails,
> And sometimes are more read than tales."

Mr. Spurgeon wrote that " Example is the school of mankind, and many will learn at no other. Examples preach to the eye and leave a deeper impress than counsel addressed to the ear. Children like pictures better than letter press, so do men prefer example to precept."

And when speaking directly of his grandfather's influential example he also said:

" When a little child, I lived some years in my grand-father's house. In his garden there was a fine old hedge of yew of considerable length, which was clipped and trimmed till it made quite a wall of verdure. Behind it was a wide grass walk which looked out upon the fields, and afforded a quiet out-

look. The grass was kept mown, so as to make
pleasant walking. Here ever since the old puritanic
chapel was built, godly divines had walked, and
prayed and meditated. My grandfather was wont
to use it as his study. Up and down he would walk
when preparing his sermons, and always on Sabbath
days, when it was fair, he had half an hour there
before preaching. To me it seemed a perfect paradise, and being forbidden to stay there when
grandfather was meditating, I viewed it with no
small degree of awe. I love to think of the green
and quiet walk at this moment, and could wish for
just such a study. But I was once shocked, and
even horrified, by hearing a farming man remark
concerning this sanctum sanctorum, ' It 'ud grow
a many 'taturs if it wor ploughed up.' What cared
he for holy memories ? What were meditation and
contemplation to him ? Is it not the chief end of
man to grow potatoes, and to eat them ? Such on
a larger scale would be an unconverted man's estimate of joys so elevated and refined as those of
heaven, could he by any possibility be permitted to
gaze upon them."

To the day-school, taught by Mrs. Burleigh, at
Stambourne, reference has already been made. It
appears that he learned so little, or was altogether
so inattentive or mischievous that the school never
made any very deep impression upon his memory.
It is clear that at that early day in his history, before
he was eight years old, he was not to be specially

distinguished from many other boys living in his social position and circumstances. But in his grandfather's family he necessarily saw more of books than other boys in the neighborhood would see, and heard a great deal more of literary matters and intellectual discussion than would fall to the lot of a farmer's son. He learned slowly but remembered long. A lesson once thoroughly comprehended was indelible.

He left his grandfather's manse and returned to his father's house at Colchester, where his father kept a shop, when he was seven or eight years of age, and there found an opportunity for excellent school training. But in that school there were some scholars who excelled him, and it is said that he himself did not consider it any special disgrace to be at the foot of the class, provided that it brought him in the winter season nearer the stove.

But the clearness with which these events at that time in his life impressed themselves upon his memory is wonderfully shown in the account which in later years he gave of a little incident while at school. In his "John Ploughman's Talks" he assailed debt with peculiar bitterness, and said:

"When I was a very small boy, in pinafores, and went to a woman's school, it so happened that I wanted a stick of slate pencil, and had no money to buy it with. I was afraid of being scolded for losing my pencils so often, for I was a real careless little fellow, and so did not dare to ask at home; what

then was John to do? There was a little shop in
the place, where nuts, and tops, and cakes, and balls
were sold, by old Mrs. Dearson, and sometimes I had
seen boys and girls get trusted by the old lady. I
argued with myself that Christmas was coming, and
that somebody or other would be sure to give me a
penny then, and perhaps even a whole silver sixpence. I would therefore go into debt for a stick of
slate pencil, and be sure to pay for it at Christmas.
I did not feel easy about it, but still I screwed my
courage up and went into the shop. One farthing
was the amount, and as I had never owed anything
before, and my credit was good, the pencil was
handed over by the kind dame, and *I was in debt.*
It did not please me much, and I felt as if I had
done wrong, but I little knew how soon I should
smart for it. How my father came to hear of this
little piece of business, I never knew, but some little
bird or other whistled it to him, and he was very soon
down upon me in right earnest. God bless him for
it; he was a sensible man, and none of your chil-
dren-spoilers; he did not intend to bring up his
children to speculate and play at what big rogues
call financiering, and therefore he knocked my getting
into debt into the head at once, and no mistake. He
gave me a very powerful lecture upon getting into
debt, and how like it was to stealing, and upon the
way in which people were ruined by it; and how a
boy who would owe a farthing, might one day owe
a hundred pounds, and get into prison, and bring

his family to disgrace. It was a lecture indeed; I think I can hear it now, and can feel my ears tingling at the recollection of it. Then I was marched off to the shop like a deserter marched into barrack, crying bitterly all down the street, and feeling dreadfully ashamed because I thought everybody knew I was in debt. The farthing was paid amid many solemn warnings, and the poor debtor was free, like a bird let out of a cage. How sweet it felt to be out of debt. How did my little heart declare and vow that nothing should ever tempt me into debt again. It was a fine lesson, and I have never forgotten it. If all boys were inoculated with the same doctrine when they were young, it would be as good as a fortune to them, and save them wagon-loads of trouble in after life. God bless my father, say I, and send a breed of such fathers into old England, to save her from being eaten up with villainy, for what with companies, and schemes, and paper money, the nation is getting to be as rotten as touchwood.

" Ever since that early sickening, I have hated debt as Luther hated the Pope, and if I say some fierce things about it, you must not wonder. To keep debt, dirt, and the devil out of my cottage has been my greatest wish ever since I set up housekeeping; and although the last of the three has sometimes gotten in by the door or window, for the old serpent will wriggle through the smallest crack, yet, thanks to a good wife, hard work, honesty, and scrubbing brushes, the other two have not crossed the threshold. Debt is so degrading that if I owed a man a penny, I would walk twenty miles in the depth of winter, to pay him, sooner than feel that I was under an obligation. I should be as comfortable with peas in my shoes, or a hedgehog in my bed, or a snake up my back as with bills hanging over my head at the grocer's, and baker's, and the tailor's. Poverty is hard, but debt is horrible; a man might as well have a smoky house and a scolding wife, which are said to be the two worst evils of our life. We may be poor yet respectable, which John Ploughman and wife hope they are, and will be; but a man in debt cannot even respect himself, and he is sure to be talked about by his neighbors, and that talk will not be much to his credit. Some persons appear to like to be owing money; but I would as soon be a cat up a chimney with the fire alight, or a fox with the hounds at my heels, or a hedgehog on a pitchfork, or a mouse under an owl's claws. An honest man thinks a purse full of other people's money to be worse than an empty one; he cannot bear to eat other people's cheese, wear other people's shirts, and walk about in other people's shoes; neither will he be easy while his wife is decked out in the milliner's bonnets, and wears the draper's flannels. The jackdaw in the peacock's feathers was soon plucked, and borrowers will surely come to poverty—a poverty of the bitterest sort, because there is shame in it."

From 1841 to 1844 he attended that excellent school at Colchester taught by a conscientious and able instructor who interested himself greatly in his students, yet until near the middle of 1844, when he made a summer visit to his grandfather at Stambourne, there was nothing specially remarkable noted either by his parents or his teacher.

But the event of that summer, of which an extended account will be made in the next chapter and which partakes so strongly of the miraculous, appears to have made an entire change in his mental constitution and in his ambitions. It is possible that we know very much more concerning his life from that special period on, because his family and friends began at that point to expect greater things of him, and consequently did notice more closely his characteristics and doings.

In 1844 when he was ten years of age he had progressed favorably in writing, reading, arithmetic, and spelling. He had also begun the study of the Greek grammar and Latin grammar and received some lessons in philosophy. But he never became in school an expert scholar in the ancient languages, although he afterward gave considerable attention to New Testament Greek and Hebrew at such odd times as he could secure, in order that he might gain a better understanding of the original languages in which the Bible was written.

In 1846 he received a prize in an examination and competition in the school, although he was several times defeated in the same attempt. His classmates say that he was characterized at that time by unusual practical observation among common things. He saw what no other boy appeared to notice. Valuable instruction was gained from the wayside, from the household scenes, from the fields of grain, from the most ordinary circumstances in the annals of the country people. Things dead to others were alive to him. Inanimate bodies were instinct with life. The trees had their messages, the rocks their lessons, and the lurking wild beasts their proverbs. He would have obtained a thorough useful education at that time had he lived in a desert. The most helpful education often is found in the examination of every-day events, and in the close scrunity of the most ordinary things.

In 1849 his father by great sacrifices secured him a place in New Market under care of Mr. Swindell, who was then a noted instructor and especially devoted to the preparation of young men for college.

He was obliged to live in a most meagre way and was acutely conscious of the sacrifice his father and mother were making to secure him an education. Hence he worked with a devotion and persistency born more of the heart than of intellectual ambition.

His father, as we have seen, had but little time to devote to the personal care or instruction of his children because he was in the shop in the day and preached evenings in some chapel or mission, and regularly on Sunday as the pastor at Tollesbury. But the father improved every opportunity to secure any interesting and good book for the use of his

children, and in that way often placed in Charles'
hands very valuable helps in securing a comprehensive education.   When his father gave up business
altogether and accepted the call of the Congregational Church at Cranbrooke, Kent, he made use of
his added income to secure several instructive
periodicals for the use of his sons, Charles and
James.   His fatherly generosity was returned to him
a hundred-fold through the indirect influence of
Charles, when his popularity began in London, for
the church at Fetter Lane having heard of the son,
sent a unanimous call to the father to come and be
their teacher in London, where he remained until 1876, in a prosperous and affectionate pastorate.

It is, however, often remarked that Mrs. Spurgeon,
Charles' mother, was as truly and effectively a pastor
in the Church and congregation as her husband, although she was a very quiet old lady, yet she was
so continuously engaged in good deeds that the sum
of them brought to her great affection and to her
husband no small honor.   It was a special comfort
and delight to Charles thus to have his father
and mother near him, to which came an added satisfaction when his brother James was also settled in
London as his assistant pastor.

No comprehensive view can be obtained of the
education of Charles H. Spurgeon without carefully
allowing a large space for the silent influence of the
example which such a mother and such a father con-

tinually presented for many years after he had actually become a preacher himself.

Many of the public charities, profitable deeds and kindness, as well as the great institutions which will through the coming generations bear his name, owe their origin, unquestionably, to the instruction by precept and example which he received from his parents, independent of any institution of learning.

His school-life necessarily held a prominent place in his early career and was always so connected with his religious training that even on days of examination when he had an oration or essay his subjects were generally upon some questions relating to the Church or upon the subject of missions.

He has given us himself a very clear account of the causes which led him to abandon the idea of entering college. It will be most interesting if given in his own words:

"Soon after I had begun, in 1852, to preach the Word in Waterbeach, I was strongly advised by my father and others to enter Stepney, now Regent's Park College, to prepare more fully for the ministry. Knowing that learning is never an incumbrance and is often a great means of usefulness, I felt inclined to avail myself of the opportunity of attaining it, although I believed that I might be useful without a college training, I consented to the opinion of friends that I should be more useful with it. Dr. Angus, the tutor of the college, visited Cambridge, where I then resided, and it was arranged that we should meet at the house of Mr. Macmillan, the publisher. Thinking and praying over the matter, I entered the house at exactly the time appointed, and was shown into a room, where I waited patiently for a couple of hours, feeling too much impressed with my own insignificance and the greatness of the tutor from London to venture to ring the bell and inquire the cause of the unreasonably long delay."

"At last patience having had her perfect work, the bell was set in motion, and on the arrival of the servant, the waiting young man of eighteen was informed that the doctor had tarried in another room, and could stop no longer, so had gone off by train, to London. The stupid girl had given no information to the family that any one called and had been shown into the drawing-room, consequently the meeting never came about, although designed by both parties. I was not a little disappointed at the moment; but have a thousand times since thanked the Lord very heartily for the strange providence which forced my steps into another and far better path.

" Still holding the idea of entering the Collegiate Institution, I thought of writing and making an immediate application; but that was not to be. That afternoon having to preach at a village station, I walked in a meditating frame of mind over Midsummer Common, to the little wooden bridge which leads to Chesterton, and in the midst of the Common,

I was startled by what seemed to be a loud voice, but which may have been a singular illusion ; whatever it was, the impression it made on my mind was most vivid ; I seemed very distinctly to hear the words, ' Seekest thou great things for thyself, seek them not.' This led me to look at my position from a different point of view, and to challenge my motives and intentions. I remembered my poor but loving people to whom I had ministered, and the souls which had been given me in my humble charge ; and although at that time I anticipated obscurity and poverty as the result of the resolve, yet I did there and then renounce the offer of collegiate instruction, determining to abide, for a season, at least, with my people, and to remain preaching the Word so long as I had strength to do it. Had it not been for those words, I had not been where I am now. Although the ephod is no longer worn by ministering priest, the Lord guides His people by His wisdom, and orders all their paths in love ; and in times of perplexity, by ways mysterious and remarkable. He says to them, ' This is the way, walk ye in it.' "

A little later he wrote, "I have all along had an aversion to college, and nothing but a feeling that I must not consult myself, but Jesus, could have made me think of it."

" I am more and more glad that I never went to college. God sends such sunshine on my path, such smiles of grace, that I cannot regret if I have forfeited all my prospects for it. I am conscious I held

5

back from the love of God and His cause ; and I had rather be poor in His service than rich in my own."

If at the time when he abandoned the idea of going to college, he had surrendered his intention to secure all the education those do obtain who go to college, then the position of those simple people who assume that it is just as well to preach without an education, would be clearly established. But the fact remains that he was none the less determined to have all the instruction possible and necessary to equip him for his great life-work ; and that he devoted himself to it most assiduously in all his spare hours. Hundreds of young men have entered the ministry thinking they were copying Spurgeon's example by refusing to attend an institution of learning, or pursue at home a systematic course of study, wholly forgetting all that other side of his history wherein he secured his advanced instruction, but under specially unfavorable circumstances.

Perhaps the conditions ought not to be considered unfavorable after all, when we remember that the very difficulties he so bravely encountered only added greatly to his mental power and furnished him with the especially superior weapons in the great difficulties of his after experience. It is never best to secure an education easily ; and scholars ought always to pursue those studies which are the most difficult to them. For the discipline of mind and the enlargement of mental power is of far more consequence than the collection of facts.

Mr. Edward Leeding, who for a time was Mr. Spurgeon's tutor, declared that Charles could have received the University degree on examination at any time after reaching manhood, had he chosen to make the application. The college degree is a label which is often displaced, but which in Mr. Spurgeon's case would have reflected more honor upon the institution than it could upon him.

CHAPTER III.

BEGINNING OF MIRACLES.

These are miraculous things, who can hear them? Strong meat is here given which only the believer or the most careful student can digest. Please keep out of these sacred precincts every one who will not enter them with reverence, or with a conscientious determination to weigh carefully the facts and deduce reasonably the simple truth. It is a garden of roses to affectionate friends and a field ripe for the harvest to the trusting believer, but a dangerous bog to the skeptic. Yet a skeptical spirit is by no means a crime, provided it be attended by an investigating disposition. It is a curious thing that we often find men of great genius spending years of time investigating the origin of the universe and the first causes of "modes of motion" in the development of animal life, who would regard it as foolishness to spend even a day in looking for the first causes of great moral and religious reforms.

Yet the origin of important social and religious changes and wonderful advances in civilization, are often traceable to a point as infinitely small and inscrutable as that which the mind ever reaches, which seeks for the origin of life.

It requires just as scientific and careful methods to trace the genesis of impulses or ideas as it does to find the first living celule in protoplasmic existence.

The mysterious influences which were brought to bear in such unusual ways upon the character and work of Charles H. Spurgeon, deserve the closest scrutiny of the deepest thinkers of the age. If they could be better understood than they are, they would make great changes in our systems of education, in our researches for the philosophy of history, and in nearly every relation of social and religious life.

We do not expect to explain these things, but we are trying to so present them as to win the attention of greater minds to this important matter. Can the mysteries be cleared up without attributing the causes directly to miraculously Divine interposition? Let us consider, first, the celebrated "Knill's Prophecy." That is placed here before the other marvelous incidents in Mr. Spurgeon's story simply because it occurred earliest in his history. We will give two accounts of the prophecy, for, like the New Testament records of the Saviour's life, they agree in all essentials, yet present the facts from different points of view. In Mr. C. M. Berrill's life of Rev. Richard Knill, is found the following account, which is copied *verbatim:*

"During his residence at Wotton-under-Edge, he visited the Rev. James Spurgeon, the minister of an ancient chapel at Stambourne, Essex; on walking in the garden with his host's grandson, then about ten years old, he felt, he afterward said, a prayerful concern for the intelligent and inquiring boy, sat with him under a yew tree, put his hands on his head, and prayed for him; telling him at the close that he believed 'he would love Jesus Christ, and preach His gospel in the largest chapel in the world.' When this curious prediction obtained something like fulfillment in the young preacher of the Surrey Music Hall, both parties in a short correspondence, referred to the old garden incident with feelings akin to wonder. Who can trace the subtlety of such suggestions on the tenor of one's life? All will at least be able to appreciate the aspiration prompted by these occurences—O Lord God omnipotent! Thine is the kingdom, and the power, and the glory. Help me as Thy servant, to go on laboring and rejoicing. These are tokens of Thy favor too great to be left unrecorded. What would thousands of gold and, silver be, compared to the conversion of souls and the calling out of preachers?"

We will now turn studiously to the other account, given in writing by Mr. Spurgeon himself. He said: "When I was a very small boy, I was staying at my grandfather's, where I had aforetime spent my earliest days; and, as the manner was, I read the Scriptures at family prayer. Once upon a time, when reading the passage in the Book of Revelation which mentions the bottomless pit, I paused and said, 'Grandpa, what can this mean?' The answer was kind, but unsatisfactory: 'Pooh, pooh, child, go on.' The child intended, however, to have an explanation, and therefore selected the same chapter morning after morning, Sunday included, and always halted at the same verse to repeat the inquiry. At length the venerable patriarch capitulated at discretion, by saying: 'Well, dear, what is it that puzzles you?' Now the child had often seen baskets with very frail bottoms, which in course of wear became bottomless, and allowed the fruit placed therein to fall upon the ground. Here then was the puzzle; if the pit aforesaid had no bottom, where would all the people fall who dropped out at its lower end?—a puzzle which rather startled the propriety of family worship, and had to be laid aside for explanation at a more convenient season. Questions of the like simple and natural character would frequently break up into paragraphs at the family Bible-reading, and had there not been a world of love and license allowed to the inquisitive reader, he would have soon been deposed from his office. As it was, the Scriptures were not very badly rendered, and were probably quite as interesting as if they had not been interspersed with original and curious inquiries.

"On one of these occasions, Mr. Knill, whose name is a household word, whose memory is precious to thousands at home and abroad, stayed at the minister's house on Friday, in readiness to preach at Stambourne for the London Missionary Society on the following Sunday. He never looked in a young face without yearning to impart some spiritual gift. He was all love, kindness, earnestness, and warmth, and coveted the souls of men as misers desire the gold their hearts pine for. He heard the boy read and commended; a little judicious praise is the sure way to a young heart. An agreement was made with the lad that on the next morning, Saturday, he should show Mr. Knill over the garden, and take him for a walk before breakfast; a task so flattering to juvenile self-importance was sure to be readily entered upon. There was a tap at the door, and the child was soon out of bed and in the garden with his new friend, who won his heart in no time by pleasing stories and kind words, and giving him a chance to communicate in return. The talk was all about Jesus, and the pleasantness of loving Him. Nor was it mere talk; there was pleading too. Into the great yew arbor, cut into the shape of a sugar loaf, both went, and the soul-winner knelt down; with his arms around the youthful neck, he poured out vehement intercession for the salvation of the lad. The next morning witnessed the same instruction and supplication, and the next also, while all day long the pair were never far apart, and never out of each other's thoughts. The mission sermons were preached in the old Puritan meeting-house, and the man of God was called to go to the next halting place in his tour as deputation for the Society. But he did not

leave until he had uttered a most remarkable prophecy. After even more earnest prayer with his
little *protégé*, he appeared to have a burden on his
mind, and he could not go till he had eased himself
of it. In after years he was heard to say that he felt
a singular interest in me, and an earnest expectation
for which he could not account. Calling the family
together, he took me on his knee, and I distinctly
remember his saying, 'I do not know how it is, but
*I feel a solemn presentiment that this child will
preach the gospel to thousands*, and God will bless
him to many souls. So sure am I of this that when
my little man preaches in Rowland Hill's chapel, as
he will do one day, I should like him to promise me
that he will give out the hymn commencing,—

> "'God moves in a mysterious way,
> His wonders to perform.'"

"This promise was of course made, and was
followed by another, namely, that at his express
desire I would learn the hymn in question and think
of what he had said."

"The prophetic declaration was fulfilled. When
I had the pleasure of preaching the Word of Life
in Surrey Chapel, and also when I preached in
Mr. Hill's first pulpit at Wotten-under-Edge, the
hymn was sung in both places. Did the words of
Mr. Knill help to bring about their own fulfillment?
I think so. I believed them, and looked forward to
the time when I should preach the Word. I felt

very powerfully that no unconverted person might dare to enter the ministry. This made me the more intent on seeking salvation, and more hopeful of it; and when by grace I was enabled to cast myself on the Saviour's love, it was not long before my mouth began to speak of His redemption. How came that sober-minded minister to speak thus to and of one into whose future God alone could see? How came it that he lived to rejoice with his younger brother in the truth of all he had spoken? The answer is plain. But mark one particular lesson; would to God that we were all as wise as Richard Knill in habitually sowing beside all waters. Mr. Knill might very naturally have left the minister's little grandson on the plea that he had other duties of more importance than praying with children; and yet who shall say that he did not effect as much by that simple act of humble ministry as by dozens of sermons addressed to crowded audiences? To me his tenderness in considering the little one was fraught with everlasting consequences, and I must ever feel that his time was well laid out."

It will be noticed that there is no necessary discrepancy between these two accounts, although Mr. Knill remembered having said "that the boy would love Jesus Christ and preach His gospel in the largest chapel in the world," while Mr. Spurgeon's account of the same incident declares: " I distinctly remember his saying, " I do not know how it is, but I feel a solemn presentiment that this child will preach the gospel to thousands, and God will bless him to many souls. So sure am I of this that when my little son preaches in Rowland Hill's chapel, as he will do one day, I should like him to promise me that he will give out the hymn commencing :

> " 'God moves in a mysterious way,
> His wonders to perform.' "

Mr. Spurgeon seems to have given the general import of a lengthy conversation, while Mr. Knill presents the exact words of a part of his prophecy. There is no question probably in any candid mind but that this scene at the arbor and this wonderful prophecy are matters of fact. Assuming then that no discussion can arise concerning the general accuracy of these reports, we have presented to us the question : How did Mr. Knill then know that Charles would preach in "the largest chapel in the world?"

It might be said by those who believe only in the consecutive course of nature's cause and effect that Mr. Knill may have been unusually wise, and that he judged the future by the past or that he only surmised what would be probable from what he had known in his own experience of the history of other boys. Or it may be assumed by the more skeptical that it was altogether a wild guess, such as any person might make and would forget if it was left unfulfilled. If this had been the only strange incident of the kind in the life of Mr. Spurgeon, or even had it been the most mysterious incident connected with his strange history, it might more readily be passed by as a mere coincidence—where a shrewd guess was accidentally as true as prophecy.

But other incidents to which reference is yet to be made, present such cumulative evidence that there was working at this very time a mysterious spirit beyond human scrutiny, that very few people who believe in a spiritual agency, doubt but that Mr. Knill was in this a veritable prophet. The religious world will believe that he was given a supernatural foresight, and that a gleam of divine light opened to him the future of this servant of the living God.

Neither the prophecies of the Old or the New Testament, nor the strange foretelling of subsequent events on the part of great and saintly Christian men since that day, can be reduced to any system or adjusted to any known law of the natural or spiritual world.

That under a certain inspiration and condition human beings do in a measure foresee coming events is well established, and needs no confirmation in this place. In fact, a close consideration of the subject leads one to the conclusion that, in a greater or less degree, every person has a certain amount of foresight and that such a foresight is not altogether the result of previous experience.

Premonitions are among the most common things in daily life, and their fulfillment does not especially surprise any one.   To be a divine prophet after the manner of Isaiah or Agabus appears to be only this that they were given a higher degree of foresight or what is called " exalted spiritual vision."   But after all discussion is passed, the whole matter assumes again the form of a belief, and persons will accept or reject it as a matter of faith, and be influenced but little by the argument.

So many persons who have not the gift of prophecy judge other people by themselves, and deny that power to every other person ; yet it is easily seen by the candid mind that it is not positive proof that the gift of prophecy is not held by any person, because another lacks the same gift.

The days of prophecy are not passed, neither is the period of miracles closed ; yet, because the subject is not understood and is necessarily in the domain of the mysterious, many deceivers have waxed bold and surrounded the thought with so many shams and falsehoods as to cause good people to greatly mistrust even the most clearly established facts.   But it is the part of men of sense to allow no prejudice to sweep them to absurd extremes, or compel them to take the foolish position that because so many men falsify no man tells the truth.

There under those closely trimmed yews, in the shady arbor of Stambourne, God revealed Himself, and, for a purpose higher than that which man can fully comprehend, impressed his servant's mind with the events which must necessarily come to pass.   It was irrevocably fixed that the boy would grow to become a man and preach in the largest chapel in the world. Listeners to such incidents from the mouth of men whose life, and whose words have ever been noted for truth and calm good sense should attend reverently when the same persons relate even miraculous things. But we are all of us far too much inclined to regard such statements as wholly or partially illusionary, and so dismiss them with but slight thought, and make no account of them whatever in summing up the causes or results of a human life. Science digs deep, but it has not yet thrust its shovel low enough to unsettle the foundation of things, nor has any philosopher been able to present by the law of material things a comprehensive, conclusive reason for the most ordinary events.

We are strangers after all, and in a strange world. We surmise but do not know. Simple belief is finally the sum of all the results which the most analytical mind secures. We believe Mr. Knill's prophecy was supernatural; so do the many hundred thousands of living men who knew Mr. Spurgeon. Then it reasonably follows that while many doubters will not accept the conclusions we draw as infallibly proven, yet we do believe Charles was then selected of God as a special apostle to do a definite religious work.

We will look back again to the experience related in the last chapter concerning Mr. Spurgeon's decision to go on with his preaching, without a college education. In that it will be seen that he stated, "That afternoon having to preach at a village station, I walked slowly in a meditating frame of mind, over Midsummer Common, to the little wooden bridge which leads to Chesterton, and in the midst of the Common I was startled by what seemed to me to be a loud voice, but which may have been a singular illusion; whatever it was, the impression it made on my mind was most vivid; I seemed very distinctly to hear the words, 'Seekest thou great things for thyself, seek them not!' This led me to look at my position from a different point of view, and to challenge my motives and intentions."

This experience reminds one very strongly of the "Genius" of Plato. He is said by the classical historian to have heard a voice suggesting to him which way he should go, and the ideas it would be wise to adopt.

Many persons have trusted the record and declared their belief that Plato did actually hear some voice which was superhuman, or which, if not, was an impression beyond the understanding of natural philosophers. But the greater number of classical scholars have assumed at once, without investigation, that Plato's Genius was an imaginary creature, and that the voice was only heard "echoing in his soul." Yet it is clearly impossible to prove the negative in this case and place beyond controversy or doubt the theory that Plato could not have heard any communication save that of the voice of some living man. But many superstitious people have drawn their own extreme conclusions, and some of them by their very absurdity, have driven minds away from that careful investigation which it is at least reasonable to give to a matter of this kind.

That the Apostle Paul heard a voice when on his way to Damascus has sometimes been denied by most profound theologians, and the whole scene explained as being an inner impression, made outwardly from the soul, rather than inwardly from any external shining light. Such is the interpretation put upon the voice heard at Christ's Baptism, and heard when the Greeks in the Temple said "it thundered."

But that theory explains nothing. It is no less supernatural or wonderful even if that interpretation were correct. But the millions of Christians who take the Bible to be the spiritual word of God and an infallible guide to heaven, believe that Paul heard a real voice, and they believe it was the voice of Jesus the Christ.

Augustine heard strange voices. Luther heard supernatural voices. But their historians and philosophers have never come to any clear decision whether the voices they heard were imaginary or real.

Thousands of other Christians have related how, at their conversion or at other times, messages have

SPURGEON AT THE AGE OF NINETEEN.

come to them which seemed to be spoken in tones of a human voice, and which turned the whole current of their lives into a channel toward which no previous application of the "law of association of ideas" would lead them. We would teach no superstition, nor advocate the trustworthiness of strange impulses nor approve of the hallucinations which come to minds often more or less unbalanced. But with calmness and conservatism, and yet with firmness in the right as God gives us to see the right, let us frankly face this question, Did Mr. Spurgeon hear a voice, or did he not?

The great profit to be obtained in the study of such a matter is that it prevents thoughtful minds from sweeping into that materialistic condition which leads them to trust more to the sectarian bigotry of some modern scientists than to the eternal truth of revelation, or the judgment of good common sense.

On the other hand, examination will tend to prevent the acceptance of wild and reckless conclusions concerning such matters, and offset the foolish "inspirations" which have led astray so many weak Christians in these later years.

Mr. Spurgeon was unquestionably a man of strict integrity, he would not intentionally misrepresent the slightest circumstance in connection with any event, and the logical conclusion to which he came concerning the voice he heard at Midsummer Common, is one of great importance to the Christian world.

6

He said "which may have been a singular illusion."
He does not venture to assert the supernatural.
He might be mistaken as to the origin of the voice,
But the same impression was received by his mind,
which human language makes through vibration
in the ear. It would require in order to truthfully deny that any real voice was heard, that
the person denying it should have infinite knowledge. For he who says that such a thing could not
occur, thereby claims to be acquainted with all the
laws of nature, and above nature, and that he is so
fully able to measure their powers and possible com-
binations as to mathematically figure out of all the infinite possibilities the impossibility of such an event.

Any person could declare that he did not believe
it, and might be truthful in his statement. But he
who asserts that such a thing is actually impossible
assumes a divinity of knowledge which is sublimely
absurd. Yet, on the other hand, so many voices are
said to have been heard by those who are wholly untrustworthy in other matters and so many of them
have been used to prop up so many of the most silly
superstitions that it is reasonably difficult for the
superficial thinker to decide that any real voice of
this kind is ever heard in modern years.

The sanctified common sense of Mr. Spurgeon is
beautifully shown in his expression, given in his account, that the loud voice "may have been a singular
illusion." Such illusions are not rare and certainly
are to be most carefully investigated before being

accepted as established truth. But it is certain that
Mr. Spurgeon evidently believed that it was the
voice of God. At all events, he allowed it to guide
him to the most important decision of his life and
ever after kept the saying of that voice vividly
before his mind to determine his actions in situations
of great difficulty.

As Henry Ward Beecher said of Abraham Lin-
coln's belief in signs, "even if it was an illusion, it was
still the voice of God." What difference does it make
if the right impression is made upon the mind,
whether it be the result of a trumpet blast, or of a
still small voice whispering in the soul? God is not
confined to any particular agency in making His
chosen communications; and however weak may be
our speculations concerning the channel through
which God conveys His divine will, it is perhaps
enough for us to know that He does communicate
with His own in some way, and impresses upon them
His will in a manner akin to that which He used
with the saints of old.

Impressions of great variety are continually being
made upon the wicked, going into deeper wrong,
which to the Christian are clearly warnings from
a great and good spirit, which would turn them
back from their evil ways, before their souls
are utterly lost. And in the same way, spiritual
voices, though perhaps using no mechanical instrument for expression, are continually encouraging the
soul which is struggling after the truth, and are help-

ing upward by mysterious suggestions the servant of God who would know more of Christ and be better fitted to perform His will.

If we were to surrender this position, we would suffer complete defeat as defenders of the Christian principles that God still saves and impels by His Holy Spirit.

We declare unhesitatingly our unshaken belief in the fact that the voice which Mr. Spurgeon heard at that time was the voice of the Holy Spirit of God. We also declare, that it must have been the same Divine agency which afterward followed him from that point on, and in the most miraculous ways answered his prayers and furthered his efforts for the salvation of men.

Only a few of the uncounted number of singular events in his history are probably known to any writer. And if they all could be known, it would be impossible to write the books which should contain their narration. We will gather here as many as we feel are perfectly trustworthy, being sadly conscious, however, of the fact that any collection of the Providential visitations of God to Mr. Spurgeon and his work will be but a hint to the great aggregation of unwritten events. We believe in the miraculous agency of the Holy Spirit in connection with the conversion of every soul which he saw turn from the world unto God. No known natural law accounts for the revolution in disposition and the change in relation to God and Godly things, which comes to the heart that surrenders itself to a belief in Jesus the Christ.

Accompanying this religious work he found, as many other servants of Christ have found, that there are ever at work mysterious, unaccountable, providential causes leading to the definite result. Our religious libraries are filled with books giving accounts of marvelous answers to prayer, of the most strange turning about in the lives of bad men, of the building of churches, the beginnings of missions, of power in revivals, healing of diseases and the hundred other transformations of human character or human circumstances. All of these help to confirm the idea that Mr. Spurgeon's life was one specially led by a supernatural spirit. Yet so interwoven with this record are the natural results of the well-understood human agencies that no one may hope to draw a clear line of division and say this was supernatural, and that was natural.

How difficult then is the task of the historian, working in human limitations, lacking the infallibility of divine inspiration. The writer can at the best, only touch upon the facts here and there, catching but occasional glimpses of the plan which Mr. Spurgeon lived out, the main features of which are hidden with God. Only when the books are opened beyond this present existence, can there be presented a true record of all the supernatural influences which worked with the natural ones in the making up of his romantic career.

CHAPTER IV.

EARLY RELIGIOUS EXPERIENCES.

We must tread again the border-land of the known and the unknown, as we try to present a truthful narration of Mr. Spurgeon's earliest religious life. It was as remarkable and startling as many of the other things in his strange career. Yet it may be that we ought not to regard his religious experiences as beginning at the time when he thought he was converted; for he was a child of religious parents and was ever under the influence of Biblical teachings, from the day he began to learn anything.

The Church and Sabbath-school were as familiar to him as was his grandfather's sitting-room. The Bible was a book which was kept in mind by continual quotation and by daily reading, both morning and evening. Thus he lived through all his early years in the atmosphere of a religious and holy home-life. A hatred of evil and a love for the good were inculcated by teachers and friends, both in precept and example, until it must have been a kind of second nature to him to be religious in an external sense.

He has told us how the *Pilgrim's Progress* and

the *Lives of the Martyrs* were among the first books that he ever read, and the impression they made upon his thoughts and feelings never disappeared.

He lived in the Church as some boys do on the streets, he was as much at home with the Sunday-school classes and books as some boys are with the billiard-rooms and dram-shops. If careful and conscientious training could ever be of advantage to a child, he could not fail to be a good boy.

While he does not appear to have been precociously intellectual, he does appear to have been precociously religious.

His grandfather never wearied of telling the incidents connected with Charles' evangelistic tendencies, and with great delight used to relate how the boy once went into an ale-house on an errand, and having found there, drinking and carousing, a member of the church, indignantly rebuked him by exclaiming, "What doest thou here, Elijah!" Then, too, he inherited that deep emotional nature, that large philanthropic spirit, which would lead him to most tenderly sympathize with sorrow and pain, and would arouse him to lion ferocity to witness cruelty or injustice. He was an upright youth and no hint of anything immoral, no suggestion of vice comes to us concerning him, in all the traditions connected with his early years.

His forceful utterances from the pulpit were never

afterward weakened by the remembrance of wrongs committed in his youth. He was never compelled to meet in his pastoral duties or works of mercy the bitter insinuations which surround the preacher whose previous life is a matter of sorrow or shame.

Men often proclaim, and with an appearance of pride, that they have descended to the lowest experiences of vice and debauchery, and that they have been lifted from the horrible pit and the miry clay by the especial and miraculous interference of God in their behalf. Many such testimonies seem to state the truth ; but it would appear as though the man who had never tasted evil nor committed an act of which he had reason to be ashamed, should praise God with the loudest voice or with the most sincere emotion. For the stain and scars of a life once evil are never erased beyond recognition.

A wasted life or wasted half a life! How sad it must be to reflect upon it continually, and to think how much more good might have been done, had religious life began in childhood, instead of opening in volcanic eruptions or in purifying thunder-storms.

The startling conversions and thrilling experiences of which we hear, perhaps none too much, are after all not so much the subject of praise or congratulation as to have led an entire life under the influence and in the service of the Saviour. Yet Mr. Spurgeon, notwithstanding his moral uprightness of character, had the same struggle with Satan, and the same

turmoil of spirit which has characterized a large portion of the religious conversions recorded in the
books. He has told us about it himself and in language so plain and interesting that we will give his
statement here in his own words, and for conveni-
ence, combine two different accounts. He was
converted at Colchester, in Essex, England, when he
was between fifteen and sixteen years of age, and
while he was attending school.

He said: "I can remember the time when my
sins first stared me in the face. I thought myself to
be most accursed of all men. I had not committed
any very great open transgressions against God ; but
I recollected that I had been well trained and tutored,
and I thought my sins were thus greater than other
people's. I cried to God to have mercy, but I feared
that He would not pardon me. Month after month
I cried to God, but He did not hear me, and I knew
not what it was to be saved. Sometimes I was so
weary of the world that I desired to die ; but then I
recollected that there was a worse world after this,
and that it would be an ill matter to rush before my Maker unprepared. At times I wickedly
thought God a most heartless tyrant, because He did
not answer my prayer ; and then at others I thought,
'I deserve His displeasure ; if He sends me to hell,
He will be just.' But I remember the hour when I
stepped into a place of worship, and saw a tall thin
man in the pulpit; I have never seen him from that
day, and probably never shall until we meet in

heaven. He opened the Bible and read in a feeble voice, 'Look unto me and be ye saved, all the ends of the earth; for I am God, and beside me there is none else.' Ah! thought I, I am one of the ends of the earth; and then turning around, and fixing his gaze on me, as if he knew me, the minister said: 'Look, look, look!' Why, I thought I had a great deal to *do*, but I found it was only to *look*. I thought I had a garment to spin out for myself; but I found that if I looked, Christ would give me a garment. Look, sinner; that is the way to be saved. Look unto Him, all ye ends of the earth, and be saved." * * *

"I will tell you how I, myself, was brought to the knowledge of this truth. It may happen the telling of that will bring some one else to Christ. It pleased God in my childhood to convince me of sin. I lived a miserable creature, finding no hope, no comfort, thinking that surely God would never save me. At last the worst came to worst—I was miserable; I could scarcely do anything. My heart was broken in pieces. Six months did I pray, prayed agonizingly with all my heart, and never had an answer. I resolved that in the town where I lived I would visit every place of worship in order to find out the way of salvation. I felt I was willing to do anything and be anything, if God would only forgive me. I set off determined to visit the chapels, and I went to all the places of worship; and though I dearly venerate the men who occupy those pulpits now, and did so then, I am bound to say that I never heard them once fully preach the gospel. I mean by that, they preached truth, great truths, many good truths that were fitting to many of their congregation who were spiritually-minded people; but what I wanted to know was, How can I get my sins forgiven. And they never once told me that. I wanted to know how a poor sinner, under the sense of sin, might find peace with God; and when I went I heard a sermon on, 'Be not deceived. God is not mocked,' which cut me up worse, but did not say how I might escape. I went again another day, and the text was something about the glories of the righteous; nothing for poor me. I was something like a dog under the table, not allowed to eat of the children's food. I went time after time, and I can honestly say, I don't know that I ever went without prayer to God, and I am sure there was not a more attentive listener in all the place than myself, for I panted and longed to understand how I might be saved.

"At last one day—it snowed so much that I could not go to the place to which I had determined to go, and I was obliged to stop on the road, and it was a blessed stop for me—I found rather an obscure street, and turned down a court, and there was a little chapel. I wanted to go somewhere, but I did not know this place. It was the primitive Methodists' chapel. I had heard of these people from many, and how they sang so loudly that they made people's heads ache; but that did not matter. I wanted to know how I might be saved, and if they made my head ache ever so hard I did not care. So sitting down, the service went on, but no preacher came. At last a very thin looking man, Rev. Robert Eaglen, came into the pulpit and opened his Bible and read these words: 'Look unto me and be ye saved, all ye ends of the earth.' Just setting his eyes upon me, as if he knew me all by heart, he said: 'Young man you are in trouble.' Well, I was, sure enough. Said he, 'you will never get out of it unless you look to Christ.' And then lifting up his hands he cried out, as I think only a Primitive Methodist could do, 'Look, look, look.' 'It is only look,' said he. I saw at once the way of salvation. Oh! how I did leap for joy on that moment. I know not what else he said. I did not take much notice of that—I was so possessed with that one thought. Like as when the brazen serpent was lifted up, they only looked and were healed. I had been waiting to do fifty things, but when I heard this word, 'look,' what a charming word it seemed to me. Oh! I looked until I could almost have looked my eyes away, and in heaven I will look on still in my joy unutterable.

"I now think I am bound never to preach a sermon without preaching to sinners. I do think that a minister who can preach a sermon without addressing sinners does not know how to preach."

The change of heart and faith which this incident marks was so great, notwithstanding his previous unimpeachable character, that all his friends and acquaintances who had not heard of his conversion, recognized the great transformation. Life took upon itself a new robe. His entire ambition concentrated in the thought of doing good. He had decided to be a Christian teacher, and felt that he could not possibly keep back the message, even should he bring all his naturally stubborn disposition to bear upon the repression. An irresistible desire to proclaim the new gospel he had found impelled him on with such speed that he had no opportunity to even look back. The very next day found him visiting the poor and talking to his classmates concerning their religious life, and heard him declare to his teacher, "it is all settled, I must preach the gospel of Christ." Yet he was by disposition very timid, had always trembled at the sound of his own voice in public declamation, and up to that period had shown a discouraging disposition to stutter and choke when suddenly called upon to answer a question or make a remark in a public assembly. But nearly all that timidity disappeared before his very first experience as a preacher.

It is a matter of no little surprise to many early friends of Mr. Spurgeon that he should have departed from the faith of his fathers' and instead of uniting with the Congregational body, should enter into the fellowship of a Baptist Church. It is said that his decision to enter the Baptist Church was caused entirely by his own independent conscien-

tious convictions concerning the principles of the
Church and the form of baptism. He read his Bible
with great care, and insisted with great enthusiasm
on literally complying, as far as possible, with the
actual example of the Saviour. He had been drawn
into association with some students connected with
the Baptist Church at Isleham and so had occasionally attended worship in that church. When he decided that it was his duty to unite with that denomination he pleaded most strenuously with his father
and mother and grandfather for their consent. They
were, in no sense, bigoted sectarians, and when they
found his heart so strongly fixed upon that Church,
they withdrew their first objections and bid him
heartily "God speed."

He was baptized by the Rev. Mr. Cantlow, of
Isleham Baptist Church, May 3d, 1850, celebrating
at the same time as he often afterward claimed, the
birthday of his mother. The Isleham pastor was
one of the old vigorously protestant Baptist teachers
who insisted most persistently in declaring the principle that "every person shall have the right and
ought to exercise it, to worship God according to the
dictates of his own enlightened conscience."

The remark of his mother concerning his baptism
and his reply has been running through the newspapers for a great many years, wherein she said, "I
have often prayed the Lord that you might be converted, but never asked Him that you might be a

Baptist." To which Charles replied that God had answered her prayer with His usual bounty, and had " given her more than she had asked."

Connected with the church at Isleham was a young schoolmate who was also closely connected with the "lay preachers' association" of the Baptist Church in Cambridge. Through him Charles was introduced to the pastor and some of the deacons of the Cambridge Church. He joined that church soon after his baptism, either by letter from the Isleham Church or upon a letter of commendation from the Rev. Mr. Cantlow. His purpose in uniting with the church at Cambridge seems to have been specially to identify himself with the "lay preachers' association," which was an organization of young men who devoted their Sabbaths largely to missionary and personal Christian work. There he found most congenial companionship and very agreeable religious employment, entering into it with all his heart and soul and winning the hearts of many of the poor and the sinful. It was in connection with this association that he preached his first sermon. It was entirely an impromptu address, about which he had but a few minutes to think in advance. He entered the pulpit a boy, dressed in a round jacket and a broad turned-down collar. Perhaps it will add to the interest if we should give in his own language the manner in which the address was thrust upon him.

"I had been asked to walk out to the village of

7

Taversham, about four miles from Cambridge, where I then lived, to accompany a young man whom I supposed to be the preacher for the evening, and on the way I said to him that I trusted God would bless him in his labors. 'Oh! dear,' said he, 'I never preached in my life; I never thought of doing such a thing. I was asked to walk with you and I sincerely hope God will bless *you* in *your* preaching.' 'Nay,' said I, 'but I never preached, and I don't know that I could do anything of the sort.' We walked together until we came almost to the place, my inmost soul being all in a tremble as to what would happen. When we found the congregation assembled, and no one else there to speak of Jesus, although I was only sixteen years of age, I found that was I expected to preach, so I did preach."

The sermon is said by some of those who heard it, to have been most truly amusing, because it was so serious, practical, and earnest, and given by a mere boy, amid such dignified surroundings. He was in earnest to the verge of fanaticism, and soon lost all consciousness of self, and all embarrassment on account of his age, and threw himself into the delivery of the message with an abandon which to the preacher is the keenest, richest joy. Some of his hearers afterward compared his youthful appearance and his unaccountable wisdom to the scene of Christ among the doctors, while skeptical or envious ones, said "the boy is wildly bold." He was wholly, unreservedly in earnest, and that covered a multitude

COTTAGE WHERE MR. SPURGEON PREACHED HIS FIRST SERMON.

5091

of faults, and forced to defeat all of his theological and literary critics.

His first practical Christian work, was, as a matter of course, very largely among the humble people, and his first experience was connected with the leadership of small prayer-meetings. Some of these meetings did not number more than, as he said, " he could count on his hands," and were often held in the kitchen or sitting-room of some humble dwelling. But he was young, vigorous, and enthusiastic and often walked ten miles to attend a short evening service. He removed his school relations from New Market to Cambridge, where his father had employed a tutor, and, with his comrades of the Lay Preachers' Association, took up the most systematic course of house visiting, ascertaining who were Christians, and exhorting most earnestly those who were not. The boys connected with that society became very well known in the course of a very few months, and Charles was recognized by them all as a leader. He was often compared with Peter by his companions because of his impulsiveness and his strong inclination to chastise himself for any neglect or seeming sin.

He arose early with the sun, studied his lessons hard until the hour for school, he then remained in school until four o'clock in the afternoon, and for one year attended some kind of religious service almost every evening in the week, and preached the gospel on Sunday. His pulpit in the week was sometimes a chair, at other times a barrel, while frequently he stood in the open road and occasionally he found his way into the pulpits of the smaller churches. He taught a Sunday-school class, which soon grew out of all proportion with the rest of the school, but he reduced it by urging the scholars to go out and become evangelists, in the distribution of tracts, caring for the poor, and praying for the sick.

There were two young men connected with the Lay Preachers' Association who were far more eloquent than he, but there was a conspicuous lack in their character of that impulsive power, that influence over the action of others, that ability to organize them into effective work which was then and has been his chief characteristic ever since that day.

He often volunteered to assist the children of the village in their studies at home, frequently making their acquaintance on the street or at school, and thus found his way into the families as a Christian evangelist, to the great delight of the parents and to the profit of the children.

Religious work became with him a positive passion, inspiring all his thought and the object of his entire ambition. He was bright, active, and at times very witty. His fun was exuberant, natural, and contagious. He was often seen running races with the children, rolling the hoop for their amusement, and performing feats in youthful athletics to the surprise and admiration of the boys whose souls he desired to win to the Lord Jesus Christ.

He studied his Bible constantly, and was often overheard repeating chapters of it by heart, that he might so fasten them upon his memory as to make them indelible there.

It appears that from the very first he was so positively in earnest in the work himself that he took little time to listen to the preaching of others. This may in a measure account for his singular originality, and may have aided him greatly in reaching the eminence on which he stood at the time of his death. If he had been less anxious to engage at once in some practical work, and had spent more time listening to the preachers of that day, he would have been inclined to copy their forms of expressions, their gestures, intonations, or dress.

But all his life he was so perpetually busy about something in which his own personality was needed that he rarely ever had time to listen to a sermon or address by any other person.

He read sermons, lectures, and books by the hundred, and thus secured the best ideas of his time on theological matters. But he copied no one, and carved for himself such an independent place as an orator and teacher that even his blunders and extravagances added greatly to his attractiveness and power. He had no Oxford airs, no aristocratic affectations, and was often mentioned by those who spoke of him as one who was "different from every other man on earth."

In this way he adjusted himself to all the circum

stances in which he was placed and went directly toward the object he had in view. His language and his entire appearance were the products of his own age and time, and were adjustable to the variety of his present needs. He lived in his own time and for his own generation, and consequently was especially fitted for the personal and public Christian work which he was so anxious to perform.

There are practical machinists, there are theoretical machinists, there are theoretical farmers, and there are practical farmers, even so there are theoretical ministers and practical ministers. As the practical farmer and mechanic make all the money, while the theorists spend it all, just so the practical preacher wins all the souls, while the theorist drives them away.

He loved greatly to attend Sabbath-School conventions and anniversaries, and while making no pretensions to oratory was always called upon to speak whenever he was present. He was simple as a child, consequently the children delighted to hear him. His fund of anecdotes, traditions, stories, and illustrations were positively inexhaustible. Every anecdote or description which he read in a periodical or a book seems to have remained with him subject to instant call.

But he was colloquial and often awkward. He did not hesitate to use expressive local phrases which would be regarded by the polished scholars as partaking altogether too largely of slang. But he scrupled not to use any sort of effective weapon in his contest with evil, and hastened to throw to the sinking sinner a window-frame or a cabin table in the absence of handy life preservers. The effect of his teaching was immediately felt in the entire vicinity, to such an extent that he was called for on every side to pray with the sick and counsel the dying, although he was but a mere boy in years or experience.

In the year 1851, which was the first year of his preaching experience, he was invited to deliver an address in the church at Waterbeach, not far from Cambridge, and is said to have had less than a dozen at his initial service. But the Waterbeach Baptist Church was composed of very poor people and paid a salary of but $100 per year to the really distinguished men who had presided over its religious services. The church was small, built of composite, plastered outside and in, with rude benches and a very high pulpit. The best description we have been able to obtain of the old church, which has since been destroyed by fire, reports it to have been a barren and sterile place except when filled with the devoted Christians, to many of whom it was a veritable Mecca. The old ladies who heard him preach his first sermon regarded him as a "dear good boy," but would not have dreamed of accepting him as their pastor until he began to make his influence felt in their homes and among their children.

He was always diligently at work. They often asked him if he ever slept.

He had no thought, however, of beginning a pastorate at Waterbeach during the first two or three months of his active work in that neighborhood as an evangelist, but the thought at first absurd soon became possible, then arose to the probable, and finally was a certainty. The church unanimously called him to be their pastor, when he was about eighteen years of age, and probably the youngest ordained preacher of any denomination in England. He accepted the position after a great deal of hesitation and many hours spent by himself in prayer.

It was then that he was compelled to come to the important decision to which we have referred in a previous chapter, concerning the pursuit of his education through a college course. He felt that he belonged to the Lord. His body, his soul, his talents, and his time. He believed that the Lord could use him without an education, if his Heavenly Father was so inclined; and he cut himself off from educational opportunities and entered directly into the work of saving souls, assured that in some way the Lord would make up for the deficiency.

Many persons regarded him as a fanatic, and tried their best to discourage him by calling his attention to the fact that he was so young. Some even wrote to his father, saying that it was a shame to allow a bright boy like that to throw himself away in such a foolish manner. But he was ready to go through fire and water, and had determined to sacrifice everything and anything in the cause he had espoused.

Yet he entered upon it with the most deliberate thought, with most broad common sense, and combined with these such skill and tact in the management of others, and in the declaration of truth, as to establish himself quickly with the oldest and most conservative of his hearers. The fire in his soul which many feared would become a hard master he ever kept within proper bounds and compelled it to be a good servant.

Unstinted praise was heard on every side and the extremest flattery was spoken unblushingly to his face. It is a marvel that the boy was not completely destroyed by egotism. But he had the natural tact to consult with old men, and to follow their advice rather than to give heed to flatterers, who would have led him so sadly to overestimate his forces.

Many say that during his youth he did at times exhibit considerable self-importance, and there are those who seem to recognize that trait, though largely in abeyance, in the entire history of the man.

Mr. Spurgeon has also left an account of his first pastorate, in which he said: " Well I remember beginning to preach in a little thatched chapel, and my first concern was, would God save any souls through me? They called me a ragged headed boy; I think I was—I know I wore a jacket. I preached and I was troubled in my heart because I thought, ' This gospel has saved me, but then somebody else preached it; will it save anybody if I preach it?' Some

Sundays went over, and I used to say to one of the deacons, 'Have you heard of anybody finding the Lord?' My good old friend said, 'I am sure there has been, I am quite sure about it.' 'Oh!' I said, 'I want to know it, I want to see it.' And one Sunday afternoon he said, 'There is a woman who lives over at so-and-so who found the Lord three or four Sundays ago through your preaching.' I said, 'Drive me over there, I must go directly,' and the first thing on Monday morning I was driving down to see my first convert. Many fathers recollect their first child; mothers recollect their first baby—no child like it, you never had another like it since. I have had a great many spiritual children born of the preaching of the word, but I do think that woman was the best of the lot. At least, she did not live long enough for me to find many faults in her. After a year or two of faithful witness-bearing she went home to lead the way for a goodly number since. I have had nothing else to preach but Christ crucified. How many souls there are in heaven who have found their way there through that preaching, how many there are still on the earth, serving the Master, it is not for me to tell; but whatever there has been of success has been through the preaching of Christ in the sinners' stead."

A glimpse of the domestic side of his life is afforded us in a humorous off-hand line he sent about this time to his sister, which Mr. Bliss has given to the public :—

"Cambridge, Thursday.

"To Miss Carolina Louisa Spurgeon :—

"Your name is so long that it will almost reach across the paper. We have one young gentleman in our school, whose name is Edward Ralph William Baxter T———. The boys tease him about his long name, but he is a very good boy, and that makes his name a good one.

"Everybody's name is pretty if they are good people.

"The Duke of Tuscany has had a little son. The little fellow was taken to the Catholic cathedral, and had some water put on his face, and then they named him—you must get Eliza to read it— 'Giovanni Nepomuceno Maria Annunziata Giuseppe Giovanbattista Ferdinando Baldassere Luigi Gonzaga Pietro Allesandro Zanobi Antonio.'

"A pretty long name to go to bed and get up with. It will be a long while before he will be able to say it all the way through.

"If any one is called by the name of Christian, that is better than all these great words. It is the best name in the world, except the name of our Lord Jesus Christ.

"My best love to you. I hope you will enjoy yourself and try to make others happy too, for then you are sure to be happy yourself. Whereas, if you only look out to please yourself, you will make others uncomfortable, and will not make yourself happy. However, you know that, and I need not tell you of it. A happy Christmas to you.

"Your loving brother,

"CHARLES."

Mr. Spurgeon's personal letters have always been distinguished for their simplicity and originality of style. He had no time, even if he had the inclination, to study the copy-books for fashionable letter-writing. He lost no time, but wrote concisely and directly what he meant, omitting generally the ornamental and the flourish. In this was the great gain to him found in the omission of a classical education in the schools. No one would ever accuse him of plagiarism who understood his style or knew his habits.

Imitators never succeed, Even painters who endeavor to copy Raphael or Rubens fail as copyists, and bring shame to themselves as artists, and the literary man or public speaker who endeavors to copy any minister is doing a most conspicuously foolish thing.

When Beecher died, a host of little Beechers arose, claiming to be a second Beecher. They were all very little Beechers. Successors to John B. Gough, to John Wesley, to Martin Luther, have often been foolishly advertised, but their lack of genius and learning was in every case as notorious as was the success of the persons they attempted to imitate.

Probably no profession in the world contains as many imitators as that of the ministry. One man's success immediately brings about him a school of prophets, who regard him as a superior model, and follow him in the closest details; but every such follower is a dismal failure. The curse of the pulpit, if there be any one curse more deleterious than another, is this weak tendency to imitate some successful man. The fear of being original and the timidity with which they meet criticism after having stated something different from the declarations of other people, keep men and women from doing their duty, and suppresses the sublime natural power found in all our pulpits. Let every man remain himself. If in being individual, he blunders and flounders like a porpoise, or brays like a donkey, he will attract more respectful attention in that manner which is natural than with all the most refined sentences stolen from classical models.

If God had intended or desired that men should be all alike, He would have so constructed them, and would have surrounded each with the same influences. But He made no two men alike, and they best answer the ends of their being by keeping to the individuality and originality which God impresses upon their natures.

Mr. Spurgeon was Charles Haddon Spurgeon. No other person. His expressions were so original that his declarations are recognized anywhere. There was no danger of his being confounded with Cardinal Manning, Joseph Parker, or Henry Ward Beecher. These excellent preachers excelled him in some things, but he was their peer in originality. He was nature's nobleman, and nature had her perfect work.

When our schools and colleges can so adjust themselves to the needs of the age as to give to each student an open field for his individual genius, then shall we have a perfect system of education. Until then, many of our schools and theological institutions will serve in a measure to destroy much of the effectiveness of many persons who by nature are brilliant or gigantic.

We see, too, that his theological training in actual personal Christian work among all classes of people in all the different grades of religious teaching was a far better discipline for the real battle of his life than could have been the same number of months given him even in the halls of Cambridge or the University of Leipsic. Not that these great institutions are to be despised, but that if one must choose between the practical experience and impractical theory, reason always dictates that a person should take the practice.

Mr. Spurgeon's pastorate at Waterbeach lasted nearly two years. But it was a most valuable school, without which he could not have hoped to succeed in London. His youth and impetuosity made him a remarkable curiosity, and drew to the old church an immense audience, requiring on his part great variety of illustrations and appeal in order to win the souls of the different classes represented. His sincerity won for him the positive love of the church membership, and no matter what he might state or do, they were as blind to his faults as any lover can be.

He had not been long a pastor when there was held a Sunday-school convention at Cambridge, where he was especially invited to give a short address. But he was so busy in his own pastorate, and so anxious concerning some of the local enterprises connected with the church that he gave the address but little thought.

When his turn came to speak he felt that he had but little to say, and was wise enough to say that little in a few words and sit down. Here again we see, that, if he had taken more time and had more carefully prepared a cultured address, he would have failed to accomplish the great good which followed these few remarks. Not that any person can ever be excused from doing his best. Should a minister of the Gospel spend his time in amusement or laziness, then his impromptu remarks would be stale and disgraceful. But if his time is fully occupied with earnest practical Christian work, then in every case he can depend safely upon the promise of the Saviour, that it shall be given him what he shall say.

The best speeches, like the most noted specimens of oratory, are always inspired by the circumstances present, and are panoplied Minervas leaping forth from sudden and inspiring emotions awakened by a desire to do good. The hard worker, whose life is crowded with varied experiences in the severe conflicts with sin, is always a full man and usually ready to speak effectively on the shortest notice. His daily experience supplies him with themes and his actual practice makes him an authority on the subject.

What Mr. Spurgeon said to the Sunday-school scholars who were present at the assembly, or what advice he gave to the teachers he did not himself remember in after years, and every other person seems to have forgotten. But one listener was present who did not forget the boy, and who remembered especially his originality and independent way. That listener was the instrumentality which Providence used to take Charles to London, for a few weeks later he met one of the deacons of the church in London, of which Charles afterward became the pastor, and in conversation with the deacon, mentioned this precocious young man, stating that he was greatly impressed with his spiritual power and his excellent common sense. That conversation, though for a time forgotten by both of them, was afterward recalled by the deacon and led to the invitation of which we will speak further, in the next chapter.

It was during his first pastorate, at Waterbeach, when his name had been spread abroad far and wide as the "boy preacher," and while the aged shook their heads and the ungodly made sport, that he wrote a long and affectionate letter to his mother, the character of which may well be judged from the following extract:

"I am more and more glad that I never went to college. God sends such sunshine on my path, such smiles of grace, that I cannot regret if have forfeited all my prospects for it. I am conscious I held back from love and His cause, and I had rather be poor in His service than rich in my own.

I have all that heart can wish for; yea, God giveth more than my desires. My congregation is as great and loving as ever. During all the time that I have been at Waterbeach I have had a different hous for my home every day. Fifty-two families hav thus taken me in; and I have still six other invita tions not yet accepted. Talk about the people not caring for me because they give me so little! I dare tell anybody under heaven "tis false! They do all they can!"

CHAPTER V.

THE HISTORY OF HIS CHURCH.

The planting of a church is like the planting of a seed which is almost certain to grow into a tree, spreading its branches in beauty and beneficence at home and sending the fruit into every portion of the earth.

How incredulous the forefathers would have been had any prophet informed them that the New Park Street Baptist Church would become so influential for good and so widely known.

It had its origin far back in the days of persecution, when men paid for their opinions with property, pain, shame, and often death.

The founders of that Church over which Mr. Spurgeon eventually became the pastor were brave men who feared not the stake and who had often seen fires burning their co-religionists. It will be interesting and highly helpful in the study of Mr. Spurgeon's life to trace the history of this organization, in order that we may better understand the circumstances into which he was drawn when he went to London.

Mr. Spurgeon has himself furnished a complete and accurate history of the Tabernacle and the

Church, but he wrote at the time when many of the individuals were still living who welcomed him to London, and wrote when also conscious that the sons and grandsons of those who had acted a part in the history of that Church would read his book. No one writes without great restraint, under such circumstances, and while he need never state an untruth, yet all the truth is not to be spoken at all times.

One could heartily wish in the preparation of a story like this that some accurate records of the thoughts of Mr. Spurgeon himself might somewhere be found. But no such private diary seems to exist. The unwritten history of the Church, especially in the early days of Mr. Spurgeon's ministry, would furnish most interesting reading. The best, however, that can be done now is to gather up all the material he has left behind him into a connected and useful history.

Friends often forsook him, to which he indirectly refers. Enterprises promising well were often destroyed by some unkind act or by the foolishness of the managers. Expected gifts of money did not come at the time appointed, and some revivals did not furnish the harvest which was expected of them.

But, on the other side, he often received more than he expected in money, or friendship, and in every kind of success.

Such seems also to have been very largely the history of the pastorate which preceded his time.

It was ever the unexpected which was happening, and we may go further and say that such is the usual history of every Church, and human oversight is not able to arrange for the events which are almost certain to surprise both pastor and people, and yet without which there is no possible success in the work.

The successful church organization is the one which works on endeavoring to be guided by the Divine hand, and which regards nothing either encouraging or discouraging as at variance with the general Divine plan they may not then understand. The power which brought light out of the darkness brings harmony out of discord, and beauty out of wretchedness, also exhibits its characteristics in the conduct of the spiritual Church. That same power can often reverse the processes and send night or discord, and often does so in the spiritual history of mankind for reasons of good, unaccountable to us. Hence a glance at the condensed history of that Church as given by Mr. Spurgeon shows us a continued, but irregular series of advances and retreats. It will be well for the student of his life to read a portion of Mr. Spurgeon's statement concerning the history of the Church, before studying further his personal connection with it.

In his history of the Metropolitan Tabernacle Mr. Spurgeon said:

"When modest ministers submit their sermons to the press they usually place upon the title-page the words, 'Printed by request.' We might with emphatic truthfulness have pleaded this apology for the present narrative, for, times without number, friends from all parts of the world have said: 'Have you no book which will tell us all about your work? Could you not give us some printed summary of the Tabernacle history?' Here it is, dear friends, and we hope it will satisfy your curiosity and deepen your kindly interest."

"Dr. Stoughton tells us: 'By the Parliamentary ordinance of April, 1645, forbidding any person to preach who was not an ordained minister in the Presbyterian or some other reformed Church, all Baptist ministers became exposed to molestation, they being accounted a sect, and not a Church. A few months after the date of this law, the Baptists being pledged to a public controversy in London with Edmund Calamy, the Lord Mayor interfered to prevent the disputation—a circumstance which seems to show that, on the one hand, the Baptists were becoming a formidable body in London, and, on the other hand, that their fellow-citizens were highly exasperated against them.' Or, say rather, that the Lord Mayor's views not being those of the Baptists, he feared the sturdy arguments which would be brought to bear upon his friends, and concluded that the wisest course he could take was to prevent the truth being heard. No Lord Mayor, or even King, has any right to forbid free public speech, and when in past ages an official has done so, it is no evidence that his fellow-citizens were of the same mind : Jack-in-office is often peculiarly anxious that the consciences of others should not be injured by hearing views different from his own."

"From some one of the many Baptist assemblies which met in the borough of Southwark, the Tabernacle Church took its rise. Crosby says: 'This people had formerly belonged to one of the most ancient congregations of the Baptists in London, but separated from them, in the year 1652, for some practices which they judged disorderly, and kept together from that time as a distinct body.' They appeared to have met in private houses, or in such other buildings as were opened to them. Their first pastor was William Rider, whom Crosby mentions as a sufferer for conscience' sake, but he is altogether unable to give any further particulars of his life, except that he published a small tract in vindication of the practice of laying on of hands on the baptized believers. The people were few in number, but had the reputation of being men of solid judgment, deep knowledge, and religious stability, and many of them were also in easy circumstances as to worldly goods. Oliver Cromwell was just at that time in the ascendant, and Blake's cannon were sweeping the Dutch from the seas; but the Presbyterian establishment ruled with a heavy hand, and Baptists were under a cloud. In the following year Cromwell was made Protector, the old Parliament was sent about its business, and England enjoyed a measure of liberty of conscience."

"How long William Rider exercised the ministerial office we are unable to tell, but our next record bears date 1668, when we are informed that, 'the pastor having been dead for some time, they unanimously chose Mr. Benjamin Keach to be their elder or pastor.' Accordingly he was solemnly ordained with prayer and the laying on of hands in the year 1668, being in the twenty-eighth year of his age. Keach was one of the most notable of the pastors of our Church. He was continually engaged in preaching in the towns of Buckinghamshire, making Winslow his headquarters; and so well did the good cause flourish under his zealous labors, and those of others that the Government quartered dragoons in the district in order to put down unlawful meetings and stamp out dissent. The amount of suffering which this involved, the readers of the story of the Covenanting times in Scotland can readily imagine. A rough soldiery handle with little tenderness those whom they consider to be miserable fanatics. When the favorite court poet was lampooning these poor people and ridiculing their claims to be guided by the Spirit of God, common soldiers of the Cavalier order were not likely to be much under restraint in their behavior to them."

"Having written a book called *The Child's Instructor*, in which he avowed that children are born in sin, and in need of redemption by Jesus Christ, he was publicly tried and convicted. The merciful (?) judge pronounced upon the culprit the following sentence:—

"'Benjamin Keach, you are here convicted for writing, printing, and publishing a seditious and schismatical book, for which the court's judgment is this, and the court doth award: That you shall go to jail for a fortnight without bail or mainprize; and the next Saturday to stand trial upon the pillory at Aylesbury in the open market, from eleven o'clock till one, with a paper upon your head with the inscription: For writing, printing, and publishing a schismatical book, entitled *The Child's Instructor; or, a New and Easy Primer*. And the next Thursday to stand, in the same manner and for the same time, in the market at Winslow; and then your book shall be openly burnt before your face by the common hangman, in disgrace of you and your doctrine. And you shall forfeit to the King's majesty the sum of twenty pounds, and shall remain in jail until you find sureties for your good behavior, and for your appearance at the next assizes; then to renounce your doctrines, and make such public submission as shall be enjoined you. Take him away, keeper!'

"Keach simply replied, 'I hope I shall never renounce the truths which I have written in that book.'

"The attempts made to obtain a pardon or a relaxation of this severe sentence were ineffectual;

THE UNJUST SENTENCE.

and the sheriff took care that everything should be punctually performed.

"When he was brought to the pillory at Aylesbury, several of his religious friends and acquaintances accompanied him; and when they bemoaned his hard case and the injustice of his sufferings, he said, with a cheerful countenance, 'The cross is the way to the crown.' His head and hands were no sooner placed in the pillory, but he began to address himself to the spectators, to this effect: 'Good people, I am not ashamed to stand here this day with this paper on my head! My Lord Jesus was not ashamed to suffer on the cross for me; and it is for His cause that I am made a gazing-stock. Take notice, it is not for any wickedness than I. stand here; but for writing and publishing those truths which the Spirit of the Lord hath revealed in the Holy Scriptures.'

"Very sweetly did Mr. Keach preach the great fundamental truths of the Gospel, and glorify the name and work of Jesus. His *Gospel's Mine Opened*, and other works rich in savor, show that he was no mere stickler for a point of ceremony, but one who loved the whole truth as it is in Jesus, and felt its power. The doctrine of the Second Advent evidently had great charms for him, but not so as to crowd out Christ crucified. He was very solid in his preaching, and his whole conduct and behavior betokened a man deeply in earnest for the cause of God. In addressing the ungodly he was intensely direct, solemn, and impressive, not flinching to declare the terrors of the Lord, nor veiling the freeness of Divine grace. He was a voluminous writer, having written in all forty-three works—eighteen practical, sixteen polemical, and nine poetical. Some of them were very popular, having reached the twenty-second edition."

"Mr. Keach was of a very weak constitution, being often afflicted with illness, and once to such a degree that he was given over by the physicians; and several of the ministers and his relations had taken their leave of him as a dying man and past all hope of recovery; but the Rev. Mr. Hanserd Knollys, seeing his friend and brother in the gospel so near expiring, betook himself to prayer, and in a very extraordinary manner begged that God would spare him, and add unto his days the time He granted to His servant Hezekiah. As soon as he had ended his prayer, he said, ' Brother Keach, I shall be in heaven before you,' and quickly after left him. So remarkable was the answer of God to this good man's prayer that we cannot omit it; though it may be discredited by some, there were some who could bear incontestable testimony to the fact. Mr. Keach recovered from that illness, and lived just fifteen years afterward; and then it pleased God to visit him with that short sickness which put an end to his days. ' He fell on sleep' July 16th, 1704, in the sixty-fourth year of his age, and was buried at the Baptists' burying-ground, in the Park, Southwark. It was not a little singular that in after years the church over which he so ably presided should pitch its tent so near the place where his bones were laid, and New Park Street should appear in her annals as a well-beloved name."

"When Mr. Keach was upon his death-bed he sent for his son-in-law, Benjamin Stinton, and solemnly charged him to care for the Church which he was about to leave, and especially urged him to accept the pastoral office, should it be offered him by the brethren. Mr. Stinton had already for some years helped his father-in-law in many ways, and therefore he was no new and untried man. It is no small blessing when a church can find her pastors in her own midst; the rule is to look abroad, but perhaps if our home gifts were more encouraged the Holy Spirit would cause our teachers to come forth more frequently from among our own brethren. Still, we cannot forget the proverb about a prophet in his own country. When the Church gave Mr. Stinton a pressing invitation, he delayed awhile, and gave himself space for serious consideration; but at length, remembering the dying words of his father-in-law, and feeling himself directed by the Spirit of God, he gave himself up to the ministry, which he faithfully discharged for fourteen years—namely, from 1704 to 1718."

"Spending himself in various works of usefulness, Mr. Stinton worked on till the 11th of February, 1718, when a sudden close was put to his labors and his life. He was taken suddenly ill, and saying to his wife, 'I am going,' he laid himself down upon the bed, and expired in the forty-third year of his life. He smiled on death, for the Lord smiled on him. He was buried near his predecessor, in the Park, Southwark."

" In the beginning of the year 1719, the Church at Horsleydown invited John Gill to preach, with a view to the pastorate ; but there was a determined opposition to him in about one-half of the church. The matter was referred to the club of ministers meeting at the Hanover Coffee-house, and they gave the absurd advice that the two parties should each hear their own man turn about till they could agree. Common sense came to the rescue, and this sort of religious duel never came off. The friends with far greater wisdom, divided. John Gill's friends secured the old meeting-house for the term of forty years, and he was ordained March 22d, 1720."

"Little did the friends dream what sort of a man they had thus chosen to be their teacher ; but had they known it they would have rejoiced that a man of such vast erudition, such indefatigable industry, such sound judgment, and such sterling honesty had come among them. He was to be more mighty with his pen than Keach, and to make a deeper impression upon his age, though perhaps with the tongue he was less powerful than his eminent predecessor. Early in his ministry he had to take up the cudgels for Baptist views against a Pædobaptist preacher of Rowel, near Kettering, and he did so in a manner worthy of that eulogium which Toplady passed upon him in reference to other controversies, when he compared him to Marlborough, and declared that he never fought a battle without winning it."

"Mr. Gill, being settled in London, became more intimately acquainted with that worthy minister of the gospel, Mr. John Skepp, pastor of the Baptist Church at Cripplegate. This gentleman, though he had not a liberal education, yet, after he came into the ministry, through great diligence acquired a larger acquaintance with the Hebrew tongue. As Mr. Gill had previously taken great delight in the Hebrew, his conversation with this worthy minister rekindled a flame of fervent desire to obtain a more extensive knowledge of it, and especially of Rabbinical learning. Mr. Skepp dying a year or two after, Mr. Gill purchased most of his Hebrew works, the Baptist Fund making him a grant of eighty-seven dollars for this purpose. Having obtained the books, he went to work with great eagerness, reading the Targums and ancient commentaries, and in a course of between twenty and thirty years' acquaintance with these writings he collected a large number of learned observations. Having also, in this time, gone through certain books of the Old Testament, and almost the whole of the New Testament, by way of exposition, in the course of his ministry, he put all the expository, critical, and illustrative parts together

9

and in the year 1745 issued proposals for publishing his *Exposition of the whole New Testament*, in three volumes folio. The work meeting due encouragement, it was put to press the same year, and was finished, the first volume in 1746, the second in 1747, and the third in 1748. Toward the close of the publication of this work, in 1748, Mr. Gill received a diploma from Marischal College, Aberdeen, creating him Doctor in Divinity on account of his knowledge of the Scriptures, of the Oriental language, and of Jewish antiquities. When his deacons in London congratulated him on the respect which had been shown him he thanked them, pleasantly adding, "I neither thought it, nor bought it, nor sought it.'"

"The ministry of Mr. Gill being acceptable not only to his own people but to many persons of different denominations, several gentlemen proposed among themselves to set up a week-day lecture, that they might have an opportunity of hearing him. Accordingly they formed themselves into a society, and agreed to have a lecture on Wednesday evenings, in Great Eastcheap, and set on foot a subscription to support it. Upon their invitation Mr. Gill undertook the lectureship. He opened it the year 1729 with a discourse or two on Psalm lxxi, 16: 'I will go in the strength of the Lord God: I will make mention of Thy righteousness, even of Thine only.' Through divine grace he was enabled to abide by this resolution to the edification of many, preaching in Great Eastcheap for more than twenty·

six years, and only relinquished the lectures when the infirmities of years were telling upon him, and he felt a great desire to give all his time to the completion of his great expository works."

"As a pastor he presided over the flock with dignity and affection. In the course of his ministry he had some weak, some unworthy, and some very wicked persons to deal with. To the feeble of the flock he was an affectionate friend and father. He readily bore with their weaknesses, failings, and infirmities, and particularly when he saw they were sincerely on the Lord's side. A godly woman visited him one day, in great trouble, about the singing, for the clerk, in about three years, had introduced two new tunes. Not that he was a famous singer, or able to conduct a great variety of song, but he did his best. The young people were pleased with the new tunes; but the good woman could not bear the innovation. The Doctor, after patiently listening, asked her whether she understood singing? 'No,' she said. 'What! can't you sing?' No, she was no singer, nor her aged father before her. And though they had had about a hundred years between them to learn the Old Hundredth tune, they could not sing it, nor any other tune. The Doctor did not hurt her feelings by telling her that people who did not understand singing were the last who should complain; but he meekly said: 'Sister, what tunes should you like us to sing?' 'Why, sir,' she replied, 'I would very much like David's tunes.'

'Well,' said he, 'if you will get David's tunes for us, we can then try to sing them.' Such weak good people may be found among all denominations of Christians."

"All the stories told of Dr. Gill are somewhat grim. He could not come down to the level of men and women of the common order so far as to be jocose; and when he attempted to do so he looked like Hercules with the distaff, or Goliath threading a needle. When he verged upon the humorous the jokes were ponderous and overwhelming, burying his adversary as well as crushing him. It is said that a garrulous dame once called upon him to find fault with the excessive length of his white bands. 'Well, well,' said the Doctor, 'what do you think is the right length? Take them and make them as long or as short as you like.' The lady expressed her delight; she was sure that her dear pastor would grant her request, and therefore she had brought her scissors with her, and would do the trimming at once. Accordingly, snip, snip, and the thing was done, and the bibs returned. 'Now,' said the Doctor, 'my good sister, you must do me a good turn also.' 'Yes, that I will, Doctor. What can it be?' 'Well, you have something about you which is a deal too long, and causes me no end of trouble, and I should like to see it shorter.' 'Indeed, dear sir, I will not hesitate,' said the dame; 'what is it? Here are the scissors, use them as you please.' 'Come then,' said the pastor, 'good sister, put out

"Good Sister, put out your Tongue."

your tongue!' We have often pictured him sitting in the old chair, which is preserved in our vestry, and thus quietly rebuking the gossip."

"The comparative asperity of his manner was probably the result of his secluded habits, and also of that sturdy firmness of mind, which in other directions revealed itself so admirably. When he was once warned that the publication of a certain book would lose him many supporters and reduce his income, he did not hesitate for a moment, but replied: 'Do not tell me of losing. I value nothing in comparison with gospel truth. I am not afraid to be poor!'"

"The mighty commentator having been followed to his grave by his attached Church and a great company of ministers and Christian people, among whom he had been regarded as a great man and a prince in Israel, his Church began to look around for a successor. This time, as in the case of Dr. Gill, there was trouble in store, for there was division of opinion. Some no doubt, as true Gillites looked only for a solid divine, sound in doctrine, who would supply the older saints with spiritual food; while another party had an eye to the growth of the Church and to the securing to the flock the younger members of their families. They were agreed that they would write to Bristol for a probationer, and Mr. John Rippon was sent to them. He was a youth of some twenty summers, of a vivacious temperment, quick and bold. The older members judged him to be too young and too flighty ; they even accused him of having gone up the pulpit stairs two steps at a time on some occasions when he was hurried—a grave offense for which the condemnation could hardly be too severe. He was only a young man and came from an academy, and this alone was enough to make the sounder and older members afraid of him. He preached for a lengthened time on probation, and finally some forty persons withdrew because they could not agree with the enthusiastic vote by which the majority of the people elected him."

"John Rippon modestly expressed his wonder that even more had not been dissatisfied, and his surprise that so large a number were agreed to call him to the pastorate. In the spirit of forbearance and brotherly love he proposed that, as these friends were seceding for conscience' sake, and intended to form themselves into another Church, they should be lovingly dismissed with prayer and God-speed, and that as a token of fraternal love they should be assisted to build a meeting-house for their own conscience, and the sum of fifteen hundred dollars should be voted to them when their Church was formed and their meeting-house erected. The promise was re deemed, and Mr. Rippon took part in the ordination services of the first minister. This was well done. Such a course was sure to secure the blessing of God. The church in Dean Street thus became another offshoot from the parent stem, and with varying conditions it remains to this day as the church in Trinity Street, Borough.

" He will be best known as having prepared the first really good selection of hymns for dissenting congregations. Although a Baptist collection, it was extensively used with Dr. Watts's among both classes of Congregationalists. This work was an estate to its author, and he is said to have been more than sufficiently eager to push its sale. One thing we know, his presents of nicely bound copies must have been pretty frequent, for we have seen several greatly prized by their aged owners, who have shown them to us, with the remark, 'The dear old Doctor gave me that himself.' "

" The happy eccentricity of the Doctor's character may be illustrated by a little incident in connection with royalty. He was deputed to read an address from the Dissenters to George III, congratulating him upon recovery from sickness. The Doctor read on with his usual clear utterance till, coming to a passage in which there was special reference to the goodness of God, he paused and said: ' Please your Majesty, we will read that again,' and then proceeded with his usual cool dignity to repeat the sentence with emphasis. No other man in the deputation would have thought of doing such a thing, but from Rippon it came so naturally that no one censured him, or if they did it would have had no effect upon him."

" There are still some in the Church who cherish

his memory with affectionate and well-deserved reverence; and there are thousands in Heaven who were led first to love the Saviour by his earnest exhortations. He quarried fresh stones, and built up the Church. He molded its thoughts and directed its energies. Without being great he was exceedingly useful, and the period in which he was one of the judges of our Israel was one of great prosperity in spiritual things. It was a good sixty-three years, and with the previous pastorate of Dr. Gill, enabled the Church to say that during one hundred and seventeen years they had been presided over by two ministers only. Those who are given to change were not numerous in the community. Short pastorates are good when ministers are feeble, but it is a great blessing when the saints are so edified that all are content, and the ministry is so owned of God that vacancies are filled up even before they are felt: in such a case change would wantonly imperil the hope of continued prosperity, and would therefore be criminal."

"The next pastor of our Church was Mr.—now Doctor—Joseph Angus, a gentleman whose career since he left us to become secretary of the Baptist Missionary Society, and afterward the tutor of Stepney Academy, now Regent's Park College, has rendered his name most honorable among living Baptists. He is one of the foremost classical scholars, and is a member of the committee for producing a revised version of the Holy Scriptures.

He is the author of those standard books, *The Bible Handbook, The Handbook of the English Tongue, and Handbook of English Literature.*"

"Mr. James Smith succeeded Dr. Angus, and after a useful pastorate of eight years resigned on account of ill health. In October, 1849, he wrote: 'For a considerable time I have felt an oppression on my chest, and great difficulty in breathing. Last week I consulted a doctor upon it, and he advised me to leave London as soon as I could, and get into the country, as my lungs required a purer air. I am seeking wisdom from God: I cannot doubt but He will guide me.'"

"In February, 1850, he said: 'I have written my resignation of office, and laid it before the deacons. It is a serious and important step which I have taken. I trust I have taken it in a proper spirit, and from a right motive. My mind is now calm and peaceful, the agitation from which I have long been suffering is at an end, and I feel as if I could now leave the matter with the Lord."

"'When my resignation was accepted, the Church passed a very kind and affectionate resolution regretting that I felt it necessary to take such a step; but as I had rested it pretty much on the state of my health, they did not feel that they could refuse to accede to my wishes. I cannot say that I have labored in vain here, for many souls have been converted, some backsliders have been restored, and between four hundred and five hundred members have been added to the Church during my pastorate of eight years. Many of my poor people deeply feel the step which I have felt it my duty to take, and I have received very affectionate letters from several of them. May they soon be favored with a pastor more suitable and efficient than I have been.'"

"Mr. Smith built up in Cheltenham the strong working Church now meeting in Cambray Chapel, which was erected by his exertions. When he was lying upon his dying bed the Church at the Tabernacle sent him a heartily affectionate letter, and gratefully reminded him of all the blessings which the Lord had bestowed upon many souls by his means. To this we received a delightful answer, assuring us that our words had greatly cheered him. He died in 1861, and an account of an interview with him may interest the reader if we include it in our pages. 'I saw this week the former pastor of this Church, Mr. James Smith, of Cheltenham. About a year ago he was struck with paralysis, and one-half of his body is dead. But yet I have seldom seen a more cheerful man in the full hey-day of strength. I had been told that he was the subject of very fearful conflicts at times; so after I had shaken hands with him, I said: 'Friend Smith, I hear you have many doubts and fears!' 'Who told you that?' he said, 'for I have none.' 'Never have any? Why I understood you had many conflicts.' 'Yes,' he said, 'I have many conflicts, but I have no doubts; I have many wars within, but I have no fears. Who could have told you that? I hope I have not led any one to think that. It is a hard battle, but the victory is sure.' Then he said in his own way, 'I am just like a packet that is all ready to go by train, packed, corded, labelled, paid for, and on the platform, waiting for the express to come by and take me to glory. I wish I could hear the whistle now.'"

"In July, 1851, the Church invited the Rev. William Walters, of Preston, to become the pastor, but as he understood the deacons to intimate to him that his ministry was not acceptable, he tendered his resignation, and although requested to remain, he judged it more advisable to remove to Halifax in June, 1853, thus closing a ministry of two years. These changes sadly diminished the Church and marred its union. The clouds gathered heavily, and no sunlight appeared."

Mr. Spurgeon's record is necessarily very much condensed, and very wisely omits the most interesting incidents concerning the history of individuals connected with the Church and showing their self-sacrifices. Some of these incidents which occurred during Mr. Spurgeon's early years in the pastorate of the Tabernacle have been recorded by others and frequently related in public by persons acquainted with the circumstances.

One of the most helpful workers in the building of the Tabernacle and who secured very large subscriptions from his friends to pay the debt when the building was dedicated, was found by Mr. Spurgeon, years before, on a wretched bed in poverty, afflicted with what was considered to be a fatal disease. Mr. Spurgeon received an anonymous letter calling his attention to this sad case, and while, as a rule, he did not read such letters, or follow their advice, in that case he made the suggested visit upon the poor and afflicted young man. The young man recovered his health soon after and was secured employment by the influence of Mr. Spurgeon, and he proved to be one of the best business men in that part of London.

At another time he received a large accession to the membership from another denomination owing to a bitter quarrel which raged in the Church to which they had belonged. Mr. Spurgeon kept them waiting for some weeks, making them frequently a subject for prayer, before he would consent that they should be received by the Church; he having had a very strong suspicion that they were joining his Church more out of spite than because they loved the Lord; yet it proved to be one of the greatest blessings that ever came to the enterprise. For among the number were some of the sincerest, noblest Christian characters and some of the most generous givers in the latter years of his life.

An old fish woman frequently visited his home, after his marriage, with whom Mr. Spurgeon conversed upon the matter of her soul's salvation. She answered him abruptly, and with great rudeness declared that she had no interest in any of those things, as religion "was made for fine people, or for those who had no money to lose." That same fish woman before her death, insisted on sending her daughter to Mr. Spurgeon's Sabbath-school, where she was converted and where she joined the Church. That fish woman's son-in-law was a very influential member of this Church, a strong supporter of the college, and is often referred to by the students who leave the college as one of their dearest friends and one in whom they put the most implicit confidence whenever his advice is given.

A boatman on the Thames, whose boat sprung a leak through some accident, received a suggestion from Mr. Spurgeon for caulking it without great expense. One friend says that Mr. Spurgeon not only paid for the material but went to the boat with a caulking knife and showed the boatman how to do the work. That boatman's brother was afterward a member of the House of Commons and for months regularly worshiped at the Tabernacle.

One woman with a little child in her arms wandered into the meeting in 1856 and the baby cried so as to disturb the people, and she was kindly invited into one of the vestry-rooms by the officer of the Church. Mrs. Spurgeon and a committee of ladies were at the time in the vestry, attending to some Church matters. They entered into conversation with the woman and especially noticing the baby and assisted in quieting its cries.

The woman's report to her uncle of Mrs. Spurgeon's kindness brought him to the Church as a curious visitor, which resulted in his uniting with the Church and becoming one of the most efficient missionaries sent out for the local missions.

One woman made Mrs. Spurgeon a present of some fancy cooking, and a letter which she wrote in acknowledgment of the kindness was received by the family after the hand which had made the cookies was cold in death. The family at once sent for Mr. Spurgeon to attend the funeral, and there he had conversation with the husband, who became a member of his Church and was afterward a very effective minister in Germany, where he preached the gospel for ten years.

When the Tabernacle was being constructed, Mr. Spurgeon and some of the officers of the Church held prayer-meetings as they knelt in the midst of the accumulating material which was not yet in place. A young man standing by altogether unnoticed by them, made inquiries of a police officer concerning what was being done, and afterward related the incident to friends in New York. It was directly or indirectly from these New York friends that Mr. Spurgeon received quite a large gift in connection with the establishment of the Orphanage. We have never been able to trace the history of the young man who witnessed their prayer, but have often heard the fact referred to in England.

Mr. Spurgeon, one day in 1858, sent an old Bible

A Practical Preacher.

to be rebound. It was either a keepsake in the family or else it was a volume made valuable because it was antique. The binding was delayed for several weeks because the binder had broken his arm. Mr. Spurgeon called at last for the book, and, finding it not finished at the second visit, asked that he might take it away to some other place. It was then for the first time that he ascertained the real reason why the book had not been bound before, and when he returned to his study he wrote a letter of condolence to the binder, and told him to keep the book until he was able to bind it. That book-binder's son is one of the most eloquent graduates of Spurgeon's college, now having a Church in the United States.

One man who had been addicted largely to drink, who had reformed under Mr. Spurgeon's personal solicitation, afterward became quite wealthy and in-sisted on presenting Mr. Spurgeon with a horse and carriage. When the gift was declined, he turned the money into the treasury of the Orphanage.

An insane man entered one of their social meet-ings at the Church and created a great disturbance, one evening in 1857. Public officers were called in, and he was removed and continued calling out that the Lord had impressed upon him the necessity of killing all the people in the Church. A little later an advertisement appeared in a newspaper asking for information concerning an insane person whose de-scription seemed to show him to be the same man who had so greatly disturbed the religious meetings, and who had been declared to be insane by the authorities. A young man in Mr. Spurgeon's Sunday-school called his attention to the advertisement, and he answered it, telling the friend who advertised where to procure the information from the public authorities. The man afterward entirely recovered, went to Australia, where he prospered in business, and where his sister died, leaving in her trunk the letter from Mr. Spurgeon. When the gentleman found that letter among the effects of his much-beloved sister, he was greatly moved by it, and especially, as he had frequently heard of Mr. Spurgeon and but a few days before had listened to a sermon by one of the students from the College. He wrote to Mr. Spurgeon, expressing his great gratitude for the kindness he had done him by showing his friends where he could be found, and inclosed a check for $100 to be used by Mr. Spurgeon himself or devoted to any beneficence he might think best. His name appears twice afterward in the list of donors toward the work of the Tabernacle, but how much he contributed cannot be now well ascertained.

But his experience was not all of this fruitful character, for, like all other public men, he attracted to him a great many swindlers and beggars, who were only anxious to get from his large heartedness and open-handedness all they could and then to leave him to reflect in sadness upon the depraved character of human nature.

One man in 1861 visited him, who claimed to be from America, whose tongue was so smooth, and whose manners were so gentlemanly that he entirely deceived Mr. Spurgeon. The villain prayed most touchingly, exhorted with success, and was frequently sent out by Mr. Spurgeon to mission stations, there to assist in public and personal Christian work among the lower classes. Mr. Spurgeon recommended him without fear to the business men connected with his congregation, and by means of these recommendations he secured quite large sums in subscriptions toward the Church work, which he used entirely for his own benefit. He forged Mr. Spurgeon's signature, and even passed counterfeit money. He left Mr. Spurgeon much wiser, but very much poorer.

Thus, like a pendulum, swinging to and fro, Mr. Spurgeon's experience swept from the sad to the gay, from the sorrowful to the joyful; or from loss to gain, in such unexpected and unforeseen ways.

CHAPTER VI.

What is the highest joy? We heard that question asked once in a travelers' camp on the Tigris River, and the whole evening was most excitedly devoted to the question. No two persons agreed upon that situation or that experience which would bring to a person in this life the highest joy.

Some said it was at the marriage altar; some said it was in the accomplishment of a life-long ambition; others said it was in the peace of a contented life; a few said it was to be found in traveling; while others mentioned books, good company, wealth, fame, and intoxication. But the conditions of life which seemed to receive the most unanimous assent of the company as containing in them attributes of the supremest joy were those of the Greek racer, who at the moment of victory reaches forth and touches the goal, or he, who amidst the awful excitement of heated battle, unconscious of danger and forgetful of self, succeeds in seizing the flag of the enemy, and waves his own in triumph over the captured battlements.

150

On such a question men might well disagree, for it is with men's pleasures as with their judgments and watches,

"None go just alike,
Yet each believes his own."

The lawyer finds untold satisfaction in a successful verdict, the sailor in a safe harbor, the mechanic in the triumph of a useful invention, the author in the praise of his books, the musician in the plaudits of his listeners, statesmen in a majority of votes, and the warrior in the hour of victory. But none of these appear to touch the heights of bliss or the depths of happiness which come to the orator speaking for God, when thousands hang upon his words, and characters are changed under his influence. Can there be on this wide earth any other inspiration like it? It combines all the gratifications of achievement, all the bliss of satisfied affection, all the triumph of a soldier, all the exaltation of spirit of the religious devotee. In speaking for God, with the angels of heaven listening, when one finds that the Spirit inspires and hearts are changed, he is at the very point of the noblest victory, as life is better than meat, as purity of heart is more lovable than wickedness, as happiness is more beautiful than misery, as love is more exalted than hate, and as forgetfulness of self in the welfare of others is a sublimer feeling than is personal gratification, so is the delivery of the good tidings of peace, the deeds which save life are grander, nobler and more inspiring than those which destroy.

The disciple of Christ whose soul is filled with spiritual enthusiasm, and who sees that the multitude accepts his message as the truth, really occupies a position of the highest joy. He rises above himself, seems to become ethereal, heavenly, eternal. He feels as though he held converse with the angels, and as though the powers of God were his own. If he is ill, he forgets it; if in pain, he becomes unconscious of it; if awkward, he cares not for it; lost in his theme, conscious only of the battle and the nearness of triumph, bone, muscle, and nerves become only myriad centres of exquisite sensations, sublime and thrilling, until language is entirely inadaquate to express the feelings. Men struggle to describe such sensations in their cooler moments but utterly fail to convey an idea to one who has never experienced that highest joy.

Mr. Spurgeon's life must have been a very happy life when we remember how many thousand sermons he delivered to large audiences who hung spell-bound upon his words, as upon the oracle of a god. Who turned away from his declarations new men and women to lead a life of holiness, purity, and truth, instead of one of vice and crime.

He who writes sermons in the coolness and quietness of his study, and then presents the clean and perfect manuscript at the Church service, or who reads with manufactured emotion the sentences he has written by the calm of his fireside, is never so effective nor so happy in his delivery of the gospel to the people as he who sweeps spontaneously into the highest happiness that men ever reach. The sunset hues were never painted, nor were the Christian orator's joys ever described. Mr. Spurgeon was a true Christian orator, and often fought his battles on a different plan of campaign from those which other leaders adopted, but he won the victory.

Oratory should always be decided by its effects, and the supreme pleasure of public speaking can only be truly enjoyed by him who succeeds.

Mr. Spurgeon, as we have said, was often rude, and affected none of the ways of the schools of oratory extant in his day, but he could so speak as to cause the hearts of those who heard him to rise or sink, to fill many eyes with tears, to pull down the stubborn sinners' heads, and to send forth to the noblest deeds of self-sacrifice a host of effective workers, who when they first came under the spell of his speech were cruel to man, and rebellious against God. He was a well-directed thunder-bolt, whose course to the spectator seemed zig-zag and erratic, yet who always cleft the rock at the selected mark. Judging by the results, he was one of the greatest orators that ever lived, not exceeded by Luther, Wesley, or Webster.

The enormous moral results of his public teaching lead us to the almost unavoidable conclusion that he had behind his words an inspiration beyond that which is given to the ordinary man. It is true that he began his pastorate in London at a time in life when his boyish appearance would make attendance upon the service a novelty. It is also true that his complete confidence in himself, which was born of a confidence in God, caused him to speak as one having authority, adding greatly to the singularity of his position. Many came to scoff, but remained to pray, many sought entrance for the purpose of criticizing, but went away to praise. Some who were sent into his audience for the purpose of manufacturing especially satirical cartoons, went away to represent truthfully, in picture and writing, the remarkable scenes they witnessed.

Yet persecution helped him greatly. Those who would not hear him, regarded him with great aversion, and thought that his peculiarities were almost sacrilegious. He was for a time most mercilessly assailed by Christians belonging to other Churches, and most grossly laughed at by the lower publications of London. But nothing builds up a Church like persecution. Often in history has some most egregious error and insanely fantastic creed been established by continuous opposition and hate, beyond the power of governments to overthrow it. Some evangelists understand this power, and scruple not to use it, awakening against themselves criticism, persecution, and discussion, that there may be excitement and the consequent crowd of hearers. Some men who have accomplished a great deal of good make it their habit to begin a series of religious meetings by such extreme criticisms of Christians as to attract large crowds of spectators from among those classes who love to hear Church members berated. Then the speakers turn upon these listeners, and with all their forces teach them the way and convict them of transgression.

Mr. Spurgeon adopted none of these mechanical methods, but his very vehemence and startling success awakened most bitter jealousies, and aroused a spirit of persecution which in the Middle Ages would have burned him at the stake. His sermons were often misquoted and his deeds misrepresented, and he himself personally caricatured in most repulsive forms. He appeared in some of the periodicals as a monkey, as a fly-trap, as a serpent, as a pig, and once as Satan himself. But all these advertised him largely, and proved ultimately to be of great good to the cause. His friends loved him more sincerely, and rallied around him with greater determination. The converted scoffers, revilers, and persecutors became naturally most daring workers in defense of the cause they had before despised.

Persons sought Christ at almost every service, and it would have caused great surprise if a week had passed at any one time without a number of conversions.

In the preparation of his sermons, Mr. Spurgeon

seems to have practiced most thoroughly the system of reasoning from the known to the unknown. The attractiveness of his sermons and speeches is found very largely in the fact that his illustrations and subjects were intimately connected with every-day events, and were well known in the experience of his hearers. He did not borrow very largely from the ancient classics, or from some scientific theory with which his hearers were unacquainted, but made his meaning clear with illuminating figures from the homely experiences of farmers, mechanics, tradesmen, clerks, and officials. His sermons were talks, not declamations. He spoke to men in masses as he would speak to them in personal conversation. He did not often hitch his wagon to a star, but we do often find the most homely steed of daily experience running between the shafts. His *John Plough-man Talks*, exhibited the more rude and homely side of his illustrative power, and also serve to account for his genius in describing and holding the attention of the country people. He did not purchase an article in the market without associating the event of his humble experience there with some gospel truth. Every child that hugged his knees and every working man who doffed his hat taught Mr. Spurgeon more than he taught them. Men were books to him, and events were God's volumes of illustrations. While in a street bus or a hansom, he continually read in the shops which he passed, or in the throng through which he drove, the prophecies, needs, and exertions of a new dispensation. The chilly fog, the black smoking chimneys, the slow-rolling Thames, and the winter sleet were volumes to him, closely read and most carefully digested. If a man entered the Church service covered with sleet, or chilled with fog, Mr. Spurgeon would be sure to use that condition as an illustration of the position of the sinner or the backsliding Christian. If the morning sun broke suddenly through the dark clouds, brightening the windows of the chapel, he would instantly turn that good omen into a never-to-be-forgotten illustration of the nearness of God's presence. If he knocked a glass of water off the table, or was obliged to limp into his pulpit, he found in these circumstances the most piercing illustration of truth and used them in his most powerful application of Scripture teaching to the lives of his hearers. Even his finger-nails were found to contain an illuminating power which astonished those who heard him as he made the application to his thoughts.

He was one who not only found books in running brooks, sermons in stones, but one who also found good in everything, when applied to his profession. The daily paper with its regular record of births, deaths, marriages, accidents, crimes, and markets was to him a whole volume from which he could select the most wonderful and helpful illustrative incidents. He lived among men, he sympathized with them. He felt as they feel, and he talked as they talk, thus connecting the most ordinary affairs of every-day work with some gospel truth in a way which made it impossible for them to pursue their usual vocation and forget what he had said.

The regular worshiper at Spurgeon's Tabernacle, if she were a woman, would be reminded of his exhortations by almost every instrument she afterward used in the kitchen, and by nearly every dish or preparation she set upon the table. One old lady while living in Halifax, Nova Scotia, actually named the dishes used upon the table after some of the sermons, lectures, or talks of Mr. Spurgeon, so that the teapot suggested one phase of election, and the soup-dish brought to mind a sermon on God's sovereignty. He put a halo upon common things, making home life and shop life more interesting and delightful because of the associations into which he drew the tools and articles there in constant use. The farmer puts on his frock and calls to mind Mr. Spurgeon's illustration of Elijah and Elisha, he puts his hand to the plow, and cannot forget Mr. Spurgeon's ringing exhortation not to look back. The sailor reefing the sails in expectation of a coming blow, reads in every knot which he ties, and every fold which he gathers about the beam some section of Mr. Spurgeon's sermons or lectures. The cabman names his horse and vehicle in honor of some illustration associated with them, which he has heard in the metropolitan pulpit. The school-boy takes down his hat from the peg, and smiling, quotes from

Mr. Spurgeon, "this hat fits me and I will put it on." The school-girl carefully erases the pencil marks on the margin of the well-thumbed book, saying to her playmate, "Mr. Spurgeon said the other day that 'children are like school-books, what they write in the margin is theirs, what is printed in the text is God's.'" A girl in the Sunday-school tears her dress and is almost superstitiously anxious about it, because of the association with some incident Mr. Spurgeon has given, wherein the rent garment of repentant sinners is mentioned in the Bible.

The rocker squeaks in an old man's chair, and he tells his visitors that it reminds him of what he heard Mr. Spurgeon say the last time he was at Church, as he compared bigotry to a rocking-chair, saying that "the older the chair, the greater the squeak." The banker, counting his money at the close of the day's exchanges, throws out a well-worn sovereign, and says Mr. Spurgeon tells us to beware of light sovereigns. Then he goes home from his bank meditating upon the wonderful aptness of the illustration, applies its teaching to his life. He determines to do his full duty and slight nothing, and anything which he does at all he has resolved to do well. The emigrant in Australia constructs his rude cabin upon his newly-cleared farm, and tells his family at the dinner-table that he is going to do what Mr. Spurgeon advises his theological students to do, namely: to "Go around the stumps and let them rot." The young man far from home in Canada or in the United States, who at home was a frequent listener to Mr. Spurgeon, never forgets the illustration the great preacher used when speaking of the prodigal son, wherein he said: "England's prodigals wander all over the world, but, thank God! many of them are not feeding swine." An old cripple, well-known to the writer, who has for many years regularly read Mr. Spurgeon's sermons, sits month after month by the same window, unable to leave the room, and frequently speaks to the house-keeper, saying: "Please brush the dust from this glass, for Mr. Spurgeon says: 'Specks which seem to be on the soul are often in the glass.'"

Mr. Spurgeon had a natural treasure in the most wonderful voice. He could speak so loud and clear that it has been confidently asserted that at least twelve thousand people have heard it at one time in the open air. Although his voice was so loud, it also was very sympathetic, and easily modulated to the expression of all the varied shades of meaning to which he would give utterance. His voice would sometimes rise to a trumpet blast, and in the next few sentences sink to the cooing of a dove, there was something in the very tone, which, like White-field's, was "felt to be holy," and conveyed an inspiration or elevation of thought entirely distant from the sense.

He was not a musician, and his ideas of musical culture were considered by many to be very inartistic. But his voice itself contained a fund of music, and was capable of many more musical expressions than could be found in the rise and fall or variety of a church organ. His voice was said to be as clear in its head tones as that of a soprano singer, but at will became like that of a lion in the mountain. Yet he seldom combined all its powers in any one address, and it was only to the habitual listeners that these marvelous vocal powers were fully appreciated or even known.

He was not an elocutionist. He accomplished naturally all for which the academician strived to attain by art. Few voices are capable of expressing the great variety of ideas and feelings which characterized Mr. Spurgeon's. The elocutionist is required to cover the hidden defects as much as to develop the many prominent merits of the human voice. Mr. Spurgeon's voice could not be improved.

It is interesting to compare the doctrinal statements of prominent theologians at different periods in their lives and see how in nearly every case they have been gradually but surely molded into widely differing expressions, their essential beliefs undergoing a gradual and sometimes a very remarkable change. When their first sermons are placed alongside of the last, they are found to be far from each other in all that makes up a doctrinal creed. But it is a most singular thing in the life of Mr. Spurgeon that the fundamental principles of the doctrines which he espoused in his early boyhood were adhered to with such consistency and persistency through his entire life. The denomination itself passed through many modifications and changes during his ministerial experiences, and often swung like a pendulum from one point to another, leaving him ever standing at the same middle point of vantage. The comparison of the sermons last published with those which appeared in 1856 and 1858, show no change whatever in the doctrines, and no material change in the form of presentation of the doctrines, save to make them more distinct, and express a firmer adherence to their principles. It is a matter so remarkable that it amounts to a wonder that through a life in which he delivered so many thousand sermons, he should have maintained such consistency with himself, his denomination and doctrines. He was strongly Calvinistic, and believed with positive assurance in the perseverance of the saints and in the eternal punishment of the wicked. His creed carried his whole mind with it. There was no mental reservation about it. He declared what he sincerely believed, and believed to the full all that he declared. The critics are few who have ever had the hardihood to assert that Mr. Spurgeon was inconsistent with himself. He felt sure that all the world was included in the condemnation, and that there was no escape but to believe in Jesus the Christ, and that the Saviour could only be found through that sincere repentance whose fruitage was naturally good works. He believed that the world was lost, and he taught that there was no other Saviour to redeem it but the one who died on Calvary. That thought permeates all that he writes, and is especially prominent in all that he speaks. It is his waking thought, and seems even to fill his dreams. Salvation! salvation! was his cry under all circumstances, and he would not be silent. He was able to reconcile in his own mind, and teach in the most wonderful way the free will of man and God's sovereignty. That is the most difficult problem with which the theologian has ever had to deal. Most minds simply dismiss the question as beyond the possibility of solution, and content themselves with the thought that in some future time it may be explained by means which are not now at hand. He also stood on that line of the golden mean with reference to his denominational doctrines and was most consistent in the reconciliation of the two somewhat contrary statements of belief contained in the practice and declaration of principles recognized everywhere by the Baptist denomination.

Henry VIII established the principle that the English Church had the right to declare its independence of the Roman Catholic Church. Independent Churches of England went further with the doctrine and declared that they had a right to be independent of every other Church, and of the Church of England itself. It was a principle which had long before been asserted and maintained by the Baptist Churches on the Continent.

The distinguishing feature of the Baptist denomination when placed historically in contrast with others of the independent or Non-conformist Churches, was in their adherence to the principle that Christians in practice should follow the example of Jesus Christ as closely as was practically possible in all the ordinances, and in daily behavior. Hence their insistence upon baptism by immersion, and upon the presence of disciples only at the Lord's table. These doctrines they have ever held up most prominently and have adhered to them in teaching throughout the entire history of the Baptist Church. But these principles have been scarcely more strongly asserted than has the other principle, set up as a counterpart, that every person shall have the right and ought to exercise it, to worship God according to the dictates of his own conscience. Thus setting up not only the independence of each individual Church, but the independence of each individual conscience. In the teaching of these principles, which sometimes seem to be in opposition, Mr. Spurgeon was perfectly consistent. He taught clearly and distinctly what he believed to be the truth as asserted in the Scriptures, and taught by the Baptist denomination, with reference to the necessity of belief in Jesus Christ, and the acceptance of Him as a Saviour and example. But he never crossed the line from teaching to the application of force or the use of persecution to compel other people to believe as he believed, or to practice as he practiced. He placed himself in that consistent position where the extremists on either hand were ever bound to return to his place. He could thus live in the close fellowship with other denominations and unite with them in carrying on Christian work and sincerely maintain a close spiritual communion with them all.

He believed in his Church heartily and advocated it thoroughly. He also believed in the full liberty of the human conscience and could intermingle most freely and lovingly with any other class of Christians, who he was sure were living up to the dictates of their own consciences enlightened by the Word of God. Men were to be persuaded, not driven. All men are fallible; and consequently he himself would not consider himself to be infallible.

He had a broad charity for denominational differences, and maintained a most intimate friendship with persons of other creeds, and with high officials in the Church of England itself. "Like priest, like people." The members of his Church were very like him in their strong adherence to their denominational belief, but were also very liberal, fraternal generous, and kind-hearted toward the members of any other Christian Church.

But articles of faith and matters of creed were always held in strict subordination to the noble theme of salvation through belief in the Lord Jesus

Christ. Christ was all and in all. He was a great Spirit and a part of the God-head. It was not external form, but internal faith which settled the question of each believer's salvation. In that he stood on a common platform with nearly every other Christian denomination.

If his position were once granted that every man should have the right to worship God according to the dictates of his own conscience, then would all denominations unite in one great Church and move on together against the common enemy of God and men.

Mr. Spurgeon was in no sense a sensational preacher unless it consisted in the sensation which the variety of illustrations and exceeding boldness aroused in his audience. He never condescended to the use of any sensational methods for the purpose of drawing a congregation or in the accomplishment of any other worldly purpose. If he used unusual topics or made strong speeches it was not because of any thought in his mind of personal gain to himself. His whole soul was wrapped up in the delivery of the Gospel message, and wherever he saw an opportunity to advance it he did not hesitate to use any weapon that was reasonably at hand. He once declared that when in the field if he could not get a sword he would take a fence-rail.

The divine word is everything. The means were only secondary. He never hesitated to refer to himself, and thought it as great a sacrilege to be

over-modest as it was to be over-bold. Mock-modesty had no place in his make-up. He had no fear of criticism when he felt that he was speaking under the inspiration of God, and threw away entirely all hesitancy born of the fear of people. He spoke what he meant and if he had occasion to use the personal pronoun I, he used it over and over and over again. He did not care whether people noticed it and attributed it to egotism or to his carelessness of self. Some people are so modest that they never let their right hand know what their left hand doeth, and are frequently so modest about it that often even the left hand never knows of their making an offering. So there are people who, in their giving, desire to trumpet it before them, as they did in the day of Christ's rebuke, and never give unless they can write their name upon the gift in prominent letters of gold. Mr. Spurgeon and his disciples have stood in the middle ground between these two extremes, never boasting of what they gave or did and never ashamed to let any one see either their deeds or their creeds, and he preached as Bayard lived, without fear and without reproach.

Another special feature of his ministry was in the adjustment of himself to the needs of his hearers or to the time at which he addressed them. He was all things unto all men that he might win some. There was a natural disposition to adaptation which is seldom found in any person occupying so promi-nent a position. His spirit was so sensitive to the feelings and needs of others that he would, without being conscious of it, think as they thought and feel as they felt; discovering by an unerring instinct the right current of thought and the antidote to their pains, as the wild beast when poisoned exercises that marvelous power to find an antidote, and as the chameleon changes its color without effort when associated with the changing shades of nature. So he, without disturbing his principles or in any way changing his religious nature, assimilated himself to the society in which he was placed in the most re-markable manner. He could talk interestingly to a ploughman and once won the highest favor from an audience composed entirely of hawkers or street peddlers. He seemed to be able to enter fully into their sympathies, disappointments, successes, and anxieties, and he found, while speaking, that even their language, which is local and peculiar, flowed spontaneously from his lips.

It is indeed a marvel to the student to observe how in his *John Ploughman's Talks,* and in his letters to persons of other trades and occupations he was able to speak in their own terms with the very nicest and most accurate appreciation of the meaning of common and sometimes rude localisms. In England there are four or five distinct dialects, and but for a third and more general language the citizens of one locality would be entirely unable to communicate with those of another. Yet it is said that Mr Spurgeon, when visiting any one of these

PREACHING TO THE LOWLY.

localities, where their language so greatly differed from that of London, was able to speak so naturally in their own local tongue as to mislead many of his audience as to the place of his birth or residence. Each locality which he visited claimed him as its own, as almost every auditor in his great congregation felt that each sermon Mr. Spurgeon delivered was intended especially for him. It seemed impossible for any person, even with the closest study and the highest natural genius, to accomplish by any plan such almost miraculous results. In this, as in many other things connected with his history, we come to the deliberate conclusion there was some power or influence above him which moved upon him and enabled him to accomplish these otherwise unaccountable results.

CHAPTER VII.

WONDERFUL HEALING.

Much has been written by those who are wise
and much has been said by those who are foolish
with reference to the power of Christian faith in the
healing of the sick. Silliness weakened and diluted
has grappled with this important subject as a jelly-
fish might grapple with a shark. It is a topic which
seems to furnish to the foolish and erratic a most attractive fund of speculation and misrepresentation.
Extremists and charlatans have monopolized this
subject until the world refuses to believe even that
which they themselves see. Men, women, and children are cured by the exercise of Christian faith.
But whether it be directly miraculous or the result
of natural law is a question not yet decided. In fact,
it has not been completely settled whether or not
natural law is entirely a series of miracles or every
miracle is itself in accordance with natural law. This
subject is deserving of respectful attention, and of
very close investigation, and the investigator must
travel along the boundary line of the wonderful and
the natural in such a way as not to lose his footing;
keeping ever consistent with nature. Prayers for
the sick are answered, and many persons do recover

directly in consequence of such petitions. That is made clear by unquestioned evidence. But it is still a debatable matter as to the means which Divine power uses in the accomplishment of such desired ends. With reference to the healing of the sick by prayer or by the laying on of hands, Mr. Spurgeon ever maintained a very careful reserve.

It was difficult to secure from him a direct expression of his convictions in this matter.

The writer once, when a correspondent for a prominent American newspaper, asked him the direct question, whether he believed all persons could be healed by the use of sincere prayer by persons who believed in Christ and whose lives were righteous. He announced that his experience in the matter had been quite extended, but that he needed to look very much further before he would be able to answer such a question without reservation. Yet, no man probably, in England or in America, in this century, has ever healed so many people as did Mr. Spurgeon, although he was not himself a physician and never wrote prescriptions. He felt that there was an unexplainable mystery about the whole matter. Yet, he asserted that there was some power connected with prayer which ought to be used when persons were in pain and could be relieved by it.

He once gathered a number of volumes on the subject of healing the sick in answer to prayer, and studied the matter with much persistent carefulness with the hope that the mystery might be discovered. But no research into the matter cleared the question from many complications and doubts, He often prayed for the recovery of the sick, who, instead of becoming at once convalescent, became immediately worse and soon died. Such experiences would have discouraged him entirely in the theory that there was any use in prayer, had it not been for the wonderfully direct recovery of other people, under circumstances which showed that there was no other possible solution to the mystery but in saying that the prayer had a definite and miraculous influence.

That the mind has a strong and powerful influence over the body is confirmed by the most ordinary experiences, and all persons recognize that fact intuitively, if they do not reason about it. That the body also exercises great influence over the mind is just as apparent to any everyday observer. Ordinary common sense teaches these fundamental truths. But to state how far this influence extends in all directions, or to draw up a law distinctly saying, Thus far does it go and no further, requires an almost Divine insight such as science has not yet reached.

The physician who can fully understand the use and influence of the mind to assist him in the administration of medicine has not yet been in practice. He may take advantage of it in a small way, but to reduce it to a science is something no person has yet accomplished. Consequently this vast unexplained field in the experiences and needs of men is often entered by the untrustworthy, who see only phantoms, weird ghosts, and who go out with the most extravagant stories of the most inconsistent things. As a matter of fact no man can assert with a positive assurance of truth in any case of recovery what was certainly the most influential agency in the matter. The whole testimony is indirect and circumstantial. If the person recovers without the use of the physician's prescription he immediately asserts that the remedy was entirely in his mind or spirit; when it may possibly have been connected with something that he ate, breathed, or drank, which was in the nature of a prescription, although not ordered by a physician. If a person returns speedily to health while taking certain doses ordered by the doctor, he gives the credit for his recovery entirely to the skill of the doctor and the power of the drugs, and yet he could not assert beyond the possibility of contradiction but that he would have recovered as soon and perhaps sooner if he had not taken any medicine at all.

The medical profession have made most surprising and gratifying advances in these recent years in everything pertaining to surgery, and in the preparation of medicines; but they are all still very far from the explanation for which the world is calling, which shall give the reasons for prevailing disease and show clearly to the common mind the processes required for recovery. "Heal the mind and heal the body" is the cry of some very enthusiastic scientists. "Heal the body and heal the mind" is the answering cry of a still larger class of practitioners. A still smaller class say, "Appeal unto the great Spirit, which is over all, and can see and understand all, and if we win its favorable attention and assistance, recovery is absolutely certain." Yet in this latter case, as in the others, the processes by which a disease is defeated are almost entirely out of sight, and surmisings seem to be fruitless. The astronomer can arrange a hypothesis to which he will adjust many of the facts connected with the heavenly bodies, and will assert with some degree of probability that this hypothesis furnishes the only reasonable explanation for many of the discoveries made by the telescope and by the hammer of the geologist.

But no hypothesis seems yet to be stated which will make consistent the thousands of gathered facts connected with the healing of disease. The school of medicine which is to triumph in the art of healing has not yet been established. May the Lord hasten its coming, and send His disciples about with the power of Jesus Christ to heal all manner of diseases ; that the lame may walk and the blind recover their sight.

"According to your faith shall it be unto you" has often been exemplified in the matter of sickness. That a person who is thoroughly convinced he is going to die is difficult to heal all physicians assert.

That a patient who fully believes he is going to recover is a much easier subject in medical practice is also a universal testimony of medical men, and this latter proposition may serve to account somewhat naturally for many of the incidents connected with Mr. Spurgeon's visitations among the sick.

Thousands did believe that his prayer would heal them. He prayed with them, they recovered. Such an experience to the ordinary mind would be convincing beyond any possible doubt that Mr. Spurgeon's prayers had behind them a Divinely healing power. Some have said that his prayers were of such a nature, and that he himself had such complete faith in their being answered, that they thoroughly convinced the pain-stricken listener that an answer was certain, and they would surely recover. Fully assured of their recovery, their way to perfect health would seem to be naturally opened.

Yet that transfers the question but a little to one side, and credits supernatural power with having changed their minds. If a skilled physician, with all his training, talent, and means could not change the mind of the patient, it is at least a wonderful thing that any other person without that skill or the use of any means should give such remarkable faith. Anyhow the whole matter is open to investigation, and any keen student with a thoroughly disciplined, analytical mind will not find it an easy field of study.

We will give some of the incidents which have

been related to us, and others which we have seen in print, all of which we believe to be literally true; and leave them to the meditation or examination of such persons as desire to study deeper into the philosophy of faith, or the molecular origin of disease. Perhaps back of the physical bacteria there may yet be found a spiritual bacteria requiring an Omnipotent mind to give explanation of the influences in the origin of Life or Death.

As the trembling of a leaf affects the motion of the earth, and through that disturbs the sun and the most distant stars of the universe, so any expression of life must affect all other life; and reach away and away beyond the highest imagination into the realms of the Divine, and perhaps to the throne of God itself. All telephones lead to the central office. All life reaches back to God.

There are now living and worshiping in the Metropolitan Tabernacle hundreds of people who ascribe the extension of their life to the effect of Mr. Spurgeon's personal prayers. They have been sick with disease and nigh unto death, he has appeared, kneeled by their beds, and prayed for their recovery. Immediately the tide of health returned, the fevered pulse became calm, the temperature was reduced, and all the activities of nature resumed their normal functions within a short and unexpected period. If a meeting were to be called of all those who attribute their recovery to the prayer of Mr. Spurgeon, it would furnish one of the most deserved tributes to his memory that could be possibly made.

His ministry in London began with some of these most remarkable incidents, which so confirmed the truths he uttered from the pulpit as to make persons believe in him because of his very works' sake. Stories were very current during the first year of his ministry at New Park Street Chapel of the marvelous results which had attended his pastoral visitations upon the sick. One man in 1855 arose from his bed of fever the same day in which the physician had declared his case to be very critical, and appeared at the meeting in the evening, to the astonishment of all his acquaintances, saying : " Mr. Spurgeon prayed with me this morning, I have been divinely healed." Another, in the same season, appeared one Sunday, walking decidedly and firmly down the aisle to a front seat, who for years before had always limped into the service. He was often heard to murmur and once to shout, " Glory to God !" as he was giving praise to his Divine Master for having used Mr. Spurgeon for his miraculous recovery. It was a case of partial paralysis, which physicians now say is due largely to a failure of some portion of the brain to perform its natural duties. In any case, it is a nervous disease, and can only be healed by the restoration of the nervous forces or in those avenues connected with the brain or in the brain itself. One gentleman connected with an institution of learning in London explained this matter satisfactorily to himself by saying that some unusual mental excitement had aroused the dormant brain into normal action, and had restored the nerves; and consequently had given the man renewed power to use his right side, which had been stricken in the paralytic stroke of five years before. That he was healed no one questioned; the crutch he gave away, thoroughly believing he would never have occasion again to use it, and declaring confidently that he was to live to be seventy-eight years of age. Whether he did live out the days as he so confidently expected is not known to the writer.

One man who had been unable to leave the house for many years, afflicted with a form of rheumatism somewhat akin to that common disease, the gout, insisted that Mr. Spurgeon should come and pray for his recovery, but Mr. Spurgeon, while accepting the invitation to attend and pray, said that for himself he could not have a complete faith in the power of his prayer to restore such a case. Notwithstanding Mr. Spurgeon's own unbelief in the effects of his petitions, the man asserted his perfect confidence. Mr. Spurgeon knelt with him and prayed. At the close of his prayer the man asserted very strongly that he felt very different and very much better. He urged Mr. Spurgeon to return and pray with him the next morning, which the preacher very cheerfully did. The old gentleman met him at the door and welcomed him with a hearty laugh, saying "The Lord is performing His promises and has answered your prayer." He was not entirely well, but he had so far recovered as to be able to walk about the house, and a few weeks thereafter did resume the care of a business which required no great amount of physical exercise. He was for several years afterward a regular attendant at the chapel, and neither storm nor cold hindered him from reaching his accustomed place.

Another person, who was a visitor in London from Wales, who had been sadly afflicted mentally in consequence of some physical defect or disease, pleaded most piteously with his family to send for Mr. Spurgeon, that he might pray at his bedside. They considered it the foolish raving of an insane mind. But at last they consented to ask Mr. Spurgeon to visit him. Mr. Spurgeon's prayer that day had a most soothing effect upon the poor lunatic and appeared partially to restore his mental balance. The family were so surprised and delighted at the effect of the petition that, while they accredited it entirely to natural causes, they interceded most earnestly for Mr. Spurgeon's return. He came to the house the same night, after the evening service, and remained for some time, praying with all his heart for the recovery of the patient, in which the poor invalid most piteously joined. Mr. Spurgeon, himself, stated afterward that while he prayed with all his heart and tried to believe that the patient would recover, yet he could not convince himself that his visit had been of any other use but simply to appease the feelings of the nurses, who were disturbed by the poor man's cries. Yet in the night after the prayers were offered, the sick man awoke with a start and a cry which frightened his nurses. But he was found to be entirely in his right mind. He declared he had dreamed of meeting the Saviour, and that the Saviour had assured him that the devils were cast out. A few days after he was able to go out of the house, and shortly afterward removed to Canada, where he has been a successful business man, having been carried to his grave in 1882.

An incident is recalled of a child who was very sick with a contagious disease which was declared fatal by the doctor. Mr. Spurgeon visited the home at the request of the family, knelt with them in a circle around the bed, and offered up a prayer for the child's salvation and added a petition for her recovery, if it should be in accordance with the will of God. The father and mother both followed in prayer, and when they arose from their knees the child, just then becoming conscious, asked for water and said: "I feel very much better." From that point in the child's sickness there was no break in her continual recovery. She afterward stated to her mother that during the prayer she felt a "strange sensation running all over her, as though the fever began to decline at her head and gradually passed off at her feet."

A boy who had worked in a printing-office as an

apprentice, met with a sad accident wherein his arm was broken twice; once below the elbow, and another bad fracture in the bone near the shoulder. His father had heard of others who had stated that they had recovered from disease through the power of prayer, and sent for Mr. Spurgeon to come and pray for the healing of his arm. The physician, who had heard of the request, said "the boy will recover the use of his arm without prayer, and if you intend to pray for anything, you had better pray that the upper-arm will not be deformed." The physician declared that he knew nothing in the school of surgery that would prevent the deformation, because the break was of such a singular and complicated nature. When the deacon of the Church who accompanied Mr. Spurgeon asked him if he thought it was possible for prayer to heal a case like that, Mr. Spurgeon answered, with a smile: "All things are possible with God, but," said he, "I cannot feel that it is very probable. Yet it is our duty to pray for the things we desire, even though they seem impossible." Mr. Spurgeon talked with the boy concerning Christ and his soul's salvation, until he was sure that the boy understood what it was to be a Christian, and was satisfied that he intended to accept the great gift, then he asked him to kneel in prayer. Mr. Spurgeon there prayed for exactly the thing that the physician had told them he would need to ask for. He appeared to be very much in earnest, and while in prayer was strongly impressed himself that in some way the prayer was to be literally answered. The next day the boy fell upon the stairs and fractured the bones again, making the wound apparently more dangerous than before. He was then carried to a hospital where a somewhat celebrated French physician was for the time visiting, and under his care the bones were so reset as to assume their natural position.

In 1861 it is said that this belief in Mr. Spurgeon's healing power became among some classes a positive superstition, and he was obliged to overcome the very false and extravagant impressions which were going out concerning it by mentioning the matter from the pulpit, and rebuking the theories of the extremely enthusiastic. He felt that it was becoming too much like the shrines of Catholic Europe, from which came the stories of such marvelous cures, many of which were unqestionably true. The power of faith does not seem to be in fact limited to any sect or Church. That fact adds another element to the mystery of the complicated problem.

For twenty-five years it has been one of the most frequent things at the Tabernacle to hear mentioned in meetings the request of some person, who was sick, for the prayers of the Church that God might send a speedy recovery. The very fact that the number of such applications increase year by year, is in itself satisfactory evidence that the people who were prayed for at first must have believed that the prayers of the Church were answered, and advertised the fact among their friends.

Thousands of cases like those we have related might be gathered, and a great number of them have been collected, showing the wonderful agency of some Divine power exercised in answer to prayer.

While no other Church, perhaps, in the world had the opportunity to test the matter so thoroughly as the Metropolitan Tabernacle of London, yet it is true of many other Churches in England and America that the prayer of faith does save the sick. We may speculate about it as best we may, and different individuals may view it in different lights, in accordance with the standpoint they take, yet, that it is positively effective, and accomplishes the greatest cures, it is impossible to deny, because this thing is not done in a corner, but is everywhere confirmed in the Churches by the evidence of those who have heard and who have seen. If any matter could ever be established in law or in experience by cumulative testimony, this much is certain, that prayers are answered in the expulsion of disease.

If we talk from Philadelphia to Boston through a telephone and recognize the voice of our acquaintances, we know that we are heard, but we are utterly unable to explain to any inquiring child just what electricity is. To tell a person that it is a mode of motion, akin to light, does not remove the mystery or explain the agency. In the same way we ask of God to be healed of a sad disease, with which human physicians are unable to contend, and after being restored by unaccountable processes, we draw the breath of health, we are sure that we have been healed, although we cannot understand the laws which controlled the means.

Mr. Spurgeon, like the Master whom he so faithfully served, went about teaching and healing the sick. He never took any credit to himself for the healing power which he exercised; and hundreds of persons were physically benefited by his visits, of whom he never afterward directly heard. He regarded himself, as every pastor should, as the mere agent of Divine power, and spoke of himself, in two instances, as unworthy of possessing the gift of healing.

The Christian world will account for these things in one way and the sceptical world in another way, but the facts will ever remain, that for some reason, either supernatural or natural, these people did recover their health, and are indebted to Mr. Spurgeon or to his influence with a higher power, for the comfort of body and peace of mind which they now enjoy.

Next to the supreme joy of facing thousands of people, anxious to hear the Gospel, and forgetting one's self in its earnest delivery, comes the pleasure of being an instrument or messenger of the great force lying beyond our ken, to bring breath to the asthmatic, calmness to the palpitating heart, perfect peace to the tingling nerves, strength to the tottering steps, a flush to pallid cheeks, a flash to dull eyes, a smile to trembling lips, hope to discouraged friends, and long years of useful life to the expiring invalid. Oh! what a life was that! What an inestimable privilege to occupy a position like his.

There can be no situation on earth so much to be charitably envied as that which is occupied by such a messenger of God. "How beautiful upon the mountains are the feet of them that bring good tidings, good tiding of peace."

Some idea of the spirit with which the young preacher entered upon his work may be gained from the following letters, which explain themselves.

"No. 60 Park Street, Cambridge, Jan. 27, 1854.

"To James Low, Esq.,

"My dear Sir:—

"I cannot help feeling intense gratification at the unanimity of the church at New Park street in relation to their invitation to me. Had I been uncomfortable in my present situation, I should have felt unmixed pleasure at the prospect Providence seems to open up before me; but having devoted and loving people, I feel I know not how.

"One thing I know, namely, that I must soon be severed from them by necessity, for they do not raise sufficient to maintain me in comfort. Had they done so I should have turned a deaf ear to any request to leave them, at least for the present. But now my Heavenly Father drives me forth from this little Garden of Eden, and while I see that I must go out, I leave it with reluctance, and tremble to tread the unknown land before me.

" When I first ventured to preach at Waterbeach, I only accepted an invitation for three months, on the condition that if in that time I should see good reason for leaving, or they on their part should wish for it, I should be at liberty to cease supplying, or they should have the same power to request me to do so before the expiration of the time.

" With regard to a six months' invitation from you, I have no objection to the length of time, but rather approve of the prudence of the Church in wishing to have one so young as myself on an extended period of probation, but I write after well weighing the matter, when I say positively that I cannot—I dare not—accept an unqualified invitation for so long a time. My objection is not to the length of time of probation, but it ill becomes a youth to promise to preach to a London congregation so long, until he knows them and they know him. I would engage to supply for three months of that time, and then, should the congregation fail, or the church disagree, I would reserve to myself liberty, without breach of engagement, to retire ; and you would on your part have the right to dismiss me without seeming to treat me ill. Should I see no reason for so doing, and the church still retain their wish for me, I can remain the other three months, either with or without the formality of a further invitation; but even during the second three months I should not like to regard myself as a fixture, in case of ill success, but would only be a supply, liable to a fortnight's discharge or resignation.

"Perhaps this is not business-like—I do not know; but this is the course I should prefer, if it should be agreeable to the church. Enthusiasm and popularity are often the crackling of thorns, and expire. I do not wish to be a hindrance, if I cannot be a help.

"With regard to coming at once, I think I must not. My own deacons just hinted that I ought to finish the quarter here; though by ought, they mean simply —pray to do so if you can. This would be too long a delay. I wish to help them until they can get supplies, which is only to be done with great difficulty; and as I have given you four Sabbaths, I hope you will allow me to give them four in return. I would give them the first and second Sabbaths in February, and two more in a month or six weeks' time. I owe them much for their kindness, although they insist that the debt lies on their side. Some of them hope, and almost pray, that you may be tired in three months, so that I may again be sent back to them.

"Thus, my dear sir, I have honestly poured out my heart to you. You are too kind. You will excuse me if I err, for I wish to do right to you, to my people, and to all, as being not my own, but bought with a price.

"I respect the honesty and boldness of the small minority, and only wonder that the number was not greater. I pray God that if He does not see fit that I should remain with you, the majority may be quite as much the other way at the end of six months, so that I may never divide you into parties.

"Pecuniary matters I am well satisfied with. And now one thing is due to every minister, and I pray you to remind the church of it, namely, that in private, as well as public, they must all wrestle in prayer to God that I may be sustained in the great work.

"I am, with the best wishes for your health, and the greatest respect,

"Yours truly,

"C. H. SPURGEON."

"75 DOVER ROAD, BOROUGH, April 28th, 1854.

"To the Baptist Church of Christ, worshiping in New Park Street Chapel, Southwark.

"Dearly beloved in Christ Jesus:

"I have received your unanimous invitation as contained in a resolution passed by you on the 19th instant, desiring me to accept the pastorate among you. No lengthened reply is required; there is but one answer to so loving and cordial an invitation. I ACCEPT IT. I have not been perplexed as to what my reply shall be, for many things constrain me thus to answer.

"I sought not to come to you, for I was the minister of an obscure but affectionate people; I never solicited advancement. The first note of invitation from your deacons came to me quite unlooked for, and I trembled at the idea of preaching in London. I could not understand how it came about, and even now I am filled with astonishment at the wondrous Providence. I would wish to give myself into the hands of our covenant God, whose wisdom directs all things. He shall choose for me; and so far as I can judge this is His choice.

"I felt it to be a high honor to be the pastor of a people who can mention glorious names as my predecessors; and I entreat of you to remember me in prayer, that I may realize the solemn responsibility of my trust. Remember my youth and my inexperience; pray that these may not hinder my usefulness. I trust also that the remembrance of these may lead you to forgive the mistakes I may make, or unguarded words I may utter.

"Blessed be the name of the Most High! He has called me to this office, He will support me in it; otherwise how should a child, a youth, have the presumption thus to attempt a work which filled the heart and hands of Jesus? Your kindness to me has been very great and my heart is knit unto you. I fear not your steadfastness, I fear my own. The gospel, I believe, enables me to venture great things, and by faith I venture this. I ask your co-operation in every good work, in visiting the sick, in bringing in inquirers, and in mutual edification.

"Oh! that I may be of no injury to you, but a lasting benefit! I have no more to say, only this: that if I have expressed myself in these few words in a manner unbecoming my youth and inexperience, you will not impute it to arrogance, but forgive my mistake.

"And now, commending you to our covenant-keeping God, the triune Jehovah, I am yours to serve in the gospel.

" C. H. SPURGEON."

A gentleman belonging to another denomination visited the chapel during Mr. Spurgeon's early ministry, and wrote the following quite interesting description of the appearance of the young preacher:

"His voice is clear and musical; his language plain; his style flowing, but terse; his manner sound and suitable; his tone and spirit cordial; his remarks always pithy and pungent, sometimes familiar and colloquial, yet never light or coarse, much less profane. Judging from a single sermon, we supposed that he would become a plain, faithful, forcible, and affectionate preacher of the gospel in the form called Calvinistic; and our judgment was the more favorable because, while there was a solidity beyond his years, we detect little of the wild luxuriance naturally characteristic of very young preachers."

A correspondent, writing in 1857, shows the preacher from another standpoint. In his letters he said:

"He is of medium height, at present quite stout, has a round and beardless face, not a high forehead, dark hair, parted in the centre of the head. His appearance in the pulpit may be said to be interesting rather than commanding. He betrays his youth, and still wears a boyish countenance. His figure is awkward—his manners are plain—his face (except when illumined by a smile) is admitted to be heavy. His voice seems to be the only personal instrument he possesses, by which he is enabled to acquire such a marvelous power over the hearts and minds of his hearers. His voice is powerful, rich melodious, and under perfect control. Twelve thousand have distinctly heard every sentence he uttered in the open air, and this powerful instrument carried his burning words to an audience of twenty thousand gathered in the Crystal Palace."

Still another writer of that year is quoted by Mr. Needham, in his life of Spurgeon, who said: "As soon as he commences to speak, tones of richest melody are heard. A voice, full, sweet, and musical falls on every ear, and awakens agreeable emotions in every soul in which there is a sympathy for sounds. That most excellent of voices is under perfect control, and can whisper or thunder at the wish of its possessor. Then there is poetry in every feature, and every movement, as well as music in

13

the voice. The countenance speaks, the entire form sympathizes. The action is in complete unison with the sentiments, and the eye listens scarcely less than the ear to the sweetly flowing oratory. To the influence of his powerful voice he adds that of a manner characterized by great freedom and fearlessness, intensely earnest and strikingly natural. When to these we add the influence of thrilling description, touching anecdote, sparkling wit, startling episodes, striking similes, all used to illustrate and enforce the deep, earnest home truths of the Bible, we surely have a combination of elements which must make up a preacher of wonderful attraction and marvelous power."

CHAPTER VIII.

BUILDING FOR THE LORD.

It would require as many volumes as we have allowed pages to give all the varied incidents of Mr. Spurgeon's remarkable life which would be of interest to some classes of readers; but in no division of his great work was there shown more distinctly the unaccountable power of faith than in the enlargement of the New Park Street Chapel and in the building of the Metropolitan Tabernacle.

The difference between building a Church and establishing a secular business is so widely divergent that the methods adopted in the one seem never to be applicable to the other. Yet, after all, the business principles which should conduct to success a large manufacturing concern or a commercial enterprise are necessarily blended with that faith in the unseen which makes Christian enterprises successful.

They who build a church enter into contracts and assume obligations, "seeing the invisible;" for it is a rare thing in the history of church building for such enterprises to be started with the capital all in the bank. The builders are obliged to assume that miraculous agencies will work with them in their undertaking, and accomplish in church building what would never be expected in ordinary affairs of business. They believe that somewhere in the world is the gold and the silver belonging to the Lord, which will be pushed forward, by mysterious agencies, into their hands, for the uses of the religious undertaking.

Hospitals, schools, colleges, mission houses, chapels, and churches can be counted by the score which began entirely in the faith of some individual who had far less money than enthusiasm for the good of his kind.

There seems, however, to be a limit beyond which faith in God becomes presumption, and the presumptuous sin brings its reward in failure and disgrace. Just where the line is between a sublime faith and reckless presumption is one of the most difficult matters to decide, and differs with every possible occasion.

It seems, however, clearly true that wherever a careful man or woman of calm judgment, and acquainted with business ways, sees the necessity for a great Christian charity or the construction of a church, there is always somewhere the means with which to carry on the work or to rear the structure. The demand is always accompanied with a supply, just as in, the body, there is no appetite without the existence somewhere of the means to satisfy it. It is one of the best evidences of a future state of spiritual existence that man everywhere has a de-

LONDON RESIDENCE OF MR. SPURGEON.

sire or an appetite for eternal life, and, reasoning by analogy, there is no just ground for supposing that such a universal and strong natural appetite will be left unsatisfied.

So when a community is sinking into sin and crime, or when fearful diseases rage, there is somewhere a means of reform and an antidote provided by nature's God which the faithful servant of the Lord is almost certain to find. In exceptionable cases, benevolent individuals have established alone great charities, and have supplied the capital from their extensive possessions. But usually such undertakings have been begun by some person, having himself but little money, and yet endowed with great faith, and the waiting benefactors have reinforced or sustained the movement with their gifts of money or property.

Some churches have such a worldly fear of debt as to practically declare by resolution and action that they will only trust in the Lord when they have the money in their pockets. While others, as wrongfully extreme, without measuring the need, run recklessly into debt and greatly harm the cause which they desire to sustain.

Mr. Spurgeon was one of those men who was especially endowed with broad common sense, having a much larger degree of faith in the personal care of God than many of his acquaintances; yet always most carefully conservative, weighing well the consequences and considering closely the probabilities, guided by the unerring finger of the providence of God.

If a door opened he entered in. If one debt was unexpectedly paid, it did not encourage him to contract another until he saw the need which was equal to the first, and he gathered up the fragments with most scrupulous care after every undertaking, that nothing should be lost.

The New Park Street Chapel was crowded to the door from the very opening of his pastorate, and the multitudes who could not secure admission, so persistently pressing at the portals, awakened in his mind great anxiety to reach the multitudes who so apparently desired to hear of the Saviour. An over-flow service was suggested and tried, but the people came to hear Mr. Spurgeon and not to attend an ordinary service, and consequently they returned to their homes or went to worse places, while he was preaching to the few, comparatively, who secured a seat or standing room inside.

As this crowded condition was so evidently permanent, young Spurgeon suggested to the deacons, at one of their meetings, that it might be necessary very soon to enlarge the Chapel so as to occupy the entire lot. But that first proposition was received by them as a visionary scheme, having no foundation in reason. He asked some of the members of the Church to pray over the matter, but they considered the matter altogether beyond the reach of prayer. The Church was composed largely of elderly people who stood by the old place because of its associations. Many of them were satisfied and others poor and had no ambition or desire to enter into a new enterprise of this kind. They had not faith enough in it even to ask God for direction. Many of them were in love with the old place, and had that natural conservative feeling that they would not be at home in the new Church. They could not endure the thought of having the pews they had occupied so long change in their relation to the pulpit, or have the walls or windows architecturally remodeled, lest it should make the place seem to them less home-like and sacred.

The proposition to enlarge was one of the most dangerous experiments which Mr. Spurgeon ever tried in his Church life. In all his subsequent propositions of the kind he always found a very strong party of friends so attached to him that they would have undertaken anything he suggested, however absurd it might appear to be to them. But in this case it was very different. The old deacons boasted of their forty years in Christian experience and of the great variety of their past Church work, and very naturally claimed the right of the aged to curb the ardor of the young. He was but a boy, only twenty-one years of age; they were men who had grown gray in practical service.

But the preacher brought to bear upon the Church the demands of people outside of its circle who claimed that they desired to hear the Gospel and that the Church of Christ was under sacred obligations to furnish it to those who so much needed it. This had a growing influence upon the membership, and, although beginning in a very small way, gradually increased in volume with a pride in their young pastor until quite a strong party in the Church were in favor of the enlargement. One day Mr. Spurgeon arose in the pulpit, after having spent a large portion of the previous night in prayer, and declared to the congregation that the Chapel was to be enlarged. He spoke of it with the decision of one who has already, in faith, seen the thing done. He unhesitatingly represented it to be the will of the Lord " that these walls are to be extended. God hath said it, no man can hinder it."

His audacity won friends, his faith aroused confidence, and his evident willingness to sacrifice with them to any extent in order that the Church might be enlarged soon brought over to his position almost the entire Church.

There were several, however, who regarded the matter as so preposterous that they refused to have anything to do with it, and left the Church which they believed would soon be overwhelmed in debt. A good sister, who had always been regarded as one of the pillars of the Church, having been a liberal giver and a devoted Christian, arose in the midst of one of the most enthusiastic meetings and quoted the saying of the Saviour, which urged the people to sit down and count the cost, lest they should not be able to finish, and she urged the brethren not to undertake to destroy this present Church until they had the means with which to build another.

A young man who had but little to give at the time, but afterward became a very generous donor, surprised the meeting by taking an opposite and extreme position, and declaring most excitedly that the enlargement of the Chapel would be only a waste of time, as a very much larger place would then be greatly needed after the enlargement as it was before.

When the Church was at last, led up where it voted to enter into the changes which Mr. Spurgeon desired, there was not a shilling on hand toward the enterprise. To undertake so expensive a matter without capital would appear to a careful business man to be very reckless, if there was not to be taken into consideration in connection with such a movement the fact that the providences of God are always to be counted as partners.

The time was set for the remodeling to begin and Exeter Hall was engaged in which to hold the services during the enlargement, before the subscriptions or gifts were sufficient even for the removal of the furniture. But the money came as it was needed and paid the debts as they became due. Like the manna in the wilderness, there was a supply for each day, but none left for the morrow. Often when the accounts were settled and the workmen paid, there was left in the treasury of the Church less than five dollars, and at two different times only one shilling. Yet at no time did the work cease, or was it hindered for lack of funds. They were obliged to enter into contracts, which of course would place them under great obligations, provided no money should come in before the stipulations were due, yet no obligations did mature without there being money on hand to pay. It was the needed discipline for the Church—a most valuable instruction, fitting them for the greater work they had still before them. It taught faith in God. Possibly none of them could have been persuaded in reason to have undertaken the greater work which followed a few years later had they not been so remarkably sustained by God's providence in this, the lesser undertaking.

The walls were torn out, enlarged foundations put in, and the structure carried upward day by day to the surprise of the unbelieving, but to the great delight of those engaged therein.

In the meantime enormous crowds, numbering more than the enlarged Chapel would hold by four or five times, were regularly in attendance upon the preaching in Exeter Hall. The external walls of the enlarged building were not firmly in place before it was clear to the larger part of the Church that they had undertaken altogether too small things for God. When they returned to the refitted structure there was an apparent sense of disappointment on the part of the congregation, because their inability to accommodate the anxious inquirers at the door was far greater than it had been before they "lengthened their cords."

At the close of the first service, after Mr. Spurgeon's very powerful sermon, which was a sublime expression of the congregation's thanksgiving, it was heard on every side among the people as they passed out, "this Chapel is too small after all, we must begin anew and construct a tabernacle."

On Mr. Spurgeon's twenty-first birthday he received a small gift accompanied by a letter, saying, "I would much enjoy the thought of being the first contributor toward the purchase of a hall, or the building of a tabernacle which should accommodate as many hundreds as our Chapel now holds scores."

A gentleman now living in America, who was at that time a regular worshiper at Mr. Spurgeon's Chapel, says that Mr. Spurgeon told him after an official meeting, that he regarded that communication as the voice of God, and that a larger building was then more certain than had been the remodeling a few months before. His faith was positive, there was no weakness nor doubt in it. He was as sure of a new and larger building then as he was after he saw its capstone laid. It was a confidence in the unseen that partakes of the miraculous, and is as unaccountable as are many other events in his strange history.

He began at once himself to lay aside for the new

enterprise and quietly dropped a hint in the ears of his closest friends, who quietly spread the thought through the Church, until nearly all participated in his own unshaken faith. He seemed to be inspired and we may as well state the whole fact, and say, *he was inspired.*

He looked back upon the undertaking in connection with the Metropolitan Tabernacle after its completion with a fluttering of heart and with trembling, often saying that it impressed him as having been an almost reckless presumption to have supposed such a thing possible. But never during the raising of the money or the construction of the building did he have any such impressions or even a suggestion of doubt or hesitation. When the occasion for his faith had passed, he sank back again into ordinary things, and the great enterprise appeared to him as it had appeared to the unbelieving before. Even his father often remarked, "if he had not succeeded, what an awful failure it would have been."

In October, 1856, the enlarged Chapel had proved itself so entirely inadequate for the pressing crowds who were determined to hear Mr. Spurgeon preach, that the Church decided to engage the Royal Surrey Gardens, Music Hall. Even his most sanguine friends thought that a hall seating so many thousands would certainly be fully adequate for the needs of the time. But, alas! the number of excited attendants increased in greater proportion than the enlarged accommodations.

SURREY MUSIC HALL.

The first night they held service in the Music Hall, the building was packed in every portion, every inch of standing room being taken long before the service began. In the midst of the delivery of the sermon some evil disposed persons, who came to the hall for the purpose of raising a disturbance and interrupting the services, raised a cry of "Fire! fire!" It was a most murderous deed. The multitude became at once fearfully excited and pressed toward the doors, running over one another, and making a most appalling scene of havoc and death. Although Mr. Spurgeon from the desk retained his presence of mind, and loudly called upon the multitude to be calm, yet the uproar was so great, and the excitement was so intense that it was impossible for him to retain control of the assembly. Several were killed in the hall and a large number injured to a greater or less degree. He attempted to go on with the service, after the police had removed the wounded, dying, and dead, but the excitement could not be easily allayed, and so, with a few words of advice, frank and earnest, he dismissed the service. An event so inauspicious at the opening of the Music Hall and so unexpected to Mr. Spurgeon, as he reasoned upon the strange providence of God, had a most distressing effect upon his spirit, bringing upon him a fever from which he did not fully recover for several months.

But he soon afterward learned, in company with the other members of his Church, that this sad accident, although much to be regretted and awakening deep sympathies, yet did indirectly exercise an enormous influence in securing the great Metropolitan Tabernacle. The demand for a safer place, and one exclusively devoted to preaching was greatly increased by this accident; while the persecutions of the opposing press and of other Christian denominations, who used this accident to decry his preaching, only deepened the determination of his friends to stand by him and do the greatest thing possible.

He was greatly sustained in the proposition to construct a larger house by a great number of people whom he had visited during the previous epidemic of the awful Asiatic cholera. Some of them felt that they owed their very life to the prayers or kindness of Mr. Spurgeon, and others had learned during that scourge to greatly admire his character and love him as a friend, who eagerly sought a kind of martyrdom in his service, either in the matter of giving or in boldly offering themselves for his defense.

It will be interesting to the reader to see Mr. Spurgeon's own account of the cholera scourge and the wonderful manner in which he was sustained in his self-sacrificing labors in connection with it. It is a remarkable fact that during any season of the Asiatic cholera, those who are entirely fearless and associate with it in the greatest recklessness seldom take the disease.

Mr. Spurgeon's faith in the protection of a over-ruling Providence was so great that it scarcely seemed to him possible that he could take the dis-case. He resembled Cæsar and Napoleon then in his unshaken confidence in his own destiny.

We quote here his account of the matter:

"In the year 1854, when I had scarcely been in London twelve months, the neighborhood in which I labored was visited by Asiatic cholera, and my con gregation suffered from its inroads. Family after family summoned me to the bedside of the smitten, and almost every day I was called to visit the grave. I gave myself up with youthful ardor to the visita-tion of the sick, and was sent for from all corners of the district by persons of all ranks and religions. I became weary in body and sick at heart. My friends seemed falling one by one, and I felt or fan-cied that I was sickening like those around me. A little more work and weeping would have laid me low among the rest. I felt that my burden was heavier than I could bear, and I was ready to sink under it. As God would have it, I was returning mournfully home from a funeral, when my curiosity led me to read a paper which was wafered up in a shoemaker's window in the Dover Road. It did not look like a trade announcement, nor was it, for it bore in a good bold handwriting these words: 'Be-cause thou hast made the Lord, which is my refuge, even the Most High, thy habitation, there shall no evil befall thee, neither shall any plague come nigh thy dwelling.' The effect on my heart was immediate. Faith appropriated the passage as her own. I felt secured, refreshed, girt with immortality. I went on with my visitation of the dying in a calm and peaceful spirit; I felt no fear of evil, and I suffered no harm. The Providence which moved the tradesman to place those verses in his window I gratefully acknowledge, and, in the remembrance of its marvelous power, I adore the Lord my God."

These sincere friends, won by such personal acts of self-sacrifice, formed a very strong party and believed that anything was possible which Mr. Spurgeon would undertake. Hence he found that the very first proposition for the construction of a church large enough to hold fully 5,000 people found many supporters. It does not appear that there was any opposition at all on the part of the membership of his Church. But the idea was taken up with great enthusiasm. There were of course many influential people in the community who ridiculed the undertaking as completely preposterous, and who discouraged responsible contractors who had thought to seek for the job of constructing the building. Even the workmen were approached by very busy individuals, who, under the plea of personal interest for the workmen's welfare, advised them not to engage with the contractors or work for the Church, because they would be very likely to lose their wages.

But while Mr. Spurgeon was laid aside, because

of the nervous strain connected with the awful catastrophy in the Surrey Garden Music Hall, he had an excellent opportunity to meditate upon the whole matter and to pray over it frequently. He decided that he was sent of God to carry on the building enterprise, and as soon as health permitted he entered at once upon a personal canvass in favor of the object. He went over the country, and from city to city, and village to village, preaching twice every day, and taking collections for the new Tabernacle, giving half the proceeds of each collection to the local Church where the money was given. Night and day he toiled on, receiving oftentimes only a shilling and at other times several dollars. The fund, at first so small, crept steadily upward into the thousands. As soon as persons of means became convinced that the building was an assured fact, then they came in with larger donations, and the building fund grew with most encouraging rapidity.

For two years his hours of sleep were confined to the time between midnight and sunrise, and often this was encroached upon by special work or by wakeful seasons of anxious meditation.

But on the 16th of August, 1859, he had the great joy to see the corner-stone laid, by Sir Samuel Morton Peto, on a lot which the Church had purchased at Newington Butts. It was very far from being an aristocratic neighborhood, and was located among factories and the humblest dwellings of London mechanics.

There was some difference of opinion in reference to the location, but the arguments of one of its advocates settled the question when he declared that it made no difference in what part of London they placed the Chapel, Mr. Spurgeon was sure to fill it to overflowing.

At the beginning of the construction, while the materials were piled promiscuously around, Mr. Spurgeon called a meeting for prayer, and with a number of his friends and Church officials went there, and kneeling among the timber and stone, he prayed that none of the workmen engaged upon the construction might be killed or injured. And it has been often published that during the entire work, in which so many men were engaged and in dangerous situations, there was not a workman injured directly or indirectly, so far as can be ascertained.

The entire cost was to have been $110,000, but the changes and improvements made in the plans before it was completed carried the cost up to $155,000.

The original plan also shows the intention to have been to seat 4,200 people, but the necessities created by the crowding, compelled them to occupy every possible space with a seat of some kind, and the actual seating capacity was increased to nearly 5,500.

The completed building is 146 feet long and 81 feet wide, having two galleries, as has before been seen in the quotation from Mr. Spurgeon's account.

The methods frequently adopted by Mr. Spurgeon's congregation for the raising of money for their building fund varied somewhat from that which had been used by other Churches in England, and brought down upon them no little criticism. Church fairs, bazaars, and entertainments have a very bad name in many Churches, and Mr. Spurgeon himself has often spoken very decidedly concerning the deleterious influence they often exerted. But he learned by the force of providential necessity that after all, for the worship of God, it is not so much whether it be at Gerizim, or Jerusalem, or after the manners of one country or another; but rather in the spirit in which the service is conducted. He found by experience that even a bazaar, or a Church fair may become a spiritual service rendered unto the Lord, even as a Sabbath service may be made sacrilegious, or the humblest deed made sacred by the purpose or spirit which inspires it. He saw very clearly that social entertainments held in the residences of Christian people, having a double purpose of raising money for the Church and becoming more socially acquainted, would also serve the Lord more effectively than many of the forms of Church themselves.

The fairs might bring together in close companionship a large number of people, a portion of whom were active Christians, filled with the missionary spirit. These if rightly inspired would act as a leaven in the whole lump, and turn many sinners from the error of their ways, by their social Christian example. Even persons who were prejudiced against the Church, and who were never seen inside the sacred walls, might attend one of these humbler gatherings, and there make the personal acquaintance of Christians whose influence over them would truly be eternal.

The advice of St. Paul with reference to marriage was most excellently applied to this series of Church entertainments, which were frequently held for the purpose of adding to the fund for the construction of the Tabernacle, viz. : " Be not unequally yoked together with unbelievers ;" in other words, be very sure not to associate with worldly people under circumstances where they will drag you down. If you are so unequally yoked together with an unbeliever that he has more power to pull you under than you have to lift him out, then you may be both foolish and wicked.

But in these social gatherings there was a great predominence of the religious idea, because of the purpose for which they were held, and because of the prayerful spirit which controlled the words and actions of the Christians engaged therein.

In 1861 a monster bazaar was held with the avowed purpose of raising sufficient funds to pay for the entire debt on the Tabernacle which was so soon to be finished, and the receipts exceeded even the expectations of Mr. Spurgeon himself.

This result was due very largely to the manner in

which it was conducted and the consecrated wor-
shipful spirit which appeared in all that was done.

Every gift made to the bazaar was received with
thanksgiving to God, and as an offering to His service. Everything was excluded from the proceedings which could work harm in a moral or religious
point of view. The committees engaged in the
undertaking, which often included a large number of
ladies and gentlemen who were not members of any
Church, frequently met for prayer, that they might be
guided by the hand of God. Nearly every person
engaged in it felt that it was in a religious service
and that the honor of the cause of God had been
placed in his hands.

In the series of regular religious meetings which
followed the opening of the Tabernacle, it was
again and again heard from the lips of repentent
seekers after God, "I cared nothing for religion
until that brother spoke to me concerning my soul's
salvation while engaged in the bazaar." The fair
was in itself a great revival of religion, although the
work was not publicly conducted as a Church service. No special prayer-meetings were held aside
from those of the different committees. Yet these
days furnished well-improved opportunities for personal conversation with persons who were not
Christians, but whose gift toward the cause had created within them a favorable interest in the general
subject. Such a gathering might have been a positive curse to the Church, and might have hindered the

payment of the debt, if it had been conducted in the worldly spirit which characterizes many such gatherings in other places, where the committees seemed to think of nothing but foolish display, senseless sport, or the squeezing out of their visitors as much money as possible. Where the idea is only to make money, even though it be for a Church, it usually results in far greater damage than good. But where the whole matter becomes, as it was in this case, an enthusiastic service in the name of the Saviour, and where the salvation of others was always kept most prominently in mind, while the gathering of money was made secondary; such meetings of the people become a spiritual blessing and a great financial gain.

A sincere desire to serve Christ, combined with the usual degree of hard English common sense, can be trusted to manage a Church bazaar so as to add greatly to the prosperity of the Saviour's kingdom. Mr. Spurgeon's people became well satisfied of that. And they have since used it in connection with the scores of chapels they have built, with almost unvarying success. The overshadowing and the indwelling of the Spirit of God can only account for the continued success of their undertaking, and for the manner in which many things usually deleterious became positively helpful.

It is said that the committee who cleared away the tables after the bazaar was closed were heard singing most heartily a hymn of praise to God.

The bazaar had given an opportunity to thousands of poor people to give their mite, and each giver followed his effort with affection, feeling ever afterward that he had a personal share in the Tabernacle.

As the mother loves the child for whom she makes the greatest sacrifices, so those Church members always love their Church home the most who have given toward it with the greatest generosity. The blessing of God which follows a cheerful giver is always shown in his greatly increased pleasure in attending the Church services and in his enjoyment of the Church's prosperity.

The subscriptions which followed the bazaar carried the sum up to nearly two thousand dollars above that which was needed to clear the Tabernacle from debt, and in May, 1861, when it was opened, they had paid all their bills and had a balance in the treasury.

Well might such a people sing " Praise God from whom all blessings flow."

CHAPTER IX.

MRS. SPURGEON AND HER WORK.

God saw that it was not good for man to be alone, and hence made a help that was meet for him. It is no easier to account for love than it is for taste. Like the dove which shines with all the reflected hues of heaven, it lights upon the most unseemly objects, and often without forethought or consideration, seeks apparently only a resting-place and a home.

With all our boasted free-will and pride of independence, how little we know of our future and how little we have to do with the moulding of the circumstances of life, is well demonstrated in the strange revolutions which love makes in human life.

If one could have looked down upon these two persons in 1850, seeing Susannah, an industrious, bright school-girl, in the great city, associating with city people, with city ideas and city culture; and Charles, a rude rustic at New Market, clumsy, awkward, and expressing by thought and gesture all the uncouth side of country life, they would have said that it was impossible for them to have found in each other's disposition or tastes that unity of thought which is a necessity to the most complete domestic life. Yet five years later, these two lives were so merged into each other as to make a most beautiful scene of affection in their home life, and so as to express their affection for each other in a harmony that was positively sublime.

Home is always the word which is nearest to the word heaven. The domestic love which makes home what it is, is the only sentiment on earth which makes heaven intelligible.

Miss Susannah Thompson's father was an attendant, or a member, of the New Park Street Church at the time it extended the call to Charles to become its pastor, but it is said that he was discouraged with the condition of the church, like many other members, and his family had, in a great measure, lost their interest in its meetings. He was a merchant, in prosperous circumstances, and consequently gave his family all the comforts and many of the luxuries of some aristocratic circles.

His daughter, Susanna, was of a quiet, sweet disposition, most earnestly devoted to Christian work and to silent deeds of charity. When her father mentioned in the family circle the fact that a young man from Essex was to preach the next Sunday in the Park Street pulpit, she paid but little heed to the announcement, and it is said that she could not be persuaded to attend the first service.

Mr. Spurgeon's own description of his dress, manners and feelings at the time he entered London for the first time, will show that he was at that time in no sense a person who would be naturally attractive in the eyes of the ladies. He had none of the sweet airs, and could not afford the fashionable dress, such as the beaux of the great metropolis affected. His expressions, both of countenance and speech, partook largely of his native fields. He did not know how to hold his hands, and made vain efforts to hide his feet. He states that in the boarding-house where he stopped the night before he preached for the first time in London, the boarders entertained him with marvellous stories of the learning, culture and critical disposition of the London people, and greatly frightened him by comparing him, by inference, with the celebrated preachers and learned theologians that London delighted to honor. He was so conscious of his own awkwardness and inability to fill so important a place as that at the New Park Street chapel, that he says he lay awake the entire previous night, and entered the church in the morning feeling very weary and trembling with apprehension. But he succeeded, through earnest prayer, and through the kind encouragement of the friends who attended the service, in getting through the day so acceptably as to win considerable sincere praise and feel a sense of encouragement in his heart.

When he appeared in the pulpit on his second visit to the city, he was greeted with many kindly smiles and encouraging nods, and the state of things had greatly changed in his favor.

The few members of the church who had heard him on his first visit, had taken especial pains to canvass the entire neighborhood, and bring to the service every friend over whom they had any personal influence. In this effort Susannah was induced to join, and made it her Christian duty to secure the attendance of her own acquaintances. Their pride in their church led the people to try to fill the house, in order that the place might appear less dreary and more inviting to the stranger who was to fill the pulpit.

A friend, who remembers well that day, says that Susannah said: "It would be a shame to have a man come so far and find the church so poorly attended." How little could that girl, in the simplicity of her Christian work and life, foresee how great was to be the effect upon her own happiness and usefulness of that Christian labor.

In this century, when every girl's life is to herself an enigma, because it depends so largely upon circumstances entirely beyond her control, how obscure her future must appear! To the young man, who can entertain reasonable ambitions and make probable prophecies concerning his future in business life, there is a measure of certainty which adds much to its attractiveness and much of enjoyment to his youthful studies. But a woman's life is far more uncertain, because it depends in so great a degree upon the appearance, habits and position of some man of whom, in her girlhood, she may know nothing whatever.

15

Such must have been the condition of Susanna when she saw, for the first time, this young man standing in the pulpit. That he would ever be any·thing more to her than a mere acquaintance, or possibly pastor and teacher, could never have entered her thoughts at that time, unless they wandered into the most extravagant imaginations. Their lives were so different. They were so far apart.

> " Man's love is of himself a thing apart,
> 'Tis woman's whole existence."

With Charles that day, his mind must have been entirely enveloped in the awful undertaking he had in hand, and cares which can scarcely be appreciated by any other person, must have kept his heart beating very fast and his brain crowded with conflicting anxieties. He could have cared little for the ladies that day, and could have given them but slight attention. His mind was overwhelmed with care.

What she thought has, of course, been hidden in the silent bowers of a Christian woman's modest reserve. A Providence which neither could have foreseen, but which both most reverently respected, had brought them that day into an association which was to furnish, in this life, a sweetest foretaste of Paradise, and begin an acquaintance which should not cease through all the rolling ages of a happy eternity.

While the precincts of the heart's love and the sacred realms of domestic affection are rightly regarded as holy ground, upon which the unwelcome stranger cannot tread, yet in the study of a great man's biography there is no more important event in his history than such a circumstance as this.

Many a man with a brilliant mind, with capital and social position, has been destroyed by an unfortunate marriage. Many others without capital or social position, or any especial gift of genius, have been lifted into prominence, wealth and fame, through the valuable support which they received in the potent aid of a brilliant and faithful wife. The cases are indeed very rare where a man of genius has made his mark upon his time or upon subsequent history, who was not strengthened, encouraged and supported by a persevering woman.

In some cases the husband is merely a figurehead, sensitively responsive to a power behind the throne, which dwells altogether with his wife. But view it in any light we choose, and endeavor by every possible excuse to belittle the influence of the wife, yet in every married man's history it works a very important factor in all that he accomplishes.

With a nature like that of Mr. Spurgeon's, with many defects to repair and a lack of classical education to be supplied, a cultivated and persevering wife might be considered an unquestioned necessity. It seems now to have been a part of the great Divine plan to have brought these two persons into intimate association, that the wife might supply all that was lacking in Mr. Spurgeon's outfit for the great work he was to do.

To the spectator, he had sacrificed much in giving up his college education for the purpose of carrying on the Lord's work at Waterbeach. But in the attendance of Susanna upon the service in London, we find a hand in the providential events completely making up to Mr. Spurgeon there, all that he had lost in his Christian resolution.

Intimate friends may have overestimated the loveliness of her mental character, and the writers who have mentioned her may have highly colored their representations, yet there can remain no doubt upon the most conservative mind, but that she was as remarkable a woman as he was a man.

It will readily be seen that the responsibility which he had assumed as a boy, in connection with one of the oldest and most aristocratic Baptist churches in London, would soon have discouraged him altogether, had there not entered into his life this unutterable affection and its consequent ambition to make a great man of himself.

Man is so constituted mentally, that he never reaches his highest attainments and never gives reins to the noblest ambitions, until he is aroused to the highest motives by a true and positive affection for some sweet-minded woman. There are ambitions in connection with the desire for money, with the hope of fame, and with the inspiration of a patriotic heart, but none of them will push a man on to such greatness of thought or heights of effort as a manly love, which influences all his hopes, all

his thoughts, and every attribute of his moral character.

After they had met and found in each other the companion which God had intended for them, Mr. Spurgeon would then be determined to go on with his pastoral work in London, and no discouragement whatever would be allowed to interfere with his intention there to remain.

To those biographers who have not considered how great a feature of his life his marriage must have been, the question has often been asked: "Why was not such a boy, with his attainments, a failure in such untoward surroundings?" The answer is partially found here. His love for true womanhood would lead him to sacrifice everything else but that, in order to succeed. Her eyes would inspire, and her advice confirm him under all circumstances, and lead him to the most reckless daring in anything that would be likely to please her. In a true love, such as was theirs, there could scarcely be any higher service of God than to be affectionately loyal to a God-given wife. Her home was in London. She would dislike greatly to leave it. His home must be where she was. Consequently we find a combination in this of all kinds of circumstances and motives, to determine his action in reference to the upbuilding of his new interests in London.

It is easy to see how much more carefully he would select his language, and how many more hours he would give to the study of his sermons, how much more cautious he would be in his care of the church, and how much more courteous he would be in his intercourse with the members of the church, with the feelings of a domestic love confirming his most sincere devotion to the service of God.

The man who could not be eloquent under these circumstances, would be exceedingly dull under any other. He who would not be fervent in spirit and diligent in business serving the Lord, with a providential combination, such as surrounded him then, would be a most disgraceful failure under many ordinary circumstances.

True worship, sincere patriotism and domestic love filled his heart with great ambitions and sustained him through the hours of most arduous work. "Victory or death" would be as truly his cry there, as it has been the motto of warriors in the midst of uncertain battle. He had secured a teacher who was much more than a teacher, as she supplied often motive and inspiration.

On the 8th day of January, 1856, at mid-day, Charles and Susanna were united in marriage.

That his wife must have been an unusually beloved young woman in the church, is evident from the fact that we find the marriage awakened no jealousy on the part of others, and did not stir the gossips of the neighborhood into prognostications of evil. "God bless them both," was the sincere benediction of young and old, of rich and poor, throughout their entire acquaintance.

Well might Charles then, on his knees before God, give most heartfelt thanksgiving for the blessings he had received, and pledge himself, with all his stubborn nature, to an entire lifetime devoted to the self-sacrificing service of the Saviour who had so favored him.

From their very first acquaintance, Mr. and Mrs. Spurgeon were a perpetual strength to each other. She could curb the uncouth eccentricities and correct his mistakes in language or history, and she hesitated not in the most affectionate manner to apply her criticisms where she saw they would do her husband good.

He urged her to take the place of a public critic and notice his errors that he might the more readily correct them, and as she was a lady of excellent good sense and of quite extensive reading, she was a far safer critic than any man he could have selected.

Had he married a silly woman, who would have regarded him as the perfection of sainthood, or a devotee of fashion, who would have discouraged him with her corrections, he could never have attained the eminence which he reached. Had he allied himself with a wife who was less pious and sincere, or who would not have maintained her hold upon the affections and esteem of his congregation, she would have served to injure his reputation and undermine many of the spiritual buildings he was able to construct.

But she worked with him, prayed with him, believed in him, and most affectionately loved him

through those many years of his work. The thought
of her, even when he was absent from home, was
to him a subtle rest of spirit. He could travel many
days and preach several times a day, finding a rest
in the thought that at home she was hourly praying
for him, and was awaiting him with a welcome he
could anticipate with a sense of divine peace.

Once when absent in Yorkshire, ten years after
their marriage, he wrote to her this characteristic
letter in poetry :

> Over the space that parts us, my wife,
>   I'll cast me a bridge of song,
> Our hearts shall meet, O joy of my life,
>   On its arch unseen, but strong.
>
>   *   *   *   *   *   *
>
> The wooer his new love's name may wear
>   Engraved on a precious stone ;
> But in my heart thine image I wear,
>   That heart has long been thine own.
>
> The glowing colors on surface laid,
>   Wash out in a shower of rain ;
> Thou need'st not be of rivers afraid,
>   For my love is dyed ingrain.
>
> And as every drop of Garda's lake
>   Is tinged with sapphire's blue,
> So all the powers of my mind partake
>   Of joy at the thought of you.
>
> The glittering dewdrops of dawning love
>   Exhale as the day grows old,
> And fondness, taking the wings of a dove,
>   Is gone like a tale of old.
>
> But mine for thee, from the chambers of joy,
>   With strength came forth as the sun,
> Nor life nor death shall its force destroy,
>   Forever its course shall run.

All earth-born love must sleep in the grave,
  To its native dust return;
What God hath kindled shall death out-brave,
  And in heaven itself shall burn.

Beyond and above the wedlock tie
  Our union to Christ we feel;
Uniting bonds which were made on high,
  Shall hold us when earth shall reel.

Though He who chose us all worlds before,
  Must *reign* in our hearts alone,
We fondly believe that we shall adore
  Together before His throne.

When his assailants spoke of him with sad falsehoods, and when friends forsook or betrayed, there was always one who stood like a shield between him and the arrows of wickedness, quenching their fiery darts most easily with the shield of domestic love.

Wherever in his busy life he could not go, she was there to supply the lack. Whenever there was a book needed, she was first to diligently search for it. Economical, neat, careful, conservative and quiet in all her relations to the public, she supplied to him so much of nerve, instruction and vigor as to make him what his brother often claimed he was, "two men, instead of one."

"How do you manage to do two men's work in a single day?" was the question asked of him by the great traveler, Dr. Livingstone.

"You have forgotten that there are two of us," said Mr. Spurgeon, "and the one you see the least of, often does the most work."

Stray gleams of the glory which filled his home are sometimes caught in a study of his sermons, and especially in many of his comments upon Scripture. Heaven is ever to him a Christian's affectionate home.

Mr. and Mrs. Spurgeon had but two homes after their marriage. One was in Nightingale Lane, Chapham Common, where they occupied a dwelling to which was attached a fruitful garden. There they lived for nearly twenty-five years. The very thought of it fills the reader with a reverent sensation. It was there that their twin sons, Charles and Thomas, were born ; it was there that pain and sickness often came ; it was there that the trials and cares of life were often discussed ; it was there that sermons were thought out and partially rehearsed before their delivery ; but it was also there that was always found a cheerful trust in God, unshaken love for each other, and a domestic peace, such as only the most perfect of English homes enjoy.

Mrs. Spurgeon, herself, in speaking of their "moving-day" from that first home in London, afterwards wrote : "What a stirring up of one's quiet nest this removal is ! and how tenderly one yearns to look on familiar objects from which we are to be parted forever ! The heart yearns over a place endeared by an intimate acquaintance of twenty-three years, and full of happy or solemn associations. Each nook and corner, both of house and garden, abounds with sweet or sorrowful memories, and the remembrance of manifold mercies clings like a rich tapestry to the walls of the desolate rooms. On this spot nearly a quarter of a century of blissful wedded life has been passed, and though both husband and wife have been called to suffer severe physical pain and months of weakness within its boundary, our house has been far oftener 'a Bethel' to us than a 'bochin.' The very walls might cry out against us as ungrateful did we not silence them by our ceaseless thanksgiving; for the Lord has here loaded us with benefits and consecrated every inch of space with tokens of His great loving kindness. The sun of His goodness has photographed every portion of our dear homes upon our hearts, and though other lights and shadows must be reflected there in coming days, they can never obliterate the sweet images which grateful memory will jealously preserve. Tender remembrances will render indelible the pictures of the sick-chamber, which so many times has almost been 'the gate of heaven' to our spirit; the little room, tenderly fitted up by a husband's careful love, and so often the scene of a scarcely-hoped-for convalescence; the study, sacred to the pastor's earnest work, and silent witness of wrestlings and communings known only to God and his own soul; the library, where the shelves gladly suffered a constant spoliation and renewal for the blessed work of the Book-Fund.

"It's hard to leave all these sympathetic surroundings and dwell in the house of a stranger; but we believe we have seen the cloudy pillar move, and heard our Leader's voice bidding us 'go forward,' so, in trustful obedience, we strike our tent, and prepare to depart to the 'place of which he has told us.' And our new home may be to us a 'Tabor' if our Lord will but dwell with us there! On our first view of it we were strongly reminded of Bunyan's description of the 'delectable mountains,' and every subsequent visit deepens that impression. '*A pleasant prospect on every side,*' said he, '*these mountains are Immanuel's land; they are within sight of His city; the sheep also are His, and He laid down His life for them.*'

"The shepherds show the pilgrims the gates of the Celestial City '*if they had the skill to look through their prospective glass.*' It may be that the Lord, our Shepherd, has called us to the top of this hill to show us '*something like the gate, and some of the glory of the place,*' beforehand, that our hearts may be set a-longing for the bliss of our eternal home. 'O Lord, if thy spirit go not with us, carry us not up hence!'"

The following inscription, written by Mr. Spurgeon, was left in the house:

"Farewell, fair room, I leave thee to a friend;
Peace dwell with him and all his kin.
May angels evermore the house defend
Their Lord hath often been within."

With such a home no external conflict could be too severe and no persecutions be unendurable. As the hearthstone of home gleams with a brighter and more cheerful ray when storms sweep without and rattle on the pane, so the presence of such a wife as Mrs. Spurgeon proved to be, makes the dwelling a paradise amid the weeds and briery deserts of a wicked world.

He could take home the basest calumnies and the most spiteful caricatures and there courageously laugh at their weakness most heartily.

> " Man may trouble and distress me,
> 'Twill but drive me to thy breast;
> Life with trials hard may press me,
> *Home* will bring me sweeter rest."

As the afflictions of life and the persecutions of our fellow-men make heaven dearer and fit us for its supreme enjoyment, so in this life, although it may be upon a smaller scale, the hard work and the cares of a man are at his home transmuted into the most precious joys, by the wife's sweet welcome which he receives at his door.

When through his wife's management and the liberality of kind friends and the unexpected rise in the value of his house, he was able to move from the smaller home into the large and beautiful villa at Westwood, with its lawn, shade trees, flower gardens and fountains, there was a strong feeling of regret and sadness on the part of them both as they stepped forth for the last time from their early home.

Mr. Spurgeon always regarded the old house as a dear friend, and often expressed his thankfulness that he was able to leave it in the hands of a dear acquaintance.

Although Mr. Spurgeon ever appeared to be a hearty, robust man, of unusual health, yet he was frequently compelled to take to his bed through illness, and there received the kind ministrations of his patient, affectionate wife. But a far greater trial to him than his own frequent sickness, was the gradually increasing infirmities which afflicted his wife through the major part of their married life. For a few years she was wholly an invalid, and became the subject of his most earnest prayers and most affectionate care. Her pitiful imprisonment by disease made her much dearer to him, as such an experience always affects the heart of any noble man. He could find no words to express his admiration for her benevolent Christian character, and was continually dissatisfied with himself that he was not able in some form or another to do more for the relief of her distress.

Day after day, and week after week, she sat in that easy chair, hoping against hope that she might be able to go forth once more to the active duties of the church, or at least to care for the domestic duties of the home. But years came and went, and she was still there. Her spirit yearned to be of more use to mankind, and she prayed the Lord to permit her to share in some direction in her husband's labors for the salvation of the souls of men. In answer to that prayer, she was directed to the establishment of that important enterprise, called the Book-Fund.

By that undertaking, she secured gifts of money and books from Christian donors, which she used in supplying the scant libraries of poor preachers in the country places.

Her own record of that undertaking furnishes a somewhat comprehensive idea of the work, and at the same time gives a more excellent estimate of her own character than anything any stranger could write. Hence we turn to what she has herself written, and present here such portions of it as will give the reader a full insight into her life as an invalid, and also into the marvellous results of the work she undertook.

Mr. Spurgeon, in 1886, in an introduction to a book containing a record of Mrs. Spurgeon's Book-Fund, very tenderly said :

"I gratefully adore the goodness of our Heavenly Father, in directing my beloved wife to a work which has been to her fruitful in unutterable happiness. That it has cost her more pain than it would be fitting to reveal, is most true ; but that it has brought her boundless joy, is equally certain. Our gracious Lord ministered to His suffering child, in the most effectual manner, when He graciously led her to minister to the necessities of His service. By this means, He called her away from her personal grief,

16

gave tone and concentration to her life, led her to
continual dealings with Himself, and raised her
nearer the centre of that region where other than
earthly joys and sorrows reigned supreme. Let
every believer accept this as the inference of experience, that for most human maladies the best relief
and antidote will be found in self-sacrificing work
for the Lord Jesus.

"If I said a word in praise of the worker herself,
my preface would not be acceptable to the author of
these reports, and therefore I must content myself
with expressing my conviction that the work is sadly
needed, has been exceedingly useful, and is still
urgently called for. How can many of our ministers
buy books? How can those in the villages get them
at all? What must their ministries become if their
minds are starved? Is it not a duty to relieve the
famine which is raging in many a manse? Is it not
a prudential measure, worthy of the attention of all
who wish to see the masses influenced by religion,
that the preachers who occupy our pulpits should be
kept well furnished with material for thought?

"By the Book-Fund, not less than twelve thousand
ministers of all denominations have been supplied
with at least a few fresh books. Sometimes men
have been aided in somewhat unusual studies for
which they had special predilection. Not long ago
I had to become an adviser to the Fund, as to a
grammar, etc., for the study of Syriac, for the use
of one who had a call in that direction. The Fund

does not profess to grant works other than those needed for the special work of the ministry, but even this gives a wide range, especially in the case of missionaries. I think great discretion has been used in the distribution of the bounty. I am sure it has been blended with the utmost sympathy and Christian love."

From that record we will try to collect those interesting facts which are german to this history, and quote, as far as possible, from her own words. When asked how the Book-Fund began, she said:

"It was in the summer of 1875 that my dear husband completed and published the first volume of his 'Lectures to my Students.' Reading one of the proof copies, I became so enamored with the book, that when the dear author asked, 'Well, how do you like it?' I answered with a full heart, 'I wish I could place it in the hands of every minister in England.' 'Then why not do so? How much will you give?' said my very practical spouse. I must confess I was unprepared for such a challenge. I was ready enough to desire the distribution of the precious book, but to assist in it, or help to pay for it, had not occurred to me; but 'John Ploughman' drives a straight furrow to one's heart, and knows how to turn over the thick clods of selfishness which lie there choking up the useful growths; and very soon his words set me thinking how much I could spare from housekeeping, or personal matters, to start this new scheme. I knew it would necessitate a pressure somewhere, for money was not plentiful just then; but to see dear John's face beam so radiantly at the idea of my scattering his books far and wide, was worth any effort; and love, even more than obedience, constrained me to carry out the suddenly formed plan. Then came the wonderful part; I found the money ready and waiting! Upstairs, in a little drawer, were some carefully hoarded crown-pieces, which, owing to some foolish fancy, I had been gathering for years, whenever chance threw one in my way; these I now counted out, and found they made a sum exactly sufficient to pay for one hundred copies of the work! If a twinge of regret at parting from my cherished, but unwieldy, favorites passed over me, it was gone in an instant, and then they were given freely and thankfully to the Lord, and in that moment, though I knew it not, 'The Book-Fund' was inaugurated.

"All last winter, in the sunniest corner of the south window of our especial sanctum, there stood a common garden flower-pot containing a little plant which we deemed a marvel of grace and beauty. We had sown some lemon pips the preceding autumn with a lively hope that one or more of them might possess the wonderful life-germ, and we were well rewarded for our confidence. In due time a frail little stem and two of the tiniest leaves that ever coaxed their way through the dark mould made their appearance, and from that moment it was watched, and watered, and tended with assiduous care. So

METROPOLITAN TABERNACLE, C. H. SPURGEON, PASTOR.

frail at first, and delicate, that a drop of dew would
have overwhelmed it, it nevertheless soon gained
courage, the tender stem strengthened, one by one
other and larger leaves unfolded themselves, and the
little plant stood perfect and complete. It was a
very little thing; but it gave great pleasure; and
though some of the younger members of the household would occasionally ask, with just a suspicion of
sarcasm in their tone, 'If there were any lemons
yet?' we cherished our little plant even more lovingly, and thanked God who, with infinite tenderness
towards His suffering children, often deepens and
intensifies their enjoyment of daily mercies, throwing
a special charm around their common comforts, and
causing a leaf, a flower, or the song of a bird, to
whisper sweet 'comfortable thoughts' in their
hearts.

"But this winter our Heavenly Father has given
us a better plant to care for. The little tree of the
'Book-Fund' sprang from as small a beginning as
the lemon plant itself, and we fondly hope it is as
surely a creation of the Lord's hand. Great was the
lovingkindness which brought *this* plant into our
sick-chamber, and gave us the loving commission to
'dress and keep it.' With what joy we received the
charge, and how happy the work made us, words
fail to tell; but since the little tree has grown rapidly
under the sunshine of the Lord's blessing, we
thought our friends would be interested to know
how much and what manner of fruit it bears.

"At first we intended only to distribute one hundred copies of Mr. Spurgeon's 'Lectures to my Students,' but we received so many kind donations from friends who sympathized with our wishes, that we soon became ambitious, and, without discontinuing the distribution of 'Lectures,' we longed to supply needy ministers with the precious volumes of 'The Treasury of David,' 'Sermons,' etc. This we have been enabled to do, and the work goes on daily. Without any solicitation, friends have sent in £182, and though our dear Mr. Editor thinks they might not like their names to be published, yet if he should one day change his mind, they are all ready for him, faithfully registered, and would look very nice in his *Sword and Trowel.* We keep also a strict debtor and creditor account, in which said dear Mr. Editor takes great interest, being quite as delighted as ourselves when any increase to the fund is announced. Better still, the Lord's 'book of remembrance' is open, and therein assuredly the names of all those who aid his toiling servants will be recorded. We are still prepared to give the 'Lectures' to all ministers who apply direct to us. Up to this date we have sent out five hundred and fifty 'Lectures,' each one with an earnest prayer for God's blessing, and we have had many delightful proofs that this has been bestowed.

"Perhaps, in closing this short statement, my dear Mr. Editor would graciously accord me the privilege of laying aside for a moment that formal and perplexing 'we,' and allow me to say how deeply I am personally indebted to the dear friends who have furnished me with the means of making others happy. For me there has been a *double* bless-ing. I have been both recipient and donor, and in such a case as this it is hard to say which is the 'more blessed.' My days have been made in-describably bright and happy by the delightful duties connected with the work and its little arrangements, and so many loving messages have come to me in letters, such kind words, such hearty good wishes, such earnest, fervent prayers have surrounded me, that I seem to be living in an atmosphere of bless-ing and love, and can truly say with the Psalmist, 'My cup runneth over.' So, with a heart full of gratitude to God, and deep thankfulness to my dear friends, I bid them for the present a loving fare-well."

"My 'Few Words' in the February number of *The Sword and Trowel* were received with so much tender sympathy and consideration, that I feel encouraged to present you with another slight sketch of the work which the Lord's love and your kindness have made so prosperous. I then told you from how small a matter the fund rose, and how pitifully and graciously the Lord dealt with me in giving me so blessed a work to do for Him when all other service was impossible. *Now* I have the same song to sing, but the notes are higher and more assured, and the accompanying chords deeper and fuller; for the 'little one has become a thousand,' and the mercy which was so great before has grown exceedingly, until my heart echoes the poet's words:

> ' For if thy work on earth be sweet,
> What must thy glory be?'

I have very much to tell you, and I shall do it in the best way I can; but as all my friends know that my pen is 'unaccustomed to public speaking,' I think I may crave special indulgence for all failures and shortcomings.

"We will discuss money matters first, because I want you to sing 'Laus Deo' with me. John Ploughman says that 'Spend, and God will send, is the motto of a spendthrift.' Now, I must not dispute this, for dear John is always right, and, moreover, knows all about everything, but I may say I consider it singularly inappropriate to the spendthrift, and should like it handed over to me at once and forever for my Book-Fund; for again and again has it been proved most blessedly true in my experience. I have 'spent' ungrudgingly, feeling sure that the Lord would 'send' after the same fashion, and indeed he has done so, even 'exceeding abundantly above what I could ask or even think.' I have received now upwards of £500, and the glory of this is that it is all spent, and more keeps coming! I never tell you, dear friends, when my store is slender, but I am sure the Lord does, and opens your hearts to give just when it is most needed; for never since I first began the work have I had to refuse an application for want of funds. I must tell you, too, that this £500 represents quite £700 or £800 in books; for Mr. Spurgeon's good publishers let me purchase on such liberal terms that by their delightful magic my sovereigns turn into thirty and sometimes forty shillings each! This, also, is of the Lord, and I bless Him for it. I often look with intense pleasure on the long list of subscribers' names spread out before the Lord, and before him only; for your kind deeds, my dear friends, are unpublished to the world, but are, per-haps, for this reason all the more precious in His sight, who 'seeth not as man seeth.' It is, indeed, pleasant to look down the long columns and note how many strangers have become dear friends, and former friends have grown dearer through this loving link of sympathy for Christ's servants be-tween us."

"But it is time I gave you some details of the work accomplished. The number of books given up to this moment is 3,058, and the persons receiv-ing them have been pastors of all denominations. But ah! dear friends, when I look at the list of names, I see the only shadow of sadness that ever rests upon my Book-Fund. It is the grief of know-ing that there exists a terrible necessity for this ser-vice of love; that without this help (little enough, indeed, compared with their wants) the poor pastors to whom it has been sent must have gone on famishing for lack of mental food, their incomes being so wretchedly small that they scarcely know how to 'provide things honest' for themselves and their families, while money for the purchase of books is absolutely unattainable."

"It is most touching to hear some tell with eloquence the effect the gift produced upon them. One is 'not ashamed to say' he received his parcel with 'tears of joy,' wife and children standing around and rejoicing with him. Another, as soon as the wrappings fall from the precious volumes, praises God aloud and sings the Doxology with all his might; while a third, when his eyes light on the long-coveted 'Treasury of David,' 'rushes from the room' that he may go alone and 'pour out his full heart before his God.'"

"Now this is very beautiful and admirable, but is there not also something most sorrowfully suggestive to the church of God? Surely these 'servants of Christ,' these 'ambassadors for God,' ought to have received better treatment at our hands than to have been left pining so long without the aids which are vitally necessary to them in their sacred calling. Books are as truly a minister's needful tools as the plane, and the hammer, and the saw, are the necessary adjuncts of a carpenter's bench. We pity a poor mechanic whom accident has deprived of his working gear, we straightway get up a subscription to restore it, and certainly never expect a stroke of work from him while it is lacking; why, I wonder, do we not bring the same common-sense help to our poor ministers, and furnish them liberally with the means of procuring the essentially important books? Is it not pitiful to think of their struggling on from year to year on £100, £80, £60, and some (I am ashamed to write it) on less than £50 per annum? Many have large families, many more sick wives, some, alas! have both; they have heavy doctors' bills to pay, their children's education to provide for, are obliged to keep up a respectable appearance, or their hearers would be scandalized; and how they manage to do all this and yet keep out of debt (as, to their honor and credit be it said, the majority of them do) only they and their ever-faithful God can know! I never hear a word of complaint from them, only sometimes a pathetic line or two, like this: 'After upwards of sixteen years' service in the Master's vineyard, I am sorry to say that, with a small salary, and a wife and five daughters to provide for, my library is exceedingly small, and I am not in a position to increase its size by purchasing books.' Or again, like this: 'My salary is small (£60), and if I did not get some little help from some benevolent societies, I should have very great difficulty in keeping the wolf from the door.' Are these men to be kept in poverty so deep that they positively cannot afford the price of a new book without letting their little ones go barefoot? 'The laborer is worthy of his hire;' but these poor laborers in the gospel field get a pittance which is unworthy both of the workmen and the work, and if their people (who ought to help them more) either cannot or will not do so, we at least, dear friends, will do all in our power to encourage their weary hearts and refresh their drooping spirits. This is a digression, I dare say, from my authorized subject; but I was obliged to say what I have said, because my heart was hot within me, and I so earnestly want to do these poor brethren good service. Now I return to the details of my work."

"I have been doing a brave business in Wales through the magnificent generosity of a stranger, whom now we count a friend. This gentleman first introduced himself to us by sending £100 to Mr. Spurgeon, £50 of which was for my Book-Fund. I was greatly gratified at receiving so large a sum all at one time, and set about 'spending' it as quickly as possible, and here you will see how grandly true my 'motto' proved; for about six months after the first gift, the same kind friend called at our house one evening, and to our sincere admiration and astonishment, announced his intention of giving a copy of 'Lectures to my Students' to *every* Calvinistic Methodist minister, preacher, and student in North Wales (of whom there are five hundred) if I would undertake the 'trouble' of sending them. Trouble!! The word was inadmissible! With intense joy and deep gratitude to God I received the charge, and *another* £50 to meet expenses! This was on the 18th of March, 1876. Since then, to this day, the work there has flourished; for as soon as four hundred copies had been given in the northern part, I received authority from the same noble donor to continue, at his expense, the distribution throughout South Wales also. The books are very eagerly accepted by our Welsh brethren, and on May 16th, the Quarterly Association sent copies in Welsh and English of a resolution passed at their meeting at Ruthin, of 'Cordial thanks to the kind brother, whoever he may be, to whose liberality we are indebted, etc., etc., and grateful acknowledgments to Mrs. Spurgeon, for her kindness in forwarding the books.' Nor does the matter rest here; other ministers besides Calvinistic Methodists coveted the precious volume, and wrote to me asking why they should be left out? I have supplied all who have written, and at this present moment I have promised copies to all the Wesleyan ministers of South Wales, and when they are satisfied, I doubt not their northern brethren will request the same favor. These copies, of course, are provided by my Book-Fund, our friend's gift being confined to his own denomination; but you see, dear friends, I never can be the least troubled at a large expenditure, because I have the firmest possible faith in my motto, 'Spend, and God will send.'

"Some weeks since, a gentleman sent me a splendid lot of second-hand books, so well selected and suitable, that they have proved most valuable in making up parcels; but usually I would prefer that help did not come to me in that shape; for I find, as a rule, that Mr. Spurgeon's works are more eagerly sought after, and more joyfully welcomed than any others. 'His words are like the dew-drops of heaven to my soul,' writes one pastor; and to most 'The Treasury of David' seems to have been a possession long coveted and ardently desired.

"Am I not happy to have been able to send forth seven hundred volumes of this veritable 'Treasure'? I have given also a goodly number of Mr. Spurgeon's lesser works. This arises from the fact that many evangelists, colporteurs, and lay preachers apply to me for books; and, although my fund is chiefly for the aid and comfort of poor pastors, I find this other class so sorely needing encouragement and help, that I cannot pass them by. Denied the blessing of a solid education in their youthful days, they find it difficult to pick up knowledge in middle life, and when called upon to conduct cottage-meetings or open-air services, they painfully feel the strain on their mental powers. To such the 'Morning and Evening Readings' are an inestimable boon; for, open the book where they will, they may find sermons in *embryo* in every page, and nuggets of thought only waiting to be picked up and appropriated.

"Next to 'The Treasury of David,' the 'Sermons' of our very dear Editor (Mr. Spurgeon) are the objects of desire on the part of those who know their worth, and happy is he who has the set complete! I have helped very many to attain their wishes in this matter when they have already possessed many volumes ; others have to be content for the present with three, four, six, or eight volumes, as the case may be. I cannot speak of the blessing these Sermons carry with them wherever they go ; God owns and blesses them so mightily that eternity alone will reveal their power and value.

"And now, dear friends, though I have by no means exhausted my information, I think I have told you all I can remember of special interest. What do you think of your work ? It is yours as much as mine ; for without your kind and loving aid I could not carry it on to so large an extent. Does it satisfy and please you ? To me, as you know, it brings unalloyed joy and comfort, and to the Lord's poor servants it carries new life, and light, and vigor ; but I want most of all that it should promote *God's glory*, and have for its chief aim and object the uplifting of His holy name. Do, dear fellow-workers, pray very earnestly that a rich blessing may rest upon every book sent out, so that first the minister, then his church, and next of all the unsaved in the congregation, may be the better, and the Lord may receive ' the thanksgiving of many.'

"I cannot close my letter without reference to my little lemon plant ; for its history interested many, and it will ever be tenderly associated in my mind with my God-given work. It has thriven in its way as gracefully and grandly as the Book-Fund, and is now an ambitious, healthy young tree, preparing itself, I hope, for future fruit-bearing. I have always

17

cherished the fanciful idea that each leaf must rep. resent £100 ; so now you can count them, and smile at the magnificent future I anticipate for my Book-Fund. Twenty-one, are there not? That must mean £2,100, and *plenty of strength to grow more!* Well, it seems a great deal of money, certainly ; but what a trifle it must be to the God who made all the silver and the gold ! Ah ! I believe that some day,

> " When grace has made me meet
> His lovely face to see,"

the subscription list of the Book-Fund will record its thousands of pounds ; the once tiny plant will be a tree bearing fruit to perfection, and the dear old motto, "Spend, and God will send," will be found true and unfailing to the end."

Again in January, 1877, she wrote as follows :

" 'A record of combat with sin, and labor for the Lord.' These words on the cover of our magazine startled me the other day as I sat thinking over my work, and what I should say about it. I felt almost ashamed of my audacity in presuming to ask a place again amidst its pages, seeing that I am not strong enough to bear a 'sword,' and my 'trowel' is such a very little one that it can only hope to gather enough mortar to supply some few of the laborers who build up the living stones. But I remembered with exceeding comfort that, when the wall of Jerusalem was repaired, in Nehemiah's time, the work of the daughters of Shallum was as faithfully recorded as the labor of the princes and the priests.

"So I take courage to tell again of the Lord's great goodness to me, and how marvellously He has continued to help and bless the Book-Fund. As certainly as if He had stretched forth His hand from the heavens and given me a written commission for the service, so surely do I know that this work came to me through His indulgent love, and from the first moment of its existence to the present, He has guided, and supported, and blessed it, and every atom of the glory shall be His. *He* sent me the needful funds to carry it on, by moving the hearts of His people to help me ; for not one penny of the £926 received from August 11th of last year till now was solicited except from Him. And He has heard and answered the prayer that a great blessing might follow the books into the homes of His dear servants, comforting their hearts and refreshing their spirits, as well as aiding them in their preparation for the pulpit. I have *two great heaps* of letters from them, so heavy that I lift them with difficulty ; and if all the joy and gratitude to God therein expressed could be written out, it would fill some volumes. Knowing how deeply interested in these letters the readers of *The Sword and the Trowel* have hitherto been, I propose in this paper to give a series of extracts from them, a set of word pictures as it were, which I shall call a glimpse at some English interiors.

Years ago, when I had the felicity of sharing my dear husband's annual holiday, one of our chief pleasures consisted in visiting the picture gallery of every continental town we entered. There 'walking circumspectly' over the shining, treacherous floors, we spent many happy hours, and enjoyed to the full the works of the grand old masters; but I am not ashamed to confess that I at least used to linger longer and more lovingly over a 'Dutch Interior,' by Teniers or Ostade, than I cared to do over any 'Madonna and Child' that Raphael or Rubens ever painted. These latter never stirred any devotional feelings within my soul, and failing this, they ceased to interest, and even grew tiresome by constant repetition. But it was charming to be absorbed in the 'little beautiful works,' as an authority on painting calls them, which the Dutch masters loved to draw with such wonderful and tender minuteness of detail. The interior of a fisherman's hut, with its quaint wooden cradle, and its basket of freshly-caught fish, would, on close inspection, reveal unsuspected objects of interest, and the picturesque farm kitchens, with their glittering array of bright pans, their wealth of delf ware, their chubby children, and their comely Vrows, were so homelike, and so natural, that the more one gazed at them the more vividly real they became, and it was an easy task to weave a tale of family joy or sorrow around each glowing canvas.

"But now I want to show my friends, by pen in lieu of pencil, some scenes in English home-life where the tale of gladness or of suffering is even more plainly pictured, and needs no effort of the imagination to unfold it. A hasty glance into a parlor, at the moment when a gift from the Book-Fund has arrived; a peep into the study where the four portly volumes of 'The Treasury of David' have just enriched the scanty store of books; a glimpse of a figure with bowed head and clasped hands, pouring out a heart full of gratitude before his God—these, and such as these, tell their own story, and as we pass from one picture to another, will only need a word or two from me to introduce them. I could show some where tearful faces gather, and a little coffin occupies the foreground; but these are veiled and my hand dares not withdraw the covering.

"The first 'Interior' which I point out to you is shining with the brightness of domestic love. The little room may be poorly furnished, and the book-shelves, I know, are sadly bare (how can they be otherwise, when the minister's income has the very uncomfortable habit of oscillating between £40 and £60 a year?); but you can see with what intense delight that kind and happy wife is assisting to un-pack the treasure of new books which will cheer her husband's heart, and make him feel a richer man for some time to come.

"Now we come to a small but choice picture. The minister sits in his study (a cosy one), and we rejoice to see his shelves moderately stocked with books; he has just had the pleasure of adding "The Treasury of David," and Watson's "Body of

Divinity" to his store ; he is writing rapidly, and this is what he says :

'This evening I have received the four much-desired volumes. Heartily I thank you, and unfeignedly bless the Lord, joining in the prayer so kindly recorded in Vol. I. that the precious contents may avail me. Here is a mine of gold—I hope to dig up nuggets for my people. How the cream of the gospel stands thickly on this unadulterated milk ! Prayer and meditation shall churn it into butter; nay, shall I not give them butter and honey till they *all* know how to refuse the evil flesh-pots of Egypt, and choose the good things of the land where David dwelt, where milk and honey flow ? Your noble efforts for ministers will be a blessing to both mind and body. It *is* rather trying to the nerves to be clearing the ground with a borrowed axe, carving wood with one's fingers, and working at the pump when the sucker is dry. But now, through Mrs. Spurgeon's loving work, poor men whose thoughts stand still for want of gear-oil will have heart and mind set spinning like the 'Chariots of Amminadib!" '

There is one difficulty I experience in arranging this little gallery of home scenes, which arises from the loving gratitude of the sketchers themselves. Some of the most interesting and touching letters I receive contain so many gentle and gracious personalities, that I am obliged to conceal them from public view, and for this reason many a bright picture enshrined in the privacy of my 'sanctum' can never leave it to touch other hearts as it has touched mine. I hope, however, that those I am able to present to my friends will interest them greatly, and next in order I place one which has two aspects—winter and summer; for, thanks to the kindness of dear friends, I was able, for a time at least, to make the sun shine on the hitherto cheerless prospect. Would to God I could do more, not only for this 'good wife,' but for the many others who I know have terrible reason

to be 'afraid of the snow for their households.'
Just think of the dear little children patiently lying
in bed while their scanty clothing was being washed!

"Although I have scores more of such letters, I
am afraid I must close my collection here, lest I tire
my reader's patience, and trespass too far on my
Editor's precious pages. It has been a joy inexpressible to minister, even in the least degree, to
the crying needs of the pastors who have sought the
aid of the Book-Fund; but I cannot forget that
there are hundreds still unsupplied, and if the Lord
permit and spare me, I hope to do more this year
than was accomplished in the past. I depend wholly
on the Lord to move the hearts of His people to
help me, and I know He 'will not fail me,' nor 'for-
sake the work of His own hands.' 4,967 volumes
have been distributed, 701 ministers have received
grants of books, and as I am corresponding secretary,
as well as treasurer, manager, etc., my friends can
imagine I have had full employment. The only part
of the work delegated to another is the packing of
the parcels, and this service is always performed as
a 'labor of love' by the willing hands of the dear
friend to whose devoted affection I already owe
so much. Who should be my 'director in chief' and
my 'referee' in all perplexities but my dear Editor?
To him I run in search of counsel, comfort, or wise
advice, and need I say I always find it?

"For many weeks past I have had a great desire
in my heart to write out the gracious details of the

Lord's dealings with the Book-Fund during the present year; but almost constant pain has fettered both head and hand, and rendered the fulfilment of the heart's wish well nigh impossible. But even the 'school of affliction' has its 'holidays,' true holydays these, and as the 'good Master' has granted me one such to-day, I will consecrate it to His honor and glory by telling what great things He hath done for me and my work since I wrote last. The commencement of the new year was marked by an offer of six volumes of the Metropolitan Tabernacle Pulpit to every minister who had formerly been a student of the Pastors' College; and so enthusiastically was it responded to, that in three months' time 164 of our own old students had received 980 volumes! I had intended this effort to be an extra one, and to extend over the entire year; but the Lord had more work for me to do than I knew of, so He would allow of no lingering, but graciously gave me strength to accomplish easily what at first sight seemed a formidable task. During this time the usual work of the Book-Fund was not neglected, but applications were cheerfully responded to.

"For a short time during the months just flown by, it seemed as if the Lord were trying my faith by sending me more 'needs' than 'supplies,' but I am almost ashamed to speak of fears which then possessed me. Now I see that the Lord only brought a cloud over the sun to veil its brightness, lest the heat of labor should overpower His weak child, and

cause her to faint under the burden of the day. So,
blessed be His name, He 'leads on softly' as 'we
are able to bear it.' Turning over the pages of my
'day-book,' I cannot but rejoice to know that already
nearly 3,000 volumes have been distributed since
the beginning of this year ; and though this number
falls wofully short of supplying the need which exists, yet I thank God and take courage.

"The Book-Fund is the joy of my life, and ever
since the Lord gave the sweet service into my weak
and unworthy hands He has led me by green pastures and beside still waters, and crowned me with
loving kindness and tender mercies.

"The Book-Fund has received this year some
splendid additions, as gifts, to its stores of works by
other authors, and I have rejoiced greatly to have at
my disposal such standard volumes of divinity as the
works of Haldane, Dr. Hodge, and others. But the
fact becomes more and more evident to me every
day, that unless already possessed of 'The Treasury
of David,' our pastors look upon no other volumes
as my gift with complete satisfaction, and that in applying to me for books, they fix their heart's desire
upon 'The Treasury,' or the 'Sermons,' as the
summum bonum of their happiness. And I think this
is very natural and very proper, so long as the
management of the Book-Fund rests entirely in these
feeble hands ; but I trust that some day, when all
the churches awaken to a sense of the urgent need
there is that 'the poor minister's bookshelf' should

have plenty of books upon it, many a noble volume, both ancient and modern, will take its place beside 'The Treasury of David.'

"As to old books, which sometimes come to me troublously fast, I am obliged to smuggle them in with the coveted works of my dear husband, and but a very faint echo of any welcome they receive ever reaches my ear. I really fear that some people think that anything in the shape of a book will do for a minister, or they would scarcely send such things as 'Advice to Wives and Mothers,' 'Essays on Marriage,' or 'Letters to a Son,' as aids to pulpit preparation!

"On looking over the list of contributors for the last year, I find a falling-away of some old friends, which somewhat grieves me, for the work is more deeply needed than ever.

"Tell the dear friends who read *The Sword and the Trowel* that 'my mouth is filled with laughter, and my tongue with singing' at the remembrance of the gracious love which continues to give support, and sustenance, and success to me in my beloved work. I am impatient to speak of His mercy, and feel constrained now to call on all who love the Lord to rejoice in my joy, and to aid me in magnifying His dear name. It is only two years since this sweet service was gently and graciously laid on my heart and hands, and yet during that time the Lord has enabled me, though compassed with infirmity, to send forth, like seed corn, many thousands of

volumes to aid the toiling laborers in the gospel
field. More than £2,000 have been received and
expended; the money coming 'fresh from the mint
of heaven,' for God has sent it all; as the dear
friends through whom it reaches me must very well
know, seeing that I never ask them for their loving
gifts. Just as the olive trees in Zechariah's vision
constantly and silently yielded their rich streams to
feed the lights of the golden candlestick, even so,
as divinely and mysteriously, does the Lord send me
the means to provide 'oil, beaten oil, for the lamps
of the sanctuary.'

"Ah! dear Mr. Editor, sound the notes of praise
for me! I want God's people to know how very
good He is to unworthy me, that they may take
comfort and courage from my experience of His
tenderness and love. I would I had Miriam's tim-
brel in my hand to-day to 'sing unto the Lord'
withal, and lead out others to sing also; but as that
cannot be, I pray you, lift up your voice for me, and
'praise the Lord before all the people.'

"The famine is sore in the land—not a famine of
bread, nor a thirst for water, but a deeply-felt and
widespread need of mental food, by those under-
shepherds who have to 'feed the flock of God';
and I had hoped that all the friends who had so generously aided me at the commencement of my work
would have 'continued with me.' To the many who
have done so, I tender my most heartfelt thanks.
'God bless you,' dear friends, and return into your

own bosoms some of the joy, and gladness, and gratitude with which you have filled mine. New friends, too, are cordially welcomed to co-operation in the blessed work, and every gift that comes for the Book-fund is offered to the Lord as a sacrifice of thanksgiving. I am just now rejoicing over the fact that the Lord has inclined the heart of a dear friend, to whom I am already greatly indebted, to give me a large donation for the purpose of supplying all the Presbyterian ministers in Argyleshire with 'The Treasury of David,' and I have another sum of money given by one who is a great sufferer, set apart for the distribution of the same precious volumes in Ireland. For the next few months, dear friends, you may know that the 'Work of the Book-Fund' will be in the full swing of business; and I pray you to remember that you can truly and tenderly help me by asking the Lord to set the seal of His blessing on every book sent out.

"Does any one care to know that my lovely lemon tree is in vigorous health and perfect beauty? I have not dared to count its leaves lately, because I feel it has far outstripped the proportions with which my fancy fettered it; yet I never look upon it or think about it without blessing God for making it grow so wonderfully in my sick-room that winter, where it heralded and illustrated, helped forward, and finally became the emblem of the Book-Fund."

In 1877, Mrs. Spurgeon again wrote:

"In giving an 'account of her stewardship' during the past twelve months, the writer is actuated by an intense desire that every word she writes may reveal the infinite tenderness and love which the Lord has displayed towards her. She wishes above all things to call attention, not to her own doings, but to God's dealings with her; and she earnestly prays that no word of hers may in the least obscure the lovely radiance of that mercy and grace of which the following pages are a record. If any heart shall be filled with holy admiration and praise, at the wonderful condescension of the Lord to one of the least of His children, in giving her this work to do, and strengthening her to perform it; if any feeble faith shall find fresh life and power in the consideration of His unfailing faithfulness to one of the poor dependants on His bounty; if any honor and glory shall be gotten to the Lord through this little report, her 'labor will not have been in vain in the Lord.'

"The Great Master could not have chosen a 'weaker vessel' by which to convey the treasure of knowledge to His servants; nor could he have selected to minister to the wants of His toiling messengers one more needing the ministry of love on her own account; but it is sometimes His good pleasure by His choice of servants to manifest His strength and wisdom, making the very feebleness and foolishness of His chosen instruments to redound to the greater glory of His sacred name. 'Make known His deeds among the people, talk ye all of His wondrous works,' sings David; and truly, if David's God will help His child to tell in fitting words the story of His great mercy and love to her, the lips of some of His saints shall be set singing fresh psalms of praise.

"Into this dear home of mine, as any one may easily imagine, the tide of periodical literature flows pretty freely. Dailies, weeklies, monthlies, quarterlies—papers and pamphlets of all sorts and descriptions, pour in like a flood, and for a season overwhelm the pastor's study table. From thence, at ebb-tide, they drift lazily into my sanctum, and, cast up upon my coast, they yield me pleasant spoils of amusement and information. From their pages I have lately gathered, with some surprise and much pleasure, the knowledge that a very large number of God's people are seeking to accomplish, by individual effort, those works of benevolence and Christian love which in days gone by were attempted only by fully constituted agencies, and societies with vast resources. A special form of need seems to strike some particular heart with pity, and forthwith the hand is stretched forth to relieve it, not with fitful or capricious charity, but with a wise tenderness and determined constancy which lead at last to an entire consecration to the chosen service. Some of the religious periodicals above alluded to contain long lists of such 'works of faith and labors of love,' and in many I note that, while they confide in a human head for management, they lean wholly on the hand of the Lord for maintenance. A fellow-feeling for these workers prompts me to watch their course with loving interest, and often leads me to breathe a prayer for their prosperity and success. I know that the world's great need necessitates the church's organized efforts on the largest scale, and therefore I bid 'God speed' with all my heart to the grand societies which are the glory of our land; but yet I turn to the solitary sower of the seed, or to the lonely gatherer-out of stones, with the most vivid and loving sense of kin-ship and communion, because our experiences so well agree.

"My own work, so feeble and insignificant in com-parison with that of others, can claim but the most modest mention among the numberless schemes for the glory of God and the good of man to which reference has been made, and yet I may assert that its origin is as divine, its object as beneficent, its support as certain, and its success as assured as the most glorious of them all. Though but a rill among the rivers, it sprang from the same heavenly source as the greatest of them; though as yet only a sap-ling among the trees of wood, it 'giveth goodly boughs' and grateful shade in its measure; and though it be but one note in the never-ceasing song of 'Glory to God in the highest, peace on earth, and good-will to man,' it will one day help to swell the shout of rapture which shall rise when the 'glory of the Lord shall cover the earth as the waters cover the sea.'

"Hoping that this little book may fall into the hands of some who have hitherto been strangers to my work, I propose to give full information concerning it, and, yielding to that habit which I suppose is inherent in us all, of trying to imitate those we love most, I shall 'divide my discourse into four heads,' beginning with the origin."

CHAPTER X.

Continuing her interesting account, Mrs. Spurgeon said:

"The 'Fund became a fact' in the most natural manner possible to all outward seeming; for, as the kind writer of the first report says, 'the casual pleasantries of a summer's day suggested the distribution of books to poor ministers;' but faith traces the true rise and spring of this 'brook by the way' to a higher source, and humbly dares to ascribe the origin of the Book-Fund to the kind hand of the loving Father Himself, who is revealed to us as the 'God of all comfort.' No loving relative, however earnestly bent on discovering a fresh source of alleviation for constant pain, or a compensating joy for a life of comparative seclusion, would for a moment have imagined that the desired solace would have been found in this most blessed work. 'God, that comforteth those that are cast down, comforted us,' after His own peculiar manner, by putting a delightful work into our feeble charge. Tenderly, too, and gradually, as His poor weak child was able to bear it, did the Lord 'lead on softly,' until 'He brought her out into a wealthy place and established her goings,'

"An intense desire took possession of me, after reading my dear husband's 'Lectures to his Students,' to place a copy in the hands of every minister in England, and consulting with the dear author on the matter, he approved my wish, and we decided to devote a few pounds to the partial gratification of it. Before the distribution of the copies thus purchased was completed, friends heard of and appreciated the scheme, and sent gifts, some of one hundred, some of fifty volumes, some of money, to help in the work, so that very quietly and silently, but most surely, as the months rolled on, it came to be a matter of established fact that a Book-Fund existed and prospered.

"One day, in my husband's study, the four comely volumes of 'The Treasury of David' caught my eye, and the question instantly sprang to my lips, 'Why could I not send these also to poor ministers? Only think what a boon they would be!' Conjugal love feared the task would be too heavy, and the responsibility of such a work too burdensome for the often weary one; but the Lord knew better, for He fostered the desire till it became too strong to be repressed, and then He graciously gave the power and means to fulfil it. Blessed be His name, I feel that it cannot be presumption to believe that this sacred charge was given me from the Lord Himself, because the fact has been abundantly proved, both by my own weakness and the manifestation of His gracious strength.

"It is not the first time He has 'given power to the faint,' or chosen a 'thing of nought' to do Him service, and I rejoice with exceeding joy over my work, because it is His from beginning to end; all the good, and the grace, and the glory are His, His wholly and only! He has reminded His stewards of a need which they are far too apt to overlook, and He has supplied for many of His ministers a necessity which they had scarcely the courage to mention. Preachers without books are as the Israelites when required by Pharaoh to make bricks without straw; but hundreds of such poor oppressed workers are toiling on from year to year, without sympathy from any one. Some little help was needed for these servants of the Lord to give them 'a little reviving,' and that aid has come by an unlooked-for hand. It was unlikely that one who is neither bookworm nor theologian should be raised up to supply poor preachers with books; and yet so it has been, and the matter is from the Lord.

ITS OBJECT.

"The Book-Fund aims at furnishing the bare bookshelves of poor pastors of every Christian denomination with standard works of theology by various authors; books full of the glorious gospel of Jesus Christ, the study of which shall enrich their minds, comfort their hearts, quicken their spiritual life, and thereby enable them to preach with greater power and earnestness 'all the words of this life.' How deeply needed this service of love has long been, what an urgent and painful necessity it has become, is fully proved by the intense eagerness shown on every hand to obtain the proffered boon. The writer could point to many a faithful servant of the Lord, who, toiling on in secret poverty for years, has not even *seen* a new book (except in the shop windows), till a grant from the Book-Fund filled his heart with joy and his lips with thanksgiving. 'These books have brightened my hope and quickened my faith,' writes one such pastor. 'I will not trouble you with my difficulties for want of a commentary to stimulate and guide my poor thought, they are too sad to tell, but they have helped me to appreciate your gifts.' Those whose resources enable them to enjoy, without stint, the luxury of a 'new book,' can scarcely realize the longing and craving which gnaws at the heart of a poor minister when he sees—beyond his reach— the help and refreshment he so sorely needs. His brain is weary with producing unaided thoughts; his mental powers are flagging for want of stimulus and encouragement; his spirit is burdened with the pressure of cares, which stern poverty brings upon him; and yet, though a few sterling, solid books would be a specific for much of this misery, the purchase of such blessed potions is as impossible to him as would be the acquisition of the 'Elixir of Life' itself! Many a one has told me that the books sent seemed to 'put new life' into him, and it is not difficult to read in those three words a sad and sorrowful story of mental faintness and famine.

" 'Read good suggestive books,' says the President of the Pastors' College, in his 'Lectures to Students,' 'and get your minds aroused by them. If men wish to get water out of a pump which has not been lately used, they first pour water down, and then the pump works. Reach down one of the Puritans, and thoroughly study the work, and speedily you will find yourself, like a bird on the wing, mentally active and full of motion.' But what if there is no water at hand to coax the up-springing of the living stream? or, rather, what if the bookshelves are bare, and no Puritans can be reached down? This is a question which the Book-Fund seeks to answer in the only satisfactory manner, by placing as a free gift in the hands of poor pastors that nourishment for their brains which is as absolutely necessary to mental vigor as food for their bodies is essential to physical existence. 'Ten thousand thanks,' said a dear brother, writing lately, 'for sending the books when you did. Their coming brought deliverance and salvation to my mind. I was in an agony of spirit—at my wits' end for a text. I opened one and found, "The Lord liveth, and blessed be my rock." This was just what I wanted ; it took hold of me, and the Lord helped me to take hold of it.' 'I have very little to spend in books,' says another. 'My salary is only £60 per annum, so that when a new book comes it is like bread to the hungry. I do not say this to make you think I am a martyr—if so, I am a very happy one, for I have chosen willingly Christ's service, and my very wants are a means of grace to me.' Again, another pastor writes: 'I cannot tell you how much the receipt of these useful and suggestive volumes cheered me. The sight of a refreshing spring never more gladdened a weary traveler.'

" No one who knows anything of the position and means of our country pastors can doubt that the 'object' of this Fund meets, and, as far as it is able, alleviates a sadly overlooked evil. After more than two years' daily correspondence with ministers all over the land, the writer feels that she speaks with sad and serious certainty on the matter, and she is grieved to know that everywhere the want is felt, and the same cry is heard. 'Oh, for some books to help me in my pulpit preparation!' says one; 'I have to preach before the same people three, perhaps four times a week, and though the Lord has promised that my "branch shall not wither," it sometimes gets very dry.' 'I know we should depend upon the Spirit's aid,' says another, 'and so I do; but if I could read some of the burning thoughts which are recorded by God's earthly seraphs, my lips, too, might glow with holy rapture, and give forth "goodly words."' 'I never dare now to think of a new book,' writes a third, 'two or three times I have begun to save a little money towards the purchase of a long-coveted work, but every time it has gone for something else; Johnny, and little Harry, and Walter, must have boots; or mother is ill; or the girls' frocks are getting shabby; and so the precious volumes are still unattainable.' And yet a fourth most touchingly says: 'When I witness the self-denial, and hard unremitting labor to which my wife so cheerfully submits herself to keep our household moving comfortably in the sphere God has given, I cannot with any pleasure add to her difficulty by purchasing the books I often covet, though this doubtless hinders the freshness and variety of my ministry.'

"Dear Christian friends, these are no fancy pictures which I am painting, these are no silly tales of fiction, told for the purpose of exciting emotions as worthless as they are weak; but I write of living, suffering realities of flesh and blood—our brethren in Christ, and men, moreover, who claim and bear the title of the 'King's ambassadors'—and I ask, 'Ought they to be thus treated?' I want you to ponder for a moment the sad fact that throughout the length and breadth of this dear England of ours there are hundreds of Christ's ministers so poor that they can scarcely find proper food and clothing for themselves, their wives and their little ones, out of the miserable pittance which is called their 'salary!' Books, which ought to be 'common things' with them—littering their rooms in 'most admired disorder,' crowding each nook and corner with mute but matchless companionship—are, through their poverty, unattainable luxuries, vainly-coveted blessings, the very thought of which must be laid aside, lest the longing should lead to repining, and the desire deepen into distress. Such things ought not to be, but unhappily they are, and till the churches of Christ shall awaken to a sense of their responsibility in this matter, and their moral obligation to provide their ministers with mental food, I will rejoice that my Book-Fund does, at least, lighten a little of the darkness, and relieve somewhat the pressure of the famine.

ITS SUSTENANCE.

" The silver is mine, and the gold is mine, saith the Lord of hosts."

"The Book-Fund has been nourished and fed from the King's Treasury, and I must 'make my boast in the Lord' that all needful supplies for the carrying on of the work have plainly borne the stamp of heaven's own mint. I say this because I have never asked help of any one but Him, never solicited a donation from any creature, yet money has always been forthcoming, and the supplies have constantly been in due proportion to the needs. Once only during the year did the Lord try my faith by allowing the grants of books to outnumber the gifts of money, and then it was only for a 'small moment' that a fear overshadowed me. The dark cloud very speedily passed away, and fresh supplies made me more than ever satisfied with the resolution I had formed to draw only on the unlimited resources of my heavenly Treasurer. None of the friends whose hearts have 'devised liberal things' on behalf of my work will reproach me with ingratitude towards them when I lay my first loving thanks at His feet; they will rather join me in praising Him for so sweetly inclining their hearts to help His needy ones, and will joyfully say, 'O Lord, of Thine own have we given Thee!'

"I recall with very glad satisfaction the first donation which reached me, 'for sending books to ministers.' It came anonymously, and was but five shillings' worth of stamps, yet it was very precious, and proved like a revelation to me, for it opened up a vista of possible usefulness and exceeding brightness. The mustard seed of my faith grew forthwith into a 'great' tree, and sweet birds of hope and expectation sat singing in its branches. 'You'll see,' I said to my boys, 'the Lord will send me hundreds of pounds for this work.' For many a day afterwards mother's 'hundreds of pounds' became a 'household word' of good-humored merriment and badinage. And now 'the Lord has made me to laugh,' for the hundreds have grown into thousands; He has done 'exceeding abundantly above what I could ask or even think'; and faith, with such a God to believe in and depend upon, ought surely to 'smile at impossibilities, and say, 'it shall be done.'

"After praising Him 'from whom all blessings flow,' my loving thanks are due to the friends who, by their generous gifts, have co-operated with me in this blessed work. Money has come to me from all quarters, and always with congratulations and good wishes. Many dear personal friends have liberally aided me; some of my dear husband's constant and devoted helpers have been pleased when sending him a cheque, to make it a little larger for the Book-Fund; while quite a number of strangers (though strangers no longer), whose names were previously unknown to me, have sent very considerable donations to my beloved work. God bless them all! And if only a tithe of the happiness their gifts have secured to me and my poor pastors be returned into their own hearts, their cups will be full to overflowing, and their joy will abound. Oh, how sweet some of these sums of money have been to me! Real 'God-sends' I may truly call them; for the gold has seemed to lose its earthly dross when consecrated to Him, and has often shed a light as from heaven's own 'golden streets' upon my pathway! Coming sometimes in seasons of great pain and suffering, these gifts have been like precious anodynes to soothe my weary spirit, and hush my restless thought; for they plainly showed the Lord had not 'forgotten to be gracious.' They have almost charmed away my sorrow by teaching me to plan for others' joy, and ofttimes they have been truly 'means of grace' to me, leading to blessed commerce with heaven, by supplying frequent occasions of prayer and praise. Surely, after so much mercy past, if I did not bless His name, 'the very stones would cry out.'

"The twelve hundred and eighty odd pounds which stand recorded for this year in the balance-sheet do not include all the moneys which I have received from the Lord through the hands of His loving people. Herein lies a secret, very precious, and hitherto very safely guarded, but now to be revealed for the honor of God and the good of His needy ministers. The thought will naturally occur to any one who has read this far, that such an intimate acquaintance as I have made with the sorrows and trials of poor pastors must have many a time caused me a sad heartache, unless means were at hand to relieve their earthly wants and woes as well as their mental necessities; and here another note of praise to the Lord must be sounded on a very tender string; for in His goodness and loving-kindness He has provided pecuniary help for exceptional cases of extreme poverty and urgent need. Without this, I think sometimes I should have felt crushed beneath the burden which my knowledge of many pressing needs has laid upon me. The tried ministers never complain; I do not remember having ever read a solitary sentence which could be construed into a murmur; but sometimes a chance word on my part leads them to confide in me, and then the sad fact is revealed, that other shelves beside the bookshelf are in pitiful need of replenishing.

"At the commencement of 1877, a generous friend placed at my disposal a sum of money, and thus founded a private

PASTORS' AID SOCIETY,

from which I could draw such sums as occasion required and prudence directed. This money has been further supplemented by gifts from my dear husband and others ; and though not attaining any vast proportions, it has sufficed to solace many a suffering one, and has lifted very heavy burdens from care-laden hearts. Full details of this little branch of my Book-Fund are withheld from motives of delicacy and tenderness to the dear brethren whose poverty, though honorable, is as jealously concealed as if it were a hidden treasure ; but could I dare to tell of the sickness and sorrow, the straits and the struggles which have come to my knowledge during this year, many of my readers would think I was romancing, and that such a state of things could not exist in this Christian land. But alas ! dear friends, the evil is deep and wide-spread, very real, and very saddening, and I would that those of God's people, to whom He has given liberally of the ' precious things of the earth beneath,' would bestow some of their overflowing wealth upon their poorer brethren. I could promise them that from ' golden grains ' thus sown they should reap a hundredfold harvest of blessing and sweet content.

ITS SUCCESS.

"Judged by the benefits and blessings the Book-Fund has conferred, its success will be best told by extracts from letters received in acknowledgment of gifts ; and as it has become entirely unsectarian in its operation it will, perhaps, be interesting and pleasant to introduce some 'kind words' from ministers of different denominations who have joyfully accepted this service of love. It has been no easy matter to restrain my hand in making these selections from the many hundreds of letters I possess ; I have felt a veritable *embarras de richesses*, and most unwillingly have omitted many a passage brimful of joy and gladness, lest I should weary my readers ; but when they have perused with delight these thankful, loving words, they may rest assured the 'half has not been told' them. Having commenced the year by offering six volumes of Mr. Spurgeon's 'Sermons' to all ministers formerly students of the Pastors' College, first speech is accorded to one of their number :—

ˣMy dear Mrs. Spurgeon :—I feel deeply grateful to you for the six volumes of sermons which reached me this morning. When ı opened the parcel, I experienced such a rush of emotion as made me kneel down instantly and thank God for His goodness to me, as well as to pray for His blessing to descend upon you. Many times when a few brethren have met together at my house, or I have gone to theirs, have we mentioned your work in our prayers, and the best expression of my gratitude, I feel, will be in the fervency and faith of my petitions. I trust you will accept my thanks, though they were so imperfectly conveyed. My heart glows, but my pen fails.

" The extract next subjoined is also from an old student, but it claims special notice because the writer is laboring in a far distant land, and a gift of books to him is truly 'as cold water to a thirsty soul.' It is not often that the opportunity is afforded of ministering to the necessities of brethren in foreign lands, on account of the heavy expense of transit; but when friends are found to take charge of a parcel, we have the rare pleasure of receiving in due time such an answer as this :—

" Dear Mrs. Spurgeon :—I have to acknowledge, with gratitude and pleasure, the receipt of six volumes of Mr. Spurgeon's ' Sermons,' which you so kindly forwarded by Mr. ———, of this village. May the Lord reward you a thousandfold for this great, and I might almost say, unexpected kindness to a stranger in a strange land. . . . . When settling here, rather more than three years ago, I often found an American volume of the ' Sermons,' well worn, and highly appreciated; and I assure you they made me feel more at home than otherwise I should have done in this rugged country. One old man, nearly ninety, whom I buried a few months since, had a volume of that kind, and he had read it, perhaps, hundreds of times, until it was almost worn to pieces. It was nearly his sole companion for several years before his death, and none can tell how much he was cheered and comforted by reading it. You can scarcely imagine the joy I felt in receiving the sermons fresh from England; but this you may rest assured of—both yourself and your dear husband were prayed for that night with more than usual fervor and feeling, and special thanks were given to Him ' from whom all blessings flow.'

" If space permitted, I could give extracts of letters from France, Sweden, Nova Scotia, Nebraska, Cape of Good Hope, Spain, Sydney, Adelaide, Bengal, Jamaica, Barbadoes, and many other "strange lands," which would delight and interest my readers; but I must content myself and them with the following much-prized communications from Church of England missionaries, one on leave of absence for a while from India, the other just starting to his work at Palamcotta (S. India). The first-mentioned writes thus :—

"Many, many thanks for the four volumes of 'The Treasury of David'; I prize them much. I doubt not that, if not already, these volumes will soon become standard works on the Psalms. Every one knew and felt that there must be 'a feast of fat things' for mind and soul in the Psalms; but Mr. Spurgeon has dished them up in a way so superior to what anybody else has ever done, that both mind and soul receive much more from his 'Treasury' than from any other work. I am thankful to find the books in the libraries of Church of England clergymen at D—— and K——, with less dust on them than Browne 'On the Articles,' or theological works akin to Den's 'Theology,' etc. The day of Christ will reveal the great good the Lord has been doing through Mr. Spurgeon's instrumentality. When a student at —— College, I used to visit some of the Irish courts around the neighborhood. In one of these dens of villainy and iniquity there lived a man who was my terror, and who more than once sent me flying out of the court, pushing me by laying his hand to the back of my neck. My heart sank every time I entered the place if I met this man. He was all that is wicked and iniquitous. One day, to my surprise, instead of cursing me, he asked me to his filthy, dark room. I entered it with fear, not knowing what was in store for me; but, thank God, it was to tell me that he had found Jesus, and had resolved in His strength to follow Him. The message of love, and mercy, and peace, had been conveyed to this man's heart by the lips of your good husband. He heard Mr. Spurgeon preach in some public place or other, and there Jesus met him and called him. From that day till his death he lived the life of a Christian, and died glorifying the depths of Jesus' love. I do not think you can have ever heard of this case; and there must be many unknown to you who on the great day will welcome your dear husband as the one who was the means of leading them to the feet of Christ.

"Dear Madam :—The books arrived safely on Saturday night. May God bless you for your kindness and liberality to a perfect stranger. I have long been under deep obligation to your honored husband, since it was through reading a passage in one of his books in South India, that I was first awakened out of a sinner's natural self-complacency to cry, 'What must I do to be saved?' And twice during the last two years have I been greatly cheered and strengthened by two sermons that I had the pleasure of hearing him deliver in Islington. Though we may never meet on earth, though we may differ on minor points, ever shall my prayers ascend to God for you both, and we shall assuredly meet where partings are unknown.

"I may just say here that many missionaries of different denominations have, on leaving England, applied to me for 'The Treasury' to carry with them to their distant stations (Damascus, Madrid, China, the Punjaub, Ceylon, Delhi, Lagos, and Timbuctoo recur to my mind at this moment, but there are many more), and it has given peculiar satisfaction to grant the requests of these dear brethren, and to receive from them assurances of the great comfort and refreshment they have derived from the perusal of the precious volumes when toiling far from home, friends and country.

"About the middle of the year an unexpected and most delightful impetus was given to the Book-Fund by a very kind and generous friend, who desired that all the ministers in Argyleshire should possess 'The Treasury of David,' and entrusted the writer with funds to carry out his wishes. How heartily the good divines of Scotland welcomed and appreciated this gift, it would take too long to tell.

"Returning to home-work, I give a letter from a Congregational pastor, which could be supplemented by hundreds, for my Book-Fund has had the privilege of ministering to very many in the Independent denomination.

"Dear Madam :—The four volumes of 'The Treasury of David' arrived safely. This thoughtful and most generous gift has filled my heart with real delight. Perhaps the infrequency of such a windfall will account for a little of the pleasure, but I cannot help tracing much of it to the kind manner in which you have presented the gift, and to the intrinsic value of the books themselves. I am a prey to the hunger usual among my brethren for the only kind of communion open to many of us with the richest and noblest minds that have served the Saviour. The possession of your honored husband's beautiful and valuable volumes makes me feel sensibly richer, and I am sure I shall frequently turn to them, both for private profit, and the enrichment of my ministry.

"Being fearful of over-taxing the patience of my readers, I must pass without notice the epistles received from Evangelists and Home Missionaries, some of which would certainly vie in interest and pathos with any that have been already given. I, therefore, introduce but one other letter, making it do duty as the representative of kind and appreciative words from the many divisions of Methodism —Wesleyan, Primitive, and so forth. It is from the pen of a Bible Christian minister, and it tells the same 'old story' of deep need of books, and utter inability to procure them.

"Dear Madam:—Your very valuable and welcome present came duly to hand, and positively made my heart leap for joy, and outflow with a thousand blessings upon the kind donors. I can never express in words the deep feelings of gratitude I am the subject of, for your great kindness in thus shedding sunshine upon the difficult pathway of one who is trying, amid all his unworthiness, to serve his generation faithfully, and to do the work assigned him by the Master; but what I cannot put into language, I can breathe in heart at the heavenly throne—that Jehovah's benedictions in ever-increasing richness may fall upon you and your honored husband, until taken to the eternal home. The 'Psalms' have always been my favorite resort for meditation and exposition, and I should long ago have purchased 'The Treasury of David' had I been able; but a salary of £80 a year allows only a very small margin for books, and though my mind often craved for them, the luxury was not enjoyed.

"As no record of my work could be considered quite complete without some reference to the beautiful plant which has always been associated with it, I am happy to say that the lemon tree is in a most

19

prosperous condition. Meeting the gardener the other day, he observed, 'Your lemon tree is brought up to the house, ma'am, it is making a great deal of new wood,' and the Book-Fund seems to follow suit with its old friend; for buds and blossoms of unexpected promise are asserting their existence and vitality. This Christmastide has brought me a number of letters from Christian ladies, who are anxious to aid the families of poor pastors, by suitable gifts of clothing; and I have had the intense satisfaction of submitting to their loving care and consideration the names of twenty-five ministers, all of whom, I believe, have been made happier, and undeniably warmer, by the reception of seasonable garments for themselves and their little ones. And yet another new branch of my work bears promise of much good fruit to poor pastors; for through the kindness of two thoughtful hearts, *The Sword and the Trowel* is to be sent regularly during the present year to sixty ministers who could not afford to purchase it for themselves. The prospect of this indulgence has greatly cheered many hearts. 'I have not been able to take in a religious periodical for five years,' said one to whom I made the offer, 'the monthly visit of the magazine will indeed be a great boon.'

"What other work the Lord may have in store for me, or how far He intends graciously to extend that which at present fills my hands, or whether perchance He may think fit to call me away from it altogether, I know not; but this one thing is certain:

'There hath not failed one word of all His good promise' from the beginning until now; and for the future I am persuaded that the 'Book-Fund and its Work' will live and thrive vigorously in its own 'little corner' of God's vineyard, where the sunshine of His blessing shall ever rest lovingly upon it, causing it to bring forth much fruit to His glory.

"And now, the 'report' is a 'tale that is told'; but I pray that its record of God's infinite tenderness and love may not leave a merely transient impression on any heart. Poor as my words are, and destitute of all literary ability, their very poverty and deficiency should be as foils to the bright deeds of mercy and grace which they endeavor to set forth. Dear friends who have helped me, the work is yours as much as it is mine, and I hope my little report will tell you that I am deeply grateful to you for trusting me with some of your substance, and that it may also make you partakers in my joy—the joy of helping the ministers of our Lord Jesus Christ. For the present I bid you a loving and grateful farewell.

> "'Another year—*or part*—to serve Thee, Lord;
> To sleep, to rise, and always leave to Thee
> The precious seed my feeble hands have sown.
> To make it spring and grow is Thine alone;
> This takes all anxious care away from me.
> I trust *Thee*, Lord, to cause Thy seed to yield
> Full golden sheaves to deck Thy harvest field.'"

Again, in 1879, Mrs. Spurgeon wrote concerning her annual report, saying:

"With much diffidence this little book is laid before you. It has cost me considerable effort and thought, yet it but feebly represents the progress and prosperity of my work, and very unworthily records the faithfulness and love of our gracious God. I have earnestly tried to do my best; but the preparation of an annual report is the only duty connected with the Book-Fund which I find burdensome; and were it not that I hope the work will bear the precious fruit of 'glory to God,' I could not have attempted it. Last year there was no question about the matter, for extreme ill-health and weakness had brought me very low; but during the last few months the Lord has dealt so gently with me, and given me such happy cessation of suffering, that I want to devote the first efforts of partially-renewed strength to the humble and grateful fulfilment of this duty. The report for 1878 was written by a kind friend who willingly and ably supplied my lack of service, and my hearty thanks are now rendered to him for assistance given in a time of much sorrow and need. Very soon after this good friend had accomplished his task, I began to wonder how the present year would be provided for: the months roll by so quickly, that no sooner is one record given than it seems time to think about another. Musing one day on this matter, a 'happy thought' suggested itself—that, as often as opportunity presented, I should gather material for future use by jotting down, somewhat in diary-form, any subject of interest or thanksgiving pertaining to my work, and so present to my friends a report, perhaps novel in character, but less difficult for me thus to produce, and, I hope, not more unpleasant to them to peruse.

"In the following pages, therefore, I have endeavored to give frequent details of the special service which the Lord has entrusted to my care, noting down any particularly interesting incident, recording some memorable mercies, and preserving much pleasant correspondence.

"Here and there the reader will find, intermingled with *bona fide* book-work, a few domestic and more private experiences, which would insinuate themselves into the little history, and which, seeing that the dear home-life and the Book-Fund are so tenderly 'joined together' by the Lord's good pleasure, I had not the heart or the wish to 'put asunder.'

"Imperfectly as I have worked out the idea which in the first instance possessed me, I yet hope the perusal of this little book will interest my friends still further in the work they, by their kindly gifts, are sharing with me. If in any degree it helps them more clearly to perceive that in this sweet ministry I am acting for them, being truly and gladly their 'servant for Christ's sake'; that the joy, and delight, and reward are not all for me only, but are shared by them most fully, while all the 'glory' is given to our faithful God: then my difficult task will not have been undertaken in vain, nor shall I regret that I tried to put on record some of the 'goodness and mercy which followed me' during the year eighteen hundred and seventy-nine.

"It is the joy of my life thus to serve the servants of my Master, and the daily blessings and tender providences which surround my work are more precious to me than words can express. 'Some of the subjects of my thankfulness may seem small and inconsiderable to others, but to me they are of constant interest and importance;' my retired life shuts out the usual pleasures of social intercourse, but opens wide a world of glad delight in thus 'ministering to the necessities of the saints.' I have scores of friends with whose circumstances I am intimately acquainted, yet whose faces I have never looked upon. I hope to know and greet them on the 'other shore'; and, meanwhile, their love and prayers are a sweet reward for such pleasant service as the Lord enables me to render to them. In these pages will be found some of the expressive outpourings of grateful hearts, and though the letters here given form but a small portion of the great mass of affectionate correspondence connected with the Fund, they will serve to reveal some of the daily comfort and encouragement I receive through this channel. Ah! if by his grace we can but win from our Master the approving words, 'Ye did it unto me,' the joy of service is only a little lower than the supreme felicity of heaven.

"A curious little incident happened lately during a time of prolonged sickness. At the close of a very dark and gloomy day I lay resting on my couch as the deeper night drew on, and though all was bright within my cosy little room, some of the external darkness seemed to have entered into my soul, and obscured its spiritual vision. Vainly I tried to see the hand which I knew held mine, and guided my fog-enveloped feet along a steep and slippery path of suffering. In sorrow of heart I asked, 'Why does my Lord thus deal with His child? Why does He so often send sharp and bitter pain to visit me? Why does He permit lingering weakness to hinder the sweet service I long to render to his poor servants?' These fretful questions were quickly answered, and though in a strange language, no interpreter was needed, save the conscious whisper of my own heart. For a while silence reigned in the little room, broken only by the crackling of the oak log burning on the hearth. Suddenly I heard a sweet soft sound, a little, clear, musical note, like the tender trill of a robin, beneath my window. 'What can that be?' I said to my companion, who was dozing in the firelight; 'surely no bird can be singing out there at this time of the year and night!' We listened, and again heard the faint plaintive notes, so sweet, so melodious, yet mysterious enough to provoke for a moment our undisguised wonder. Presently my friend exclaimed, 'It comes from the log on the fire!' and we soon ascertained that her surprised assertion was correct. The fire was letting loose the imprisoned music from the old oak's inmost

heart! Perchance he had garnered up this song
in the days when all went well with him, when birds
twittered merrily on his branches, and the soft sunlight flecked his tender leaves with gold; but he had
grown old since then, and hardened; ring after ring
of knotty growth had sealed up the long-forgotten
melody, until the fierce tongues of the flames came
to consume his callousness, and the vehement heat
of the fire wrung from him at once a song and a
sacrifice. Ah, thought I, when the fire of affliction
draws songs of praise from us, then, indeed, are we
purified, and our God is glorified! Perhaps some
of us are like this old oak log—cold, hard, and in-
sensible; we should give forth no melodious sounds
were it not for the fire, which kindles round us, and
releases tender notes of trust in Him, and cheerful
compliance with His will! 'As I mused, the fire
burned,' and my soul found sweet comfort in the
parable so strangely set forth before me. Singing
in the fire. Yes! God helping us, if that is the only
way to get harmony out of these hard, apathetic
hearts, let the furnace be heated seven times hotter
than before."

This incident Mr. Spurgeon, in 1881, made
musical in a song, using as a foundation some verses
sent Mrs. Spurgeon by a friend. Here it is:

> At the close of a dark and cloudy day,
>   As the deeper night grew on,
> On my languishing couch I wearily lay,
>   My joy for the moment gone.

Within my room all was cosy and bright,
    Yet a shadow of night had crept
Over my soul, and had hid from my sight
    The hand in which mine was kept.

Depressed and saddened, I labored in vain
    To gaze on my loving Lord.
Oh, when will his presence return again,
    And light on my spirit be poured?

Whence comes it my Lord so bitterly chides,
    And sends me such grievous pain?
The sun, and the moon, and the stars He hides,
    And clouds return after the rain.

HE HEARD: and an answer was strangely given,
    A still small voice from the throne;
No seraphim brought the message from heaven,
    Yet it came from the Lord alone.

A while in my room reigns a silence deep;
    The only sounds in mine ear
Arise from the flames which crackle and leap,
    And flash forth a flickering cheer.

When we suddenly heard a strange, sweet song,
    Like the robin's tender trill,
A whisper, a sonnet, the flames among;
    It caused our hearts to thrill.

"Can a bird be singing this gloomy night?"
    In startled surprise, we say.
"Whence comes such an anthem of calm delight
    As from harps that are far away?"

In silent wonder we listen again,
    Till my friend in a whisper said,
"'Tis yon old oak log sings that soft, weird strain
    From amidst its fiery bed."

'Twas so; and, as once the Lord spoke out
    From the bush which burned with flame,
So now to our spirits, beyond a doubt,
    His voice from the oak log came.

From the heart of the oak fire had loosed the bands
   Of music imprisoned of yore,
When the trees of the field had clapp'd their hands
   And cried out the Lord before.

When its branches waved 'neath the heaven's blue
   Through the livelong summer day,
Full many a bird to their shadow flew
   With its carol glad and gay.

The song of the thrush and the hum of the bee,
   And the music of evening bells,
All sank in the soul of the old oak-tree;
   And now the sweet tale it tells.

The hardened growth of full many a ring
   Fettered fast the imprisoned lays,
Till these flames of fire their freedom bring,
   And they dance in the joyous blaze.

The fire which consumes has lent it a tongue,
   And the oak log sings as it dies;
It yieldeth its all while its heart is wrung—
   'Tis a song and a sacrifice.

     *   *   *   *

And thus was a message most sweetly brought
   By the old oak log to me;
It raised me aloft from each gloomy thought,
   And from sorrow it set me free.

If trial and pain be as flames to my heart,
   To fetch forth its latent praise,
With joy I accept the sufferer's part,
   And would choose it all my days.

Mrs. Spurgeon's account charmingly continues:
"When our two colored brethren, Messrs. Johnson and Richardson, were on the eve of departure
for missionary work in Africa, they came with their
wives to our dear home to bid us farewell. A very
pleasant and memorable time we spent together,

their pastor encouraging them in the work to which they had devoted their lives, and their love and sympathy overflowing to him and to me (then very sick), in return. At the request of my dear husband they sang to me some of the strange, sweet songs of their captivity, for they had once been slaves; and all who heard these plaintive melodies sung in the Tabernacle at their farewell meetings will agree with me that sweeter, yet sadder melodies could scarcely be imagined. My heart was especially attracted by a peculiar air, to which they sang as a refrain these most curious words:

> ' Keep inching along, keep inching along
> Like a poor inch worm—
> Jesus Christ 'll come bye-and-bye.'

"It is impossible to describe the weird pathos with which they invested these few sentences, and my interest was so aroused that I asked if some special history attached to this strange song. Then they told me how in the sorrowful days of their bondage they would stealthily gather together, night after night, in one of the low miserable huts they called their home, and sitting crouched on the floor, hand clasped in hand, in darkness and terror, they would pray with one another, and in muffled tones would whisper this very song. Sing it aloud they dared not, for fear of their master, who would have exacted full payment by stripes for such an assertion of nature's rights; but rocking to and fro in time to the wailing melody, they found a 'fearful pleasure' in the disobedience which brought spiritual comfort to their oppressed souls.

"The glorious hope of future deliverance excited and enraptured their hearts. 'Sometimes,' they said, 'one of our number would forget the caution and silence so essential to our safety; and a voice would ring out in the darkness, jubilant and clear, "Jesus Christ 'll come bye-and-bye."' Then all would sit trembling after such an outburst, lest they should be discovered by the shout of anticipated triumph, and angels might have wept for the poor, down-trodden souls, and have longed to bring the sweet chariot, 'coming for to carry them home.'

"'Will you sing to me in whispers as you sang then?' I asked, and they very sweetly complied with my wish, though, blessed be God, their surroundings were now so happy that they could give but a faint copy of the terrible reality. I shall never forget that pitiful hushing of their voices. There was not a dry eye in the little company when the song was ended; but we wiped our tears away, soon remembering that the cause for sorrow no longer existed. The 'poor inch worms' are now free, noble, educated men and women; they can sing, and pray, and preach as loudly and as long as they please, and are bound for the land of their fathers, with the intention of exercising these privileges to the full, and making known the gospel of the grace of God to their kindred according to the flesh. The Lord go forth with them and prosper them.

"The echoes of that singular song have lingered with me ever since, and many a time have they comforted my heart. Day by day the work of the Book-Fund has 'kept inching along,' and though prevented by my weakness from taking giant strides, how gracious is the Lord to allow His unworthy child to creep even inch by inch along the pleasant road of service for Him! I should like to send forth fifty parcels weekly—I should like each parcel to be a complete library of theological lore, so that very soon not a true minister in the land should faint and fail for lack of knowledge; but as my highest aims cannot be fulfilled, I will thankfully and joyfully do what I can, and with the Lord's blessing resting on the books sent out in His name, my ten to twenty packages a week will not fail to accomplish his good purpose. Thus cheerfully, gladly, I 'keep inching along,' and for me as surely as for the greatest saint on earth—'Jesus Christ 'll come bye-and-bye.'

April, 1879.—At the time of the Annual Conference of the Pastors' College the Book-Fund usually prepares a little present for the three hundred pastors who then assemble. This is meant to be both a memorial of a happy gathering, and a pledge of continued interest in their welfare. This year, after due consideration, I have decided to give Miss Havergal's 'Royal' books (two to each pastor) as a choice and dainty morsel for their spiritual refreshment and quickening. No commendation is needed to insure a hearty welcome to a work by this devoted

lady. Miss Havergal's pen is guided by a hand
fast clasped in that of her Master, and therefore
her simple words thrill to the inmost depths of the
soul, and touch many a hidden spring of tender,
deep, religious feeling. I anticipate not only the
pleasure with which our 'old students' will receive
these delightful little books at my hands, but the
abundant blessing they may bring to their hearts
and homes. Through the kindness of Messrs. Nis-
bet, the publishers, I have been able to purchase a
thousand copies, and having made it a matter of
special prayer that not one of these precious seeds
should be unfruitful, I shall hopefully and patiently
await the result.

" To ministers who are not quite so necessitous as
those for whom the Book-Fund was specially
founded, yet who can ill spare the published price
of 'The Treasury of David,' or the 'Sermons,' I
offer these books at a somewhat reduced rate, and I
have much satisfaction in knowing that the privilege
is warmly appreciated. Some letters which I have are
fair samples of the spirit in which the favor is sought
and the warm gratitude evoked by its accordance.

"October, 1879.—Committed to the faithful keeping of his father's God, our precious son sails to-day
for his second visit to Australia. The cold and damp
of our English winter made us fear for his somewhat delicate constitution, and if it be the Lord's
will, the more genial climate of the colonies may
develop strength and power to prosecute that

which, we trust, will be his life-work—to preach to poor sinners the 'unsearchable riches of Christ.' Give the winds and the waves charge concerning him, O Lord! Let them waft him safely to his desired haven, and then do Thou guide him all his journey through, till both he and all who hold him dear shall meet to part no more!

"I am glad to say that the Book-Fund is not altogether unrepresented in the cargo which the good ship carries, though if I had possessed the means it should have been much heavier ; for in Australia, as in other distant lands, books are vastly more expensive than in England, and more difficult to procure. The book-hunger of our most needy ministers at home may be as keen and absorbing as the appetite of a colonial pastor ; but the former has many more chances of ultimately appeasing it, while hope gives him strength to endure and to wait. In the bush, or in outlying districts, where there may be little intellectual life, a man must depend very largely on his bookshelves for friendship and communion, and when these fail him, or prove uncongenial, he is very sincerely to be pitied, and ought to be helped. I should often send books to the colonies if the Fund could bear the heavy expense of freightage ; but awaiting the kind services of friends to take charge of the parcels is so slow a method of transit, that practically my grants are few and far between. To the abundant affection which the generous people on the other side of the world showed our dear son on his first visit they added this kindness, that they have once and again helped, not only his father's many 'works of faith and labors of love,' but his mother's Book-Fund; and now that he goes to seek once more health in their beautiful country, she would like him to carry a great blessing back to them. Father and mother both fervently pray that his life there may be a devoted and consecrated one, and that 'power from on high' may be given him to win many jewels for the Master's crown."

In October, 1879, she wrote: "As part of the proceeds of his last lecture in London, I have the pleasure of receiving to-day £25 as the generous and graceful gift of Mr. John B. Gough to the Book-Fund. Such a gift from such a man is precious and noteworthy, but not unusual, as I believe it is the constant habit of Mr. Gough to bestow blessings as well as to recommend them. Long as his name has been honored in our household, and his special work admired and appreciated, it was not till his recent visit to England that we had the happiness of his personal acquaintance. Now he has been twice to see us, and a friendship has been contracted between us which, though interrupted by absence from each other on earth, will find its true fruition and best enjoyment in heaven. The hours we spent in his company have left frequent memories not only of pleasant mirth at the droll tales so inimitably told, but also of sacred joy in sweet and goodly words which 'ministered grace unto the hearers.' Cannot my friends imagine that it was a rare treat to listen to the converse of John Ploughman and John Gough?

"No 'pen of a ready writer' was there to record the good things they said, or to immortalize the brilliant 'table talk' which graced each repast; but the sweet communion which knit our hearts together will never be forgotten by us, and so deep a flood of enjoyment came in upon my usually quiet life that day, that it will forever ripple pleasantly upon the shores of memory. To our very dear friends, Mr. and Mrs. Gough in their far-away home in the West, I send loving greeting; and for this £25, which means so much joy and comfort for the Lord's poor servants, I give the warmest thanks of a grateful heart."

In March, 1883, she gives this touching statement:

"Out of the terrible tempest of sorrow which lately swept over the homes of some of our friends, and brought death and desolation to their households, there came drifting to our shores a little storm-tossed barque, driven by the contrary winds of this great adversity, to seek shelter in our 'haven under the hill.' Such a charming little child! A fair pearl of humanity washed from its bed by the troubled tides of life's ocean—a tender white dovelet tossed from its nest by a rude blast of affliction,—a 'little soul that stands expectant, listening at the gate of life,'—a sweet wee mither-less bairn, whose needs claim the shelter of warm hearts and the loving service of womanly hands. We give a fond welcome to the sweet stranger, taking him to our hearts to love, and to be loved, and have found a singular joy in renewing in some measure the experience of days long past, but not forgotten.

"It is twenty-seven years since 'our own' babies' dimpled hands stroked our cheek, or their pretty voices made unaccustomed music in the house ; but the cry of this little one awakens the long-sleeping echoes, and his tiny fingers stray among our heart-strings, touching again and again one of the old chords of purest and deepest melody. Watching his winsome ways, and noting the daily un-foldings of his exceedingly sweet and gentle disposition, I ask myself, 'What shall this darling teach us, now that the Lord Christ hath set him in our midst?' I do not think we have been disputing who amongst us should be greatest in the kingdom of heaven, but the Master's words imply that hu-mility is not the only grace illustrated in the daily example of His little ones. 'Verily, I say unto you, whosoever shall not receive the kingdom of God as a little child, shall in no wise enter therein.' So I set myself to know what special message to my soul lay hidden in that sunshiny face, or per-chance, what well-merited rebuke to my unchildlike spirit might lurk amid the charms of his lovely and confiding nature. And I find that baby has been a 'living epistle' of faith before my eyes, an unconscious exponent of the blessedness of simple dependence upon God, so that I think I understand more of its sweetness and power than I ever did before. For there is perfect faith and trust in baby's heart; absolute reliance upon those who love him; unquestioning confidence in their ability and tenderness. The tottering steps grow steady, and are ventured without fear, when his small hand is closely clasped in mine; he leans all his weight of babyhood on my arms, without the shadow of a suspicion that they could fail him: every promise that I give is echoed in sweet babblings from 'lips that know no word of doubting'; and, oh, with what glee and rapture does he throw aside his toys and stretch out his pretty hands when I call him to my side! Thus am I taught not to fear or falter while my hand is held by a 'stronger than I'; thus do I see the happiness of leaning hard on love which is omnipotent, and the wisdom of unhesitating faith in gracious words of peace and pardon; thus too, I think I can perceive, faintly shadowed forth, the joy with which I hope to obey the loving call to be 'forever with the Lord.' The very caresses I give to baby are often strangely mingled with spiritual longings, and many a loving play with him ends in a prayer that I may 'become like this little child.' Is it any marvel. that with this sweet unwitting teacher on my knee, I see earthly things

still made after heavenly patterns, and rejoice that
' out of the mouth of babes and sucklings God hath
perfected praise ' ?

"Dear, bright-eyed, glad and trustful baby ! Your
little mission here has been a sacred one ; your presence has brought a blessing with it ! Your confidence in us has quickened our faith in God, and our
love to you has given us fresh glimpses of our
Father's infinite tenderness !

"Ever through your future life, dear child, may
these precious graces of faith and love adorn your
soul ; ever may it be true of you, as it is at this moment, that—

"' Of such is the Kingdom of Heaven.' "

CHAPTER XI.

LOVELY WESTWOOD.

What a satisfaction it is to know that during the last twelve years of his life, Mr. Spurgeon and his wife were able to enjoy such a delightful residence as that which they secured at Westwood.

In August of 1880 they moved to Beulah Hill, a suburb of London, and into a residence which Mr. Spurgeon had been enabled to purchase through the rise in value of his old home at Nightingale Lane, and which he called "Westwood." This beautiful country home, with its thirty acres of lawn, gardens, fields and woodland, came to Mr. Spurgeon as a result of some sensible advice given to him by one of his deacons nearly twenty-five years before. The house in Nightingale Lane had been for sale for some time when Mr. Spurgeon moved into it. The owner offered to sell it to him on very easy terms, but he discarded the idea entirely of owning any property himself until the deacons very decidedly assured him that it would be a sin not to provide for his own, saying, "He that provideth not for his own, and especially for them of his own household, has denied the faith, and is worse than an infidel." So he purchased the residence.

Having a great horror of debt, and from the first receiving a reasonable income, he was able very soon to pay for the home, and enjoy it free of encumbrance. But the house was situated in that portion of London which was growing very fast, especially in business enterprises, and as they crowded around his little homestead they shut out the light, but increased the value of his possessions.

At last, in 1880, a growing fear that the locality was unhealthy, both for Mrs. Spurgeon and himself, led him to consider the possibility of moving to some other locality. An unexpected offer of a high price for the old homestead, combined with especially favorable opportunities to purchase the lands and house at Westwood, led him to believe that the hand of Providence was directing him for his wife's sake to a healthier and more beautiful locality.

Westwood has often been described by those who have visited it ; and *The Philadelphia Press*, as late as 1892, gave us a bit of description worth inserting here :

" He (Mr. Spurgeon) was a man of taste, even of artistic and luxurious taste in some particulars. Many a millionaire might well have envied him his home. This was at Westwood, on what is known as Beulah Hill, in Sydenham, which is one of London's fairest suburbs. Here he had a large and

handsome mansion, situated in a spacious park;
so that, although within a few minutes' ride of the
teeming streets of London, it was as rural and as
secluded as though in the heart of a wilderness.
Passing the lodge gates, the visitor found himself
amid an expanse of well-kept lawns, diversified with
shrubbery and groves.

"A small lake was near the house, and elsewhere
was a fountain containing many goldfish, of which
pets Mr. Spurgeon was exceedingly fond. Bees
were another of his fads, and a dozen or more hives
were always humming and buzzing in the garden.
There was a profusion of flowers also, mostly pinks
and other familiar varieties. These were not grown
for the bees, nor yet because Mr. Spurgeon himself was particularly fond of them, but to supply
the floral mission of his church, for distribution
among the sick and poor of the city.

"There were arbors and shaded seats in plenty
about the grounds, and there were also plenty of
open sunny spots. Of these latter Mr. Spurgeon
was most fond. He had a waterproof mattress,
which he would place on the sunniest spot he could
find, and on which he would lie for hours, simply
basking in the rays of the sun. This was the
greatest physical luxury in the world to him, and
his fondness for Mentone and the Riviera was 'because there was so much sunshine there.'

"Even indoors he sought to have as much sunlight as possible. His mansion was planned and

built with that end in view. No trees were allowed
to shade it, and the windows were as large as possible. Perhaps the most interesting room was the
library, the walls of which were lined with crowded
bookshelves. Here were forty volumes of Mr.
Spurgeon's own printed sermons, in English, and
dozens of other volumes of his works translated
into other tongues.

"Here were several volumes of collected tracts
and pamphlets, written by others about him, and
arranged chronologically. The earliest were nearly
all abusive, many of them actually scandalous in
tone. The latter were as generally eulogistic, and
the gradual transition from the one extreme to the
other presented a most interesting study. Some
large scrapbooks contained copies of all the caricatures of the preacher published since he was in the
ministry. There were thousands of them, of all
possible shades of artistic merit, and of all imagi-
nable spirits, from good-natured humor to sheer
malevolence.

Other volumes contained thousands of clippings
from newspapers about Mr. Spurgeon, presenting
the same variety of tone. In all these Mr. Spurgeon
took a philosophic interest. Praise did not tickle
him, nor abuse annoy him. And on the whole his
observations led him to regard the world with increasing kindliness of spirit."

However, the best way to look in upon domestic
scenes at Beulah Hill is to take the unique description

which Mrs. Spurgeon has herself given of their home experiences, under greatly varying circumstances. To read the extracts from her letters concerning their home life, and relating to her work at Westwood, is like passing by the windows of a home, with the invitation from the occupants to look in at each opening as we pass, and catch what glimpses we may of the arrangement and beauty within.

Mrs. Spurgeon continued her work with the Book-Fund with greater earnestness at Westwood, and there Mr. Spurgeon arranged his library, received his friends, and attended to his manifold correspondence. It was a charming ten years of domestic life. He was frequently called from it on missions in preaching the gospel, and sometimes was compelled to endure a prolonged absence at Mentone, in southern France, to which place the physician imperatively sent him.

Mrs. Spurgeon usually remained at Westwood during his absence and cared for the correspondence and managed the household, experiencing that loneliness, those fears, those anxieties, which come to every affectionate wife during the prolonged absence of her husband, especially if he be absent because of illness.

The glimpses into that home which we have gathered from her writings, not only show how they lived in comfort, peace and heavenly harmony, but also give us many hints as to their thoughts, feelings, perplexities and domestic arrangements.

December 2, 1880, she wrote: "Those dear friends who have been interested in my work from the commencement will not think the record of the year is complete without a word about the lemon tree. From the time when in a little pot, in my sick-chamber, two tiny leaves, no bigger than a pin's head, emerged from the black earth and were tenderly covered by a medicine glass, to the present day when it stands in fair proportions, and boasts a height of seven feet or more, it has been closely identified with the Book-Fund, and in some mysterious manner believed to be an emblem of my work. Friends used to cherish the pretty fancy, and send their gifts as 'a few drops of water for the lemon plant,' or 'another leaf for your tree'; but though that pleasant fashion has fallen into disuse, there are many who constantly remember my favorite, and will be delighted to hear that its removal to 'Westwood' has greatly contributed to its health and beauty. I do not, however, intend now to enlarge upon its charms, but rather to use an unpleasant peculiarity it has, in order to 'point a moral and adorn a tale' I have to tell.

"Attentively considering it the other day, I saw with some surprise that it bore a few very sharp thorns. 'Ah!' I said, 'dear emblem tree, are you so true to your mystical character as all that?' For, dear friends, Book-Fund work is not all composed of pleasant fruit and flowers; there are some thorns concealed here and there which wound the hand which inadvertently touches them. Sometimes, I receive an answer to the necessary inquiries I have to make, which hurts me sorely, and makes me wince. 'Permit me to say I have no wish to be considered a pauper,' wrote an angry man a day or two since, because I asked him kindly whether he came within the limits of my work, and possessed an income under £150 per annum.

"Ever since the 'Master' gave me this charge to keep, He knows I have tried to minister in gentle, kindly fashion to His servants; but occasionally the spirit of my service is overlooked by them, and my gifts are either claimed as a right or disdained as a charity. 'Few and far between' are these ugly thorns on my flourishing, beautiful tree; tender and loving acknowledgments of my work are the rule, and when an exception comes I can well afford to forgive and forget it. Were it not that a chronicler is required to be faithful, and give fairly both sides of the history he is writing, I should have left unrecorded this painful part of a most pleasant and blessed service. The flowers of Paradise will doubtless be thornless, but here on earth one cannot gather many roses without pricking one's fingers, nor have a splendid lemon tree without seeing and bewailing its sharp spikes, nor possess any unmingled good but God's love.

"But, apropos of skylarks' songs, I must tell you, dear reader, what happened the other day, and how beautifully a sweet singer's confidence was rewarded, when fearlessly leaving her earthly treasures in our

Father's keeping (Matt. vi., 26), she mounted upward to pay her full debt of daily orisons at 'Heaven's Gate.' You may find, perhaps, some 'linked sweetness' between the little story and our present subject, or even, failing that desired end, may not be displeased with me for introducing the homely incident to your notice.

"We were making a tour of the garden and pastures, admiring the beauty of the young year's fresh life—noting with tender interest all the charming details of newly-awakened responsibility in every living thing—marking the sweet, impatient growth of leaves still rumpled and creased from their recent unfoldings, and rejoicing in the whispered promise of golden days to come which trembled on every scented breath of the perfumed air.

"Down in the Dale field we came across a skylark's nest, built in the long grass, a lovely little soft-lined cup of cosiness, with three pretty brown eggs in it. The sweet songstress had flown at the approach of human footsteps, and thus revealed the secret place of her wee home to inquisitive but kindly eyes. We looked with profound admiration on her happy work, and then quietly retraced our steps, having loving sympathy for the poor little fluttering heart which might perchance fear the despoiling of its treasures. A day or two afterwards the visit was repeated ; but imagine our consternation when, on opening the gate of the field, we saw that the cows had been let into that pasture ! How would the great, clumsy, sweet-breath'd creatures treat the little home in the grass? Would it not be crushed and trampled by their unheeding feet? We had placed an upright stick near the nest to show its position, and very doubtfully we made our way across the field, fearing to find ruin and desolation where we had left peace and prosperity.

"When we reached the spot, our surprise and delight were great to find the home intact, and the wee birds safely hatched; for though the cows had munched the grass close down to the ground all round the nest, not a hoof had touched the little inmates. So, there they were, three cunning mites, with stubby bodies, and big downy heads, cowering close together in instinctive fear of the human presence which overshadowed them. The cows grazed quietly by, and overhead the pretty mother trilled forth her delicious carol in the morning sunshine, pouring out her heart's gratitude and gladness in libations of song! And there, till the little birds were feathered and flown, the cows were every day pastured, yet never a hurt came to the wee nest in the grass! Who watched over the mother in her peril as she sat upon the eggs? Who guarded the nestlings in their hourly danger when the slight protection of her tender body was removed? Who shielded the tiny birds from the tread of the great beasts' feet? Did Daphne know that the nursery on the ground-floor must be cared for and respected? Or did Strawberry's mother-instinct tell her that little living hearts beat as truly in that wool-lined cup as in the sweet hay-crib where her own darling was lying? I cannot tell—the matter is too deep for me; but the lark knew all about it, and it may be that, could our ears have been opened to understand the language of her hymn of praise, as she rose higher and higher in the calm blue sky, we might have caught, here and there amidst the joyous notes, some such words as these:

> Not one,
> > Not one of them,
> > > Is forgotten
> > In the sight of God.
> Not one,
> > Not one of them,
> > > Shall fall to the ground
> > Without your Father.
> FEAR YE NOT, THEREFORE,
> > Are not ye
> > > Of much more value
> > > > Than they?

Did she not do well thus to sing and trust? Oh, sighing and doubting reader, cast away your fears, and follow her fair example; you shall not only joyfully leave your earthly cares with your heavenly Father, but you shall get nearer to God's throne than you have ever been before!"

In June, 1884, she said:

"From the breezy heights of Beulah Hill we command a lovely and uninterrupted view, not of the fair earth merely, but of the fairer firmament above it; our windows are observatories whence many a longing, loving glance is cast heavenwards, and one of the chief pleasures of restful or contemplative hours is found in silently watching the ever-changing aspect of the sky, and noting the manifold glories of that wonderful cloud-land which divides our earthly home from the promised inheritance on high. I never tire of gazing on the beautiful mysteries of the clouds. I love to watch the grand and solemn rolling of black and rugged masses, when storms are abroad, and the wind is marshalling them to a dread convention of brooding tempests; and equally well I love to see them when, in summer days, the cloudlets float like flakes of driven snow across the deep blue ether, and lose themselves at the feet of mountains that rival the Alpine peaks in beauty and sublimity. Sometimes the watcher will see a cloud of such celestial beauty that to his enamored fancy it looks

> ' As though an angel, in his upward flight,
> Had left his mantle floating in mid-air.'

Or anon, with pensive pleasure, he may mark

> ' Clouds on the western side
> Grow grey and greyer, hiding the warm sun.'

But under all aspects they are enchanting and sug-gestive; their very movements are restful to my spirit; they always speak to me of the Lord's great power and love, and many a time have burdens of care been lifted from my heart, and carried away, by these celestial chariots, 'as far as the east is from the west.'

"This is rather a lengthy preface to the relation of an incident which was remarkable for its brevity; but I have been betrayed into such rambling by the fascination of the subject, and the fact that it was whilst engaged in my favorite recreation that the following pleasant portent presented itself to my admiring eyes.

"We were standing at the window, my dear husband and I, noting the splendid effects of the sunset upon a bank of fleecy clouds which skirted the horizon, when all at once we noticed an unusual object in the sky, and perceived that a winged creature of uncommon size was sailing slowly and wearily towards us from the southwest. As it drew nearer, we could see that it was a large sea-bird of some kind, and with the greatest possible interest we watched the stranger's flight, till, in passing over our house, he was hidden from view. The sight stirred my heart strangely. 'That must be our darling's harbinger,' I said, 'bringing us a message from our home-coming boy.' 'Your "Sea-gull" will be with you soon,' its brief presence seemed to say; 'the waves are bearing him swiftly home, and the God who guided me here will bring him safely to your embrace.' Surely it was a happy omen; it comforted me to think that the Hand that

'Wings an angel, guides a sparrow,'

had directed this sea-bird's course, and bidden the beat of his heavy pinions speak a language of love to my longing heart. But, please God, my "Sea-gull," when he comes, will not pass away as quickly as did this herald from the ocean. He will fold his white wings for a little while, and nestle by his mother's side, and gladden her life with his sweet presence, and bless and be blessed in his own dear home.

"Blow softly, O propitious gales,—and ye rolling billows, bear securely on your mighty shoulders the good ship which carries this beloved son across the world of waters. Let there be no 'sorrow on the sea' to this dear voyager, O Lord; but do Thou give the winds and waves a charge concerning him, to bring him safely to his desired haven; and may every ocean breeze waft the sweet message to Westwood, 'I am coming—I am coming home!'

"About 10 p. m., my darling son was in my arms, and the sweet and long-anticipated joy of seeing his dear face, and hearing his loving words, and re-joicing in his welcome presence, was granted to his waiting and expectant parents; and I really think that the pain of five years' absence was almost annihilated by the pleasure of the first fond kiss! 'Mother's Sea-gull' has returned again, the Lord has brought home His banished, and while our mouths are filled with laughter, and our tongues with singing, every word we speak seems tender with gratitude, every blissful moment of reunion bears up to God a tribute of thanksgiving for so great and choice a mercy.

"My 'Diary' may not record all the details of this rapturous meeting, for a Book-Fund report should not be altogether an autobiography; but it cannot be quite silent on the subject which has brought me such exceeding gladness, nor can it refuse to score some notes of praise, while the joybells are ringing so merrily in my heart. Sixteen thousand miles to come home to see father and mother! Weary work these long journeys are, and 'Seagull's' wings grow very tired; but goodness and mercy have followed him all the way, and the love, and light, and welcome of home more than make up for it all.

"There does not seem to be space in this month's pages for anything but the joy of this merciful home-coming. So much am I in love with 'Son Tom,' that, like David Copperfield, to whose enraptured senses 'the sun shone Dora, and the birds sang Dora, the south wind blew Dora, and the wild flowers in the hedges were all Dora's to a bud,' the charm of this long-absent son's presence sheds a new and special brightness over life and its many blessings.

"'My Sea-bird' has flown. My son's bright visit is ended. Laden with loving gifts, satisfied with favor, crowned with success in his enterprise, and followed by the fervent prayers of all who know and love him, he has gone to the land of his adoption, and if the Lord will spare his life, we look forward to a grand future of usefulness for him in Auckland.

I am 'sorrowful, yet alway rejoicing.' He is so precious that to lose him must needs be a bitterness, yet because he is so precious, the sorrow is almost turned into joy. 'Therefore also I have lent him to the Lord; as long as he liveth he shall be lent to the Lord.'

"Happy mother! whose two beloved sons count it their highest honor to 'spend and be spent' in the service of their father's God!"

In opening her annual report of the Book-Fund for 1885, she said:

"My dear reader:—Will you pay me an early visit on this first morning of the New Year, and taking the most comfortable chair to be found in my cosy sitting-room, sit by the side of the blazing wood fire, while I proceed with the business of the day— opening and answering the goodly pile of letters which are awaiting my attention? It may interest all who love the Book-Fund work to know exactly what I have to do, and how I do it; so on this auspicious morning I will take my friends into full confidence, and let them peep into every letter as I open it; sharing with me the pleasure or pain, the content or the anxiety, to which the correspondence may give rise. Before us lies a day's work we shall not get through till sundown; are you willing and able, dear friend, to spend such a busy day with me?

"A tiny square box, addressed to me in my son Charles' handwriting, first claims my notice. I wonder what it can contain, and on opening it, I find, to my great surprise and pleasure, a pretty little sovereign purse, with one of those satisfactory coins inside, and a morsel of paper with a memorandum to the following effect: 'A New Year's gift to dear Grandmamma's Book-Fund, from Susie and Dora.' It is a new and very amusing experience to have my son's little ones helping in my life-work! True, the wee mites do not know much about it at present; in the blissful ignorance of childhood, such tender, sheltered blossoms are all unaware that out in the world cold winds are blowing, and biting frosts are reigning; let them enjoy the warmth, and gladness, and *couleur de rose*, as long as possible. But at least this New Year's gift promises well for future training and bringing up in the way they should go, and —who can tell?—in days to come they may take up 'Grandma's' work when she is at rest, and carry it on more extensively, and not less lovingly, than she has done! 'Grandmamma!' Ah, me! How the days are going by! It seems but as yesterday that the father of these two little maidens was my own bonnie baby, laughing, ay, and weeping too, in what I then thought a most wonderful and exceptional fashion; yet so many years have flown away, and he has traveled so far on life's journey, that now his babies crow and cry even as he once did, and make sweet childish music in his house, and call me 'Grandmamma'!

'Growing older!
With a sigh we say it,
That the early freshness of the dawn,
Rosy-tinted, rich in thoughts and fancies,
Seemeth farther at each birthday morn.

'Growing older!
Joyously we say it,
Reaching onward to immortal youth,
And the fount of bliss that never endeth,
Promised us by Him who is the Truth.'

"It will not do, however, to grow prosy over my venerable position, as a maternal ancestor. I must 'wear my honors meekly,' I must persuade the rose-buds to lie lovingly by the side of the 'sear and yellow leaf,' and teach the dimpled fingers to smooth away the wrinkles and the coming crow's-feet, and be as wise and tender a grandmother as the Lord would have me be. So a letter is written to the dear son whose love for his mother is one of the joys of her life, thanking him for the sweet re-membrance on behalf of his wee maidens, and in-voking God's rich blessings on him and his; and thus ends the examination and reply to our first New Year's missive.

"But there lies on my table, awaiting completion, a letter to that other darling son, who at this moment is on the mighty waters, sailing away from mother and from home, to go and serve his God and his people in the distant colonies. Before I open an-other epistle, this one must be finished; it is to meet him at Naples, where his ship touches, and must carry a word of comfort and of lingering farewell, and assure him once again of mother's fervent prayers for his safety. It is with a great yearning over him in my heart, and eyes that grow dim with tears as the pen runs on, that I fill up the last pages of my love-letter to my absent boy, and sealing it with a sigh, which is, in reality, a prayer, I drop it into the post-basket, and then turn to engage resolutely in the business of the day."

In 1886, she made this memorandum : " When the master of the house—the 'houseband'—is away, we lonely ones at 'Westwood' realize in an especial manner our complete dependence on the Lord for safe guard and protection both night and day. We know that the tender committal of home and its inmates to the Father's care, when the farewells are said, is always renewed and repeated by our absent one ; and at our own evening worship the prayer that He will 'hide us in the shadow of His hand' while we sleep, and guard us from all evil, is never likely to be forgotten or omitted.

" But, notwithstanding this actual appeal to the Preserver of men, and a conscious belief in His love and power, I had lately acquired a foolish habit of lying awake in the night-watches, with ear intent to catch the faintest sound, heart ready to beat wildly if but a window-sash shook in its frame, and every nerve on the alert to assert itself in throes of painful alarm at the least indication of any unusual movement.

"What if Punchie's fierce bark were to ring through the house in the darkness, or the sharp peal of the alarum should give sudden warning of the approach of danger? What if evil men should try to 'break through and steal,' or a spark unwittingly dropped, and smouldering long, should at last burst into flame, and quickly enwrap us in a fiery and fatal embrace? To tolerate such imaginings was to be tortured by them, and I suffered greatly, till some nights ago the dear Lord ended all this for me, and sent so blessed a ray of enlightenment into my 'dark place,' that at once I laid my head down on the pillow quite comforted. My painful care for the house and its inmates was all gone, because he cared for them; my watchings were over, because He watched; my fears were all allayed, because faith in Him was triumphant and complete!

"And it came about somewhat on this wise: The two texts——'What time I am afraid, I will trust in Thee,' and 'I will trust, and not be afraid'—— had been much on my mind during my wearisome nights; but they had evidently not then found entrance into my heart. I had thought of them without fully realizing their depth of blessed meaning; they had lain on the outside of my soul as fair lilies lie on the surface of a pool; but now I was to discover that they were fast anchored by strong roots in the exceeding great and precious promises of my God.

"In a moment there dawned upon me the possibility and blessedness of being absolutely without fear because I trusted in Him. 'What time I am afraid.' 'Yes,' said I, 'that is just now, dear Lord, when the creaking of a piece of furniture startles me, and the very thought of the bark of a dog strikes terror into my heart.' 'I will trust in thee.' As I said it, deliverance came. 'Do I really trust in God?' I asked of myself; and I could steadfastly reply, 'Yes, blessed be His Name! I do trust Him; and I know He can keep us in perfect safety; moreover, I am assured that He never fails those who put their trust in Him.' There came a pause, the light had broken in, and I was wondering at the fast-fleeing shadows. 'Now surely, my heart, thou canst go on with the other text, and boldly say, " I will trust, and not be afraid." What sort of trust dost thou call this that wakens, and listens, and imagines all sorts of evil instead of calmly sleeping and resting in the sheltering arms of the Blessed One? If thou dost honestly trust Him, thou shouldest certainly not be afraid; for thy faith should deal a death-blow to all thy fears.' And it did, dear reader; then and there I gave up all my nervous apprehensions. I surrendered myself and all my belongings to the Father's keeping, and I have had no more gloomy fancies, or midnight watchings. I have laid me down in peace and slept, because He only has made me to dwell in safety; or if any wakeful hours have come, my mouth has praised Him with joyful lips, while I remembered Him on my bed, and meditated on Him in the night-watches.

"Why do I tell such a simple little tale of personal and private experience? Well, just because it was a real and blessed fact to me, and I think that the relation of such instances of God's tender care and love, in even the minor matters of daily life, not only helps some of His timid and distressed ones to cast their burdens on the Lord, but it is also graciously accepted by Him as a grain of sweet incense laid on the golden altar to His praise and glory by His grateful child.

"If any courageous and lion-hearted people fail to understand my terrors, there are others who, having groaned under the pressure of like irrational disquietude, will sympathize with me in my past bondage, rejoice in my emancipation, and take heart of grace themselves to seek from the Lord by simple faith as complete and perfect a deliverance as His mercy has accorded to me.

"There are many seasons in a Christian's life when he is 'afraid' with much more need and reason than I could urge for my nervous alarms ; but there never can be a day, or an hour, or a moment, when he may not 'trust' his God absolutely, perfectly, totally ; and, as surely as he does that, so surely will faith overcome fear—trust will lift him over the trial, confidence in God will end the conflict. Not to the night-watchers only, but to those who, day and night, find fears and foes to fight with, do I lovingly commend my two 'Songs in the Night,' to be sung in any time, and to any tune—

> 'What time I am afraid, I will trust in Thee.'
> 'I will trust, and not be afraid.'

"A very pretty and suggestive picture is this week to be seen from the windows of my sitting-room. To the uninitiated observer there might appear to be nothing more extraordinary than a dense mass of shrubbery, overhung with a canopy of trees, and exhibiting in one corner a profusion of white flowers of unusually large size; but I will tell the little story, and try to enlist your interest. This clump of evergreens has been allowed to luxuriate in unchecked growth during many years, and there is in consequence such an increase in their size and height that they are more like trees than shrubs, displaying a density and superabundance of foliage which is lovely, but undesirable in their position. Down in the heart of this miniature wood or forest, a small Syringa bush had its home, and disliking the darkness and lowliness of its dwelling-place, it took heart of grace, and for five years it has been endeavoring to gain access to the light patiently pushing its way upward, growing through the laurels, and hollies, and briers, slowly ascending in spite of every obstacle, till now, in all the glory of eighteen or twenty feet of height, it overtops the surrounding trees, joyfully hangs out its snow-white garlands of perfumed blossoms, asserts its right to the lofty place it has attained, and seems to be making up in excessive beauty and luxuriance for the long years of repression and cruel hindrance it has suffered while struggling to reach this climax of growth.

"'Are those white roses?' say our friends when their attention is called to the mass of blossom towering above the great arbutus trees. 'No, not roses,' we exclaim, 'but something quite as well worth looking at'; and then the aspiring Syringa is duly admired and applauded, while its heavy bunches of flowers nod and quiver, giving forth their fragrance to every gentle breeze that stirs them, as joyful evidence of fulfilled desire and complete satisfaction.

"Pretty, impetuous, ardent, living thing, I love to think how it persevered in its efforts to escape from the surrounding pressure and darkness, how patiently it forced its way through the fretting obstacles which barred its progress to the light; and it does my heart good to go and look at it, as now, revelling in the free and open air of heaven, and the blessed light of the sun, it blooms in unexampled beauty, and showers down its sparkling white petals in a very abandonment of joy.

"What does the Syringa say to me as I stand far below it, gazing with pride and pleasure on its loveliness?

"I think I hear a whisper from each little twig and spray, 'Learn from us to be brave and patient, think no waiting too wearisome to win a blessing,

no toil too great to obtain a triumph; ever turn
from the darkness, and seek the light, though hin-
drances throng around you, and rankling cares, like
thorns, would fain obstruct your progress; believe
wholly in God, and trust in Him to bring you through
all difficulties into the sunshine of His love and
favor in His own good time. The days were very
dark with us down there when we were growing,
and sometimes we almost despaired of obtaining
deliverance; yet inch by inch we advanced, the living
sap within us enforcing our upward growth; and
ever and anon, when the wind swayed the thick
branches of the trees above us, we had such bright
glimpses of blue sky and golden beams that the
darkness became even more distasteful, and the imprisonment more intolerable, while our inward longing for the light lent us faith and courage to struggle
bravely on! And see to what strength and beauty
our Creator has brought us!'

"Dear fellow-Christians, the Syringa has a word
for us all. 'Go thou and do likewise,' it says.
By the power of Christ's life within you, you can
rise above all your trials, and difficulties, and hin-
drances; you can get up above the darkness of any
unhappy surroundings, and walk in the light of
God's countenance. Be not content to dwell in the
depths where the galling, grieving contact of doubts
and fears will well-nigh choke your spiritual life, but,
asking God 'that He would grant you, according to
the riches of His glory, to be strengthened with

might by His spirit in the inner man,' seek to 'grow up into Him in all things,' 'forgetting those things which are behind, and reaching forth unto those things which are before,' and glorifying His dear name by bearing, not merely the fine flowers of profession, but the blessed fruit of a holy, consistent, gracious life. Sweet Syringa, now I leave you, pondering, as I go, the apostle's words, which you have so well illustrated — 'Whereunto I also labor, striving according to His working, which worketh in me mightily.

"I think it must have been through the attention we bestowed upon the Syringa, and the inquiries we made concerning it, that our eyes were first opened to the folly of our mistaken forbearance in allowing the unrestrained growth of the trees and shrubs in the garden. For it was not that clump of evergreens only, of which I have spoken in the former paragraph, that had escaped the pruning-knife; but everywhere the plantations had grown at their own sweet will, and developed an enormous amount of life and vigor during the five years of our residence at 'Westwood.' When we came to look closely around, we found that these charming neighbors had completely surrounded and shut us in, and that the splendid view we had at first enjoyed and prized was now entirely hidden from us.

"We awoke to the fact as from a dream. Where were the distant, but beautifully distinct Surrey hills? Where was the lovely stretch of landscape?

Where the ever-varying play of light and shade on all the nearer fields and meadows, and the changeful beauty of the far-off Downs and open country? They were all there truly, but we could not see them, they were effectually concealed from our eyes; and we went from window to window, vainly endeavoring to discover any opening in the leafy screen, through which we might once again gaze upon that glorious prospect which had hitherto so fascinated and delighted us. In the garden itself it was much the same. There were some charming nooks and corners where we had aforetime stood enraptured, watching the effect of every mood and variation of the atmosphere on the landscape; but these were now choked up by a dense mass of foliage, and tall trees waved their luxuriant branches in joyous defiance of the prying eyes which would fain look beyond them.

"From the windows of the pastor's study there had been most lovely peeps at the distant hills; Caterham, and Wallington, and Banstead, and Epsom Downs were all spread before the spectator as in a panorama; on a sunny summer's day quivering in a golden haze, or at night putting on a strange, solemn beauty, as one by one the lights in far-away villages and houses twinkled like stars come down to visit earth. Now one could see 'nothing but leaves'; green and beautiful, it is true, but none the less embarrassing and mischievous, since they not only excluded some of the necessary light and air from the house, but did us the great wrong of concealing the loveliest of our lovely pictures.

" ' How could you have permitted this invasion of our once cherished privilege ? ' some reader asks. Well, the trees worked subtly, you see ; they grew leaf by leaf, twig by twig, so noiselessly, so gradually, that we took no note of their encroachments till the thick barrier was formed, and our glorious view was hidden ; and I must confess, also, that the master of 'Westwood,' though a decided Liberal in politics, leans terribly to Conservatism in his own garden, and deems it almost a sacrilege to use knife or axe on any of the precious living things that have taken root in this favored and fortunate spot.

" So, even when we became aware of our enclosed condition, no small amount of coaxing and persuasion was required to induce him to allow the first gap to be made in the green barrier ; and I verily think that the passage of the saw through those tree-trunks, and the down-crashing of the severed branches, brought for the moment positive physical pain to his tender, sensitive heart.

" But, oh ! when the sacrifice was once accomplished, and an exquisite gem of a picture was revealed through a frame-work of verdure, with what exclamations of delight did he welcome the beautiful result, and with what readiness did he admit the necessity for like painful but decisive measures throughout our small domain ! This first grand and successful venture of mine, this onslaught against the aggressive vegetable kingdom, was made on the dear pastor's birthday, and such a victory did I achieve, so charmed was he with the conqueror's spoils, that he thenceforth began to wage war on his own account, and became almost as enthusiastic for the subjugation of our persevering obstructionists as I had schooled myself to be. Since that day, decidedly Liberal, not to say Radical, views obtain on the 'open space' question in our garden. Notable improvements are everywhere visible, pleasing prospects meet one at every turn; some of the trees that remain are taught to lend themselves to frame-making in the most charming manner, and through these lovely loop-holes we look across miles of hill and dale, while the larger part of our battlements of living green has been sufficiently demolished to throw open again the magnificent view which makes our Hill of Beulah into a true 'Delectable Mountain.'

"For some time past, I have been debating in my mind whether or not I should give to my readers the particulars of a pleasant circumstance, which has lately enlivened my quiet life with its interesting details. To-day has decided the question, for a donation of £5 to the Book-Fund, the 'First-fruits of the fishing-smack, "Susie Spurgeon,"' supplies the link to my dear work, which seemed needful to justify the relation of the story.

"To begin at the beginning—among the large fleet of vessels which regularly leave the port of

Grimsby for the fishing-grounds in the North Sea, there has long been one which bears my husband's honored name, and from time to time we have rejoiced to hear tidings of its voyagings and welfare, while mutual tokens of interest and good-will have passed between the owner of the ship and the owner of the name. The 'Charles Haddon Spurgeon' has done noble work, too ; for not long ago it towed a wreck into port ! The disabled schooner was a foreigner, and when the crew of the 'C. H. S.' saw her flying signals of distress, they boarded her, and found her full of water ; but they bravely agreed to tow her into Grimsby ! This took them three days and nights. During this time, the second and third hands had to remain on board the water-logged vessel, at the risk of her going to pieces any moment, and sinking under them ! The good friend who gave me these details feelingly adds, 'I like to think of the "C. H. S." doing this ! It is so suggestive ! How many wrecked and storm-tossed souls has the pastor, C. H. Spurgeon, been the means of bringing into the haven of rest ! How has he toiled to win them to the only place of safety ! '

"In this last summer, there was another vessel built for the same owner, and it was decided to call her the 'Susie Spurgeon,' to my intense gratification and delight. While she was building, Mr. E. greatly desired that I should be the first to see the 'burgee,' a large flag with the ship's name in ; so it was sent up for my inspection, and, on unpacking it, I found

22

to my great surprise a huge 'color,' eight yards long,
and two and a-half yards wide, with the smack's
name, 'Susie Spurgeon,' in great letters a foot long,
marvellously fashioned, and inlaid in the bunting. It
was too large to go up anywhere but in the largest
room in the house, and there, though it wound itself
gracefully round the book-cases, and dropped in
voluminous folds from the curtain-rods, it looked as
if it pined for the bright blue sea, and felt out of
place in a parson's library! As it hung there day
after day, waiting till the ship was fitted, a strong
desire took possession of me to use it in some way
to show my appreciation of the honor done me. But
how should I set about this? I lay awake at night,
pondering by what means I could make it my messenger to carry a word to captain and crew, of good
cheer and good wishes, and give a little evidence of
my interest in my ship! At last a 'happy thought'
visited me, and I caught it, and cherished it with
much care! It occurred to me that it would be a
delightful task to work some few words on the flag,
which should not only embody my best desires for
the brave men who would serve under it, but should
also set always before them the only way of safe
sailing over the stormy sea of life, something which
should not only attract the eye, but find an entrance
into the heart! So far, so good; but how to bring
my 'happy thought' to a happier interpretation was
another embarrassment. What should the few words
be? How I puzzled over that question! How many

things my mind suggested and then 'declined with thanks,' I cannot tell you. Then, one wakeful night, some rhymes popped into my head, and I cried 'Eureka!' But I have no gift for rhyming, and it took me an inconveniently long time to arrange my undisciplined numbers into the following lines :

> This flag shall bear
> On high my prayer,
> While playful winds enwreathe it ;
> God save the crew,
> Good men and true,
> Who worship God beneath it !

"Now, I must confess I thought this rather good and was a little bit proud of it, after all the trouble I had expended on it ; but my dear husband, being an editor, is also a critic, and rather hard on 'poets,' as a good many people know to their cost ; and so, when I, with meekness and fear, showed him this production, he smiled, and shook his dear head, and said it was 'very nice, but it would not do.' The rhymes of the third and sixth lines he could not pass—I must try again. I did so, with this result :

> This flag shall bear
> Aloft my prayer,
> As it floats in the heavenly blue ;
> God bless the 'S. S.'
> Give good success,
> And save every one of the crew !

"This time I was not surprised when I found my dear Mentor could not give his unqualified approval ; but I had done my best, and could do no better, so

he tenderly undertook to revise the lines, and put
them into proper shape for me, and from his un
fettered pen they flowed forth thus :

> This flag shall bear
> Aloft my prayer,
> That good success attend you ;
> God save each one,
> Through Christ His Son,
> And from all ill defend you.

"Hurrah! This was just what I wanted, good
wishes and the gospel of the grace of God combined! Thanks to the dear writer, and blessings on
his words!

"The lemon tree must have a word of remembrance in this closing record of my work. How it
has grown! And what a sturdy, healthy tree it is!
Yet it has never borne fruit, and in this respect has
greatly disappointed me, though it is foolish to be
impatient at Nature's dignified deliberation. If it
had been grafted, the fruit would have been forced ;
now it awaits the time of perfection as God ordered
it, and as it was arranged when He pronounced all
to be 'very good.' So it stands in the greenhouse,
flourishing, and extending its branches year by year,
and I still hold it in tender estimation as the emblem
of my Book-Fund, blessing the Lord that He has
allowed the spiritual work to outstrip the leisure of
Nature, and come into full fruit-bearing so soon and
so happily, to feed and refresh His fainting servants.
It is to me a tree of tender memories, for not only
has its simple story won sympathy and help for my

Fund, and interested friends in my work, but, whenever I look at it, I seem to see again the sick-chamber which was my pleasant prison in Nightingale
Lane; the couch where I lay suffering so many
months and years; the sunlit window where the
little flower-pot was placed, and where the 'pip'
grew slowly into a feeble plant; then, looking round
upon myself and my present circumstances, I am
amazed at the gracious contrast which the Lord's
loving hand has wrought. 'Can that fine tree, of
eight feet six inches high, be the same tiny thing
that began its frail life under such unusual conditions?' 'Can I, with this unexpected measure of
health and activity, be the same person who then
seemed to be passing quickly through the Valley of
the Shadow of Death?' 'Tis even so. Then do
you wonder that often, as I stand gazing upon this
lemon tree, happy tears of thankfulness for God's
great tenderness to me should gently blot out the
details of that past experience; and then that they
should magnify the beauty and brightness of the
present blessings?

"The Lord has made my time of loneliness to be
a season of such intensely busy labor, that the days
have not been long enough to enable me to finish
all my work; and there has not been a crevice of
time into which a dreary, cheerless feeling could
intrude itself. Then the news from Mentone has
been so encouraging and hopeful, that were it only
for that mercy, I ought to sing the Old Year out

with a 'Jubilate.' There came this sweet message to me this morning, and it will not be difficult for my readers to imagine that it has made music in my heart all the day :—

> ' From sunny lands my spirit flies to thee,
>   And doth salute thee in the chilly day :
> Long hast thou been a summer's sun to me,
>   Fain would I chase thy every cloud away.
> Though dark thy skies, I would thy light increase
>   By one short message which my pen can tell,
> It brings thy love some little light of peace
>   To know that with thy husband—ALL IS WELL.'

"Perhaps I ought not to give my 'love-letters' in the Book-Fund Report, but this one came on a post card, and by this fact proclaimed itself *pro bono publico;* besides which, my few previous home confidences have been so tenderly welcomed and cherished, that I could not refrain from sharing with my readers on this last day of the Old Year the 'little bit of sunshine' which has gilded every hour of it for me. Oh, blessed wedded love, that has grown brighter and clearer after shining on for thirty happy years! Thanks be to God for a love that 'Fonder grows with age, and charms, and charms forever.'

"Very soon, if the Lord will, there will be again the joy of the home-coming, when the happiness of reunion will efface all the heartache of separation, and the two lives which, like mountain streams parted for a while by some ponderous impediment, having passed it, meet again with tumultuous current, shall flow on once more in deep and abounding bliss. Then all the routine of the dear happy home-life will begin afresh, and the days, so full of work and service, will fly swiftly on their busy rounds, and the sweet Saturday nights—my Sabbaths—will again crown the week's labor with blessing and holy peace.

"Seeing that we began this year with a long account of the doings and the duties of its first twelve hours, I might have asked my dear readers to 'assist' in the same way at its close; for the letters of to-day have been, to the full, as many and as interesting as those we opened on January 1, 1885. Do they not say that, in a well-concerted piece of music, the final note should correspond to that on which the air commences? Even so, in composing this unpretending little tune of mine, I ought doubtless to have tried to harmonize it rightly, and have played the 'finale' on the same chords as the opening 'aria.' But I spare you and myself.

"The hand that holds this pen is very weary; and the brain, which tries to think the thoughts that guide it, is jaded and overstrained. Soon the midnight chimes will be ringing, and 'each breeze that rises from the earth be loaded with a song of heaven.' It is meet and wise to say adieu now, softly and tenderly, to those who have for so many years been partakers with me of the joy of this sweet service, and then to go alone before the Lord, and bless Him for the immeasurable love and goodness which have ensured so blessed an ending to a year of blessing.

" ' Oh! tired heart—
God knows!
Not you nor I,
Who reach our hands for gifts
That wise love must deny—
We blunder, where we fain would do our best—
Until a-weary, then we cry, ' Do Thou the rest ';
And in His hands the tangled skein we place
Of our poor blind weaving with a shamèd face—
All trust of ours He sacredly will keep;
So, tired heart—
God knows!
Go thou to work or sleep.' "

CHAPTER XII.

GOD HEARD HIM.

The prayer of the righteous availeth much. God heareth him in Heaven, his dwelling place; God answers him without hesitation. It would seem impossible for any reasonable being to study carefully the life of Mr. Spurgeon as a prayerful Christian and not come to the deliberate conclusion that God does hear and directly answer prayer. We have referred to it before in speaking of the wonderful cures which followed his prayers; but here again, we are obliged to enter into the realm of the miraculous and hear and tell of wonderful things for which no natural law gives an adequate explanation.

Hard, solid, undeniable facts remain still facts, and command the respect and faith of sensible men though they may be often partially hidden by the surging waves of theory which dash and break around them.

"God cannot answer prayer" says the unbeliever, and yet here are these facts established beyond any opportunity of reasonable contradiction.

"The Lord will not change his natural laws to accommodate any single human being," has often been asserted by the theologians who claim to believe in the teachings of Scripture. They strongly assert that the day is past when God will perform miracles at the request of any of his children ; yet here was a Godly man whose character was above reproach, whose sincerity is unquestioned and who moved among a cloud of witnesses, whose petitions to God were in hundreds of mysterious ways directly answered.

The serious investigator will find this life experience a very fascinating field of research and the humble believer in Jesus of Nazareth will find encouragement in the exercise of faith and in the command to pray. A study of his methods and the record of its results must be of great practical use to every Christian man and woman who would imitate his character or who desires the same return for their petitions. His prayer for himself was answered many thousand times from the day when he first asked God for the forgiveness of his sins to the last day when he asked that the sustaining support of the everlasting arms might be underneath him.

He was continually testifying of the wonderful goodness of God in granting to him the things for which he asked. That he petitioned for many things which he did not receive is also certain and while it complicates the problem somewhat it does not overthrow the testimony in cases where God did send to him the needed blessing.

He had a most charming habit of going to God

A Sick-Bed Prayer.

in prayer in the midst of any perplexity and asking the Lord to give him a calmness of spirit. He often testified that after such a petition his anxieties seemed to pass away. He laid them all upon the Lord and he could enter upon his work encouraged and in a most peaceful disposition. Sometimes when worry came to him as it comes to nearly every human being he would bethink himself to his Great Helper and turn aside to seek a quiet opportunity to ask the Lord to relieve him of his anxiety.

He testified in 1889 that never in his life had he worried about anything beyond the time when he could secure the opportunity to turn aside to prayer. When he was in most fearful pain and suffering with those rheumatic twinges which drew him into positive contortion he could turn away in sincere prayer and become so lost in worship as to feel no longer conscious of torture. He found that he could receive such inspiration from the mysterious spirit of God as enabled him to pass many happy hours while afflicted by one of the most terrible diseases which ever comes to a person with sensitive nerves.

At the Mildmay Conference in 1890 Mr. Spurgeon said: "After a period of continued pain, with little sleep, I sat up, as best I could, one morning in my bed in an agony of pain, and I cried to the Lord for deliverance. I believed fully that he could deliver me then and there, and I pleaded my son-ship and his Fatherhood. I went to the length of pleading that he was my Father, and I said, 'if it were my child that suffered so, I would not let them suffer any longer if I could help him. Thou can'st help me and by thy Fatherly love I plead with thee to give me rest.' I felt that I could add, 'Nevertheless, not as I will, but as thou wilt.' But I did the first thing first. I pleaded with my Father, and went first where Christ went first, saying, 'My Father, if it be possible, let this cup pass from me.' I shall never forget my success in my appeal. In real earnest I believed God to be my Father, threw myself upon him, and within a few moments I dropped back upon the pillow, the pain subsided, and very soon I slept most peacefully."

Often amid the bustle of many duties and cares, through a day of severely hard work, he would hurry to the chapel to lead the evening meeting. He naturally entered the building with his heart beating fast, his body very weary and his brain greatly disturbed in the conflict of thoughts, and the anxieties to do his duty in so many disconnected relations of life. He could then kneel in prayer for a moment alone and place himself in such harmony with the Eternal Peace or receive such unction from on High as would make it possible for him to begin the meeting as fresh in body and as calm in spirit as though he had been resting upon his couch through the day.

All this may in a measure be accounted for by

the unbeliever upon the principal that it was the effect of his own mind upon his body and that such a power is unquestionably given to any one whether he prays or not. Mr. Spurgeon stoutly asserted that such was not the case with him at other times and persons not in the habit of prayer do not find themselves exercising this great privilege.

"The Peace of God which passeth all understanding" really comes only to them who make known their request unto God by supplication with thanksgiving. But whatever may be thought of the reflex mental influence in Mr. Spurgeon's case it is certain that no human argument can reason away the facts which we are now about to state.

He prayed that God would keep him safe on his journies and many a time during his history he came into the presence of great danger, amidst most serious accidents and yet escaped without great injury; and often went free wholly, because he had such confidence in God that he lost not his presence of mind. But in other cases nothing on his part could, humanly speaking, have prevented his death had there not been a combination of providential circumstances for his protection which were beyond human control.

We have spoken already of his preservation in accordance with his prayer, through the colera and other contagious diseases, and of the wonderful way in which he was guided step by step from the rustic condition of an "Essex bumpkin," to the position of a cultivated scholar, and the most revered character perhaps in England.

The experience of Mr. and Mrs. Spurgeon as invalids is often quoted as a proof that his prayers were not answered, and these facts have led many to fear that the other cases where his prayers seem to be answered, were simply mysterious coincidences. We do not hope to explain why one prayer was answered and another was rejected, except by saying that the will of God was otherwise for the good of those who prayed. But we can only present the incidents which illustrate the power of prayer in his case and leave them to the meditation of Christian readers.

There were several different occasions on which Mr. Spurgeon was so anxious for a definite result in the service of God that he spent the entire night in prayer. In three such cases he has told us he received the answer in full to his petition. In the establishment of the Orphanage, he prayed that the Lord would influence some person having the means to come forward and supply any necessities of the case. The prayer was answered without any personal interference of his own and without the person who was most influenced in the case knowing that he had spent the night in prayer.

In three other instances in connection with the same work when their money had given out and so far as he could see the Orphans would be left within twenty-four hours in suffering need of food, there by himself or with his deacons he prayed and the answer came in each case from altogether unforseen and unexpected quarters.

Mr. Spurgeon had been praying one night that the Lord would send gifts with which to supply the necessities of the Orphanage and a stranger in London was at the same time walking its foggy streets. He had never seen Mr. Spurgeon nor read any of his sermons, but he had heard his name mentioned. The impression upon that stranger's mind that same night was so great as to cause him to visit Mr. Spurgeon and make him a gift toward his church work. He had found it impossible to break away from the facinating call. He rang Mr. Spurgeon's door-bell and insisted upon seeing Mr. Spurgeon and giving him a large sum of money. He refused at that time even to leave his name with Mr. Spurgeon, simply saying that he "lived many miles away." Afterward he sent another princely gift saying that the pleasure he had received from the other donation had made it one of the best investments of his life.

When the great Tabernacle was begun Mr. Spurgeon prayed, as we have already seen, that no workman might be injured during its construction. The prayer was so distinctly answered there that in the construction of a large business house near Ludgate Circus he was especially requested by the owners to come and offer the same prayer in connection with their enterprise. There were many old buildings to be pulled down and some very large ones to be constructed, yet in this case, as in the former no persons were injured and the buildings were completed, to use the owners expression, "with songs of grateful joy."

These cases where his prayer was offered in one place and answered by some mysterious impression being made upon minds in another place with whom there was no natural means of communication were multiplied into the thousands. The history of all the great revivals at the Tabernacle presented numerous illustrations of this fact. Mr. Spurgeon, prayed and while he was praying or immediately thereafter, some person at a distance, felt it his duty to serve God in just the way, or by giving just the amount for which Mr. Spurgeon had asked.

He did not tempt the Lord by asking foolish things or by requesting God to do anything which was not for the furtherance of His divine kingdom in the earth. Even the prayers he offered up for himself were always confined to the thought that if he was himself favored of God he would only be a more useful instrument in the Lord's hands.

It would take many volumes to contain the most condensed record of the instances where the prayers were so directly replied to as to startle those who witnessed them and to fill those who believed in prayer with most enthusiastic thanksgiving.

By far the most mysterious incidents connected

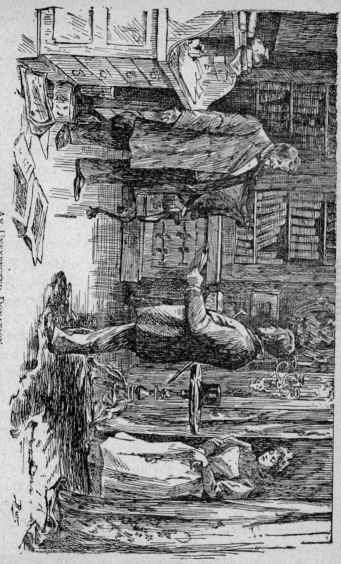

AN UNEXPECTED DONATION.

with his prayerful influence with the Almighty are shown in the conversion of individuals during the many years of his successful ministry. His prayers for the reformation and conversion of those who were not Christians who attended his service were so continually and manifestly answered and were a a matter of such public observation and discussion that it is unnecessary to follow them. They belong to the common experience of spiritual churches in other places and those who have worked in evangelistic or actual church enterprises will recognize at once the power which was exercised by him as he prayed for the descent of the Holy Spirit. But we come to more remarkable things when we find that Mr. Spurgeon's prayers for the conversion of people living at a distance who had never heard of him and knew nothing whatever of his meetings or church, were directly answered at the very time in places far distant.

.A remarkable case was mentioned in 1887 when Mr. Spurgeon at the request of friends made a special prayer in public for the conversion of a son and husband who were absent in Australia. The friends who mentioned the matter to Mr. Spurgeon were new acquaintances to him, had but a few days before moved into London. They had never by word or by letter mentioned Mr. Spurgeon or his work to their friend in Australia. He declares now that he has never read anything of Mr. Spurgeon and does not remember that he had ever heard his name mentioned, although it was barely possible that he might have seen the name in some of the newspapers. But on the very day and at the very hour when Mr. Spurgeon engaged in a most fervent prayer, this man was at work upon a building in Melbourne. He stopped while carring a timber from one portion of the building to another and said he was unable to go further, so quickly and deeply was he impressed with a sense of his responsibility to God and of his lost condition of soul. He had not attended church during his stay in Australia, and was not a regular attendant at any church or chapel before he left England. The tears came to his eyes, his hands trembled, and he felt that he was forsaken of God because he had led such an unrighteous life. He was in no sense a criminal or immoral man, but this religious impression was so deep upon him that he went to the lowest story of the building, notified the superintendent that he must go to his boarding house. He went there and fell upon his knees and prayed for God's forgiveness and there received, as he afterwards testified, the "Light of Grace which reconciled him with his God." That same night before going to bed, he wrote home to his people in London, telling them how he had, without the advice or guidance of any human being, been led to seek the Christ.

In another case, a mother came to Mr. Spurgeon in January 1872 and stated to him that her son had enlisted in the French Army, and that she was very much afraid that in such surroundings he would be influenced by the bad comany and be altogether lost to Christian principles and perhaps to his family.

Mr. Spurgeon promised to pray for him but the mother would not let him go unless he would kneel right then and there and pray with her for her son's welfare. She has since stated that it was at half-past four in the afternoon that the prayer was offered; and he afterwards said that at precisely that hour he was standing in the camp and that a strange impression ran through his body filling him with a sense of dismay and terror as though in the presence of actual death. The Army was not engaged in any conflict and there was no apparent evidence of any near engagement. His emotions were so great that his face turned pale, which called the attention of his comrades, who commented with excitement upon his fainting condition. He went to his tent and there alone called upon God for forgiveness and help. By the very next mail which left the camp, he wrote to his mother stating the circumstance and asking her to pray for him and at the same time strangely suggesting that he wished she would write to Mr. Spurgeon and ask him to pray for him.

There is related still another case. In September, 1878, Mr. Spurgeon attended the prayer-meeting at 12 o'clock which was held by a number of business men every day. One of the business men personally unacquainted with Mr. Spurgeon arose in that meeting and stated that it was his belief if Mr. Spurgeon would pray for the conversion of a brother then in Edinburgh, Scotland, that it might be accomplished that very day. Mr. Spurgeon impulsively arose and said, "I accept that challenge, let us call on God." That afternoon the brother in Edinburgh was greatly disturbed in mind throughout all the business hours which remained of the day, and went home to his family saying to them, he felt as though he had lost and wasted his life, and that he knew not what to do to reform, he was going to write at once to Mr. Spurgeon, in London. He had no acquaintance with Mr. Spurgeon except such as came through the newspapers and yet he wrote to him a long and urgent appeal that he would show him the way of salvation.

At still another time one of the sons of a deacon of the New Park Street Church, whose life had been a cause for worry to his parents because of his inclination to unbelief and wildness, had purchased a ticket to come to America intending to leave England without permitting his parents to know his purpose. The deacon knew nothing whatever of his son's intentions, but he went to Mr. Spurgeon and requested him to go into one of the ante-rooms of the church that they might there unite together in prayer for his son. Mr. Spurgeon being in haste at first refused and hurriedly started off on another errand but he had not gone far before he abruptly turned directly about and calling after the deacon went into the ante-room to pray. There both of them offered up their petitions with great earnestness for the salvation of the soul of the son. The son was at that time on the wharf in Liverpool looking at the steamer which he intended to take for America. He said afterwards in his testimony in the Metropolitan Tabernacle as related to us that a chill seized his heart and affected his whole body, that his mind become greatly excited and a sense of the sin he was committing in running away from home and leaving such affectionate parents made him to loathe himself and he wished he might die. He could not arouse sufficient courage to step aboard the steamer and it sailed away without him. He walked up and down the streets and after going to his hotel paced the room in positive misery. The temptation to take his own life was so strong that he went out of the hotel to a gunsmith's with a view of purchasing a pistol with which to shoot himself. The gunsmith's shop was closed and he returned to his room and paced to and fro until the thought that he ought to pray came to him so impulsively that he knelt by his bedside and prayed. He poured out his soul in prayer and remained in that posture of prayer until the daylight came. During the next day he was still very unhappy but he was able to surrender himself entirely to the influence of God's spirit and with a happiness he was unable afterwards to describe, he returned his ticket to the steamer office and with the money they repaid him purchased his ticket back to London and to his surprised parents.

In 1887 Mr. Spurgeon visited Yorkshire at the dedication of a small chapel and there met with a gentleman of culture and means, who was not a Christian but who was attracted to the chapel by the fact that Mr. Spurgeon was to be there. Mr Spurgeon, as was his frequent costom, asked the gentleman if he was a Christian, to which he replied distinctly, " No." Mr. Spurgeon then asked him if he did not wish to be one, to which he replied emphatically, " No." Then Mr. Spurgeon said, " God will ask you that question and I shall pray to Him tonight that He do it at once." That night Mr. Spurgeon was late at a railway station when this man came to his mind. He then, while walking upon the platform offered up repeated prayers that God would call that gentleman to himself, and use him for great Christian good. Near the same hour, if not precisely at the same time, that gentleman was in animated conversation with some friends at an inn, he had been joking concerning the chapel dedication and seemed to regard it as a subject of great sport that he should have been found in a place of worship. He had described to his friends the absurd appearance of one of his acquaintances who saw him come in and take a seat in the chapel. He broke off the conversation in the middle of a

sentence and with every appearance of great embarrassment arose and asked to be excused, hurry-
ing at once to his home ; and there, that night read
the Bible earnestly and prayed for himself sincerely,
and would not retire to rest until he felt the evident
presence of God in answer to his prayer. He himself gave a history of the affair and said he never
could account in any way for the very sudden turn
in all his sentiments and thoughts. He, however,
believed that it was a stroke of providence instantly
set upon him in answer to Mr. Spurgeon's prayer.

Another instance was related in a Sunday-school
gathering at Cambridge in 1884 wherein it was
stated that Mr. Spurgeon had been requested by a
father to pray for the conversion of his little girl,
then about twelve years of age. Mr. Spurgeon
made a note of the request upon a newspaper he
had in his hand at the time but laid the paper
aside and forgot about the request for several
weeks. One day the paper was taken out from the
library by a servant and providentially laid upon
the window sill where Mr. Spurgeon found it while
he was waiting for a friend to call. He there found
the memorandum he had made and turned away to
his libarary and knelt by his own chair and prayed
for the conversion of the child. He felt so sincer-
ly that his prayer was to be answered that he continued in prayer much longer than usual and was
aroused from it by a ring at the door. Supposing, of
course, that it was a friend he had invited, he went

directly to the door himself and what was his surprise to be met directly by the young girl for whom he had been praying and whose very first request was "Mr. Spurgeon, I have come to ask you to tell me how to be a Christian". She has since stated that she was passing the house at the time, with no previous thought of any serious nature concerning her Christian experience, but that she found it utterly impossible to pass the gate without turning in. The impulse was so great upon her to ring the door bell that she had actually pulled it before she had made up her mind what to say to Mr. Spurgeon. She has since been one of the loveliest and most effective of the Sunday-school teachers in the Tabernacle.

Mr. Spurgeon's own son was converted in the same way, in direct answer to his prayers when away from home. Mr. Drysdale felt it to be his duty to show the young man the way of righteousness and that impression to speak for Christ came to him with singular distinctness at the very hour when Mr. Spurgeon was praying the Lord that his son might be redeemed.

At a prayer meeting held in the Tabernacle a few years since which has always been remembered by the participants as one of unusual solemnity, Mr. Spurgeon requested members of the church to pray especially for the conversion of some distant friend. There were several hundred people present at the time and many of them acted upon Mr.

Spurgeon's suggestion and during a season of silent prayer asked directly for the salvation of definite persons of their personal acquaintance who could not at the time have known that they were being remembered in prayer. Four week later at a church meeting one of the Christians stated how his prayer had been most wonderfully answered that night and heartily thanked Mr. Spurgeon for having joined with him in such a request. That statement introduced the whole question again and it is said that over fifty different persons testified that night that their prayers had been directly answered. In some cases while they were praying the friends for whom they petitioned the Lord had surrendered themselves to Christ's service, and in no less than ten cases the converted persons were there present that night in the meeting.

For over twenty-five years these singular answers to prayers had been an almost daily experience in the work of the Metropolitan Tabernacle. Men know it, they see it, and yet it passes without the study or without the notice which would attach to almost any other incident thus repeating itself through such a series of years. The hopelessness of finding any explanation of it in nature's laws may have prevented the examination of the topic and the very frequency of the experiences there and in other places may serve to take it out of the list of the miraculous.

Mr. Spurgeon often stated that the day of miracles was passed and seems to have regarded these incidents as commonplace. But there such facts stand, testified to by many thousand of credible people, and their results having a present and ever-lasting effect upon the history of England itself. Prayers were offered by Mr. Spurgeon, supported by the petitions of his people, and drunkards re-formed, thieves ceased to steal, the vile forsook their vices, the dishonest turned to righteousness, the ungodly called upon the Lord, scoffers believed in Jesus Christ, the useless became useful, and in-jurious became helpful, society was cleaner, streets were safer, the laws were better administered, homes were sweeter and happier, the nation more prosperous and commerce itself becomes more stable. What a factor this has been in the life of England.

Mr. Needham in his book also gives an instance of a remarkable answer to Mr. Spurgeon's prayer. "On another occasion Dr. Brock and Mr. Spur-geon were dining together at the mansion of a beloved friend in Regent's Park when the Orphanage building was in progress, and money was wanted which was not in hand. Mr. Spurgeon suffering from feeble health, still expressed his strong faith in God that the money would come to hand in due time. Just as the dinner was ended, the servant entered the room with a telegram from his private secretary announcing that an unknown donor had sent $5,000 for the Orphanage. Dr. Brock im-

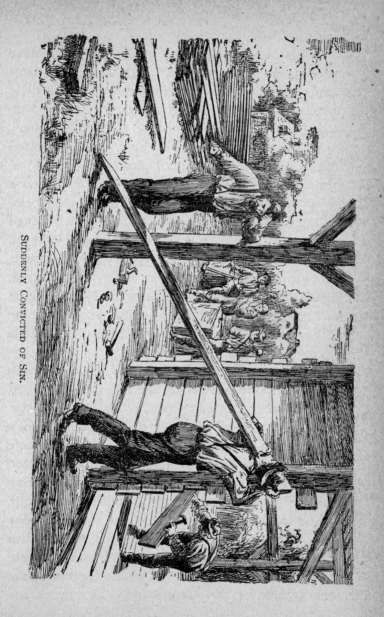

SUDDENLY CONVICTED OF SIN.

mediately arose and poured forth his utterances of gratitude in the most joyful manner, and they all united in prayer on their knees to magnify the Lord."

What a blessing to London and to the world it was to have such a saintly, praying man live and teach there for forty-seven years. He furnished an avenue of communication between earth and heaven, between the material and the spiritual, through which has flowed the vigorous influences which have blessed the world beyond estimation and made heaven itself the brighter. O, Thou mighty Ruler of the universe, send to this world many more such earnest men of prayer!

24

CHAPTER XIII.

THE PASTORS' COLLEGE.

It is divine to create; it is heroic to stand alone; and that man best exemplifies the divine and heroic who single-handed begins an enterprise for the good of his fellow-man. There are usually found plenty of people who are willing to spread a cause already under way, and the whole world will run tumultuously after a great success. As at the beginning of creation we find God, so at the beginning of any great enterprise in the earth we find the godly man or woman.

Mr. Spurgeon began many things which he intended should be a blessing to mankind, and for that characteristic he deserves the everlasting praise of humanity. Any person who goes through life laying foundation stones for new sources of delight or benefit will be remembered long after he has passed from the stage of action; for these fountains which he releases from the rocky mountain side will flow on in ceaseless rivers.

The Pastors' College is a peculiar institution, differing from anything else of its kind, and yet one greatly needed for the furtherance of the Kingdom of the Lord. Many measures connected with the practical theological training of men for Christian work have received the attention of great minds and have been discussed for many years, yet we seem as far from agreement at present concerning the proper solution of the question as we were a hundred years ago.

Just what training is necessary, and just what is to be considered a call of God is one of those important matters to which Mr. Spurgeon gave his attention, and to which many other men of equal ability ought to give their attention. As the Gospel is intended to change the heart and not to specially discipline the mind, and as it is a question of moral influence and not of scientific erudition, the preacher or teacher could make use of any event or influence which would produce the desired change, whether or not it be in accordance with theory or precedent.

As there are many different classes of people to be instructed in the way of righteousness, belonging to all grades of moral and intellectual culture, so it would seem that there is needed for their instruction a class of people especially adapted to each order of the hearers. A man may be educated altogether too much to accomplish a great work among a certain class of people; another may be far too ignorant to be of any value among the scholars whose minds he would influence and whose hearts he would touch. One person's experience may especially fit him for labors among a definite class in society which would at the same time unfit him for the accomplishment of any good in any other class in society. The poor are to be saved, as well as the rich; the ignorant need the Gospel as much as the wise; and the truths of Scripture are far better inculcated by persons who are in touch with the people they address.

Mr. Spurgeon evidently founded the Pastors' College upon the idea that God calls men to the ministry, and consequently selects them from many different grades of society. It was not in his idea to found an institution to educate them out of the very position into which God called them. But rather to supply them with better means for working in their own grade and in their own place.

He prayed much for an opportunity to do good in the name of his Master, and in response to his petition the door was opened for the establishment of this theological school. It has accomplished great things indeed in itself, but will accomplish far more in the number of other institutions like it because of the great demand.

Seeing that an intelligent devout coal miner could preach with the most effective illustrations to coal miners out of his own experience; seeing that a sailor could preach to sailors; and a teacher to teachers, he used his excellent common sense in assisting such representatives of the people to do more efficiently the work to which the Lord had apparently called them. He did not accept the testimony of every emotional or deluded individual as evidence that God had called him to be a minister, but he only accepted that inward conviction as a part of the evidence with which to judge a man's fitness for the Lord's work. He certainly required on the part of his students that they should have sincere piety and should feel convinced beyond contradiction that they must preach the Gospel. But he also had the sanctified sense to see that if God did call a man to preach the Gospel He would also call men to hear him.

When He sent Philip into the desert of Gaza He had already provided the hearer, the Ethiopian, to whom Philip was to preach.

Men are called to preach the Gospel if other men are called to hear them preach it—that is, if they preach the true and simple Gospel presented by Jesus of Nazareth. The students who have attended the College thus far have been selected from almost all different trades that could be found. They have been required to show their ability to preach and their power to convert the souls of men before they were accepted as students at the College. Hence, the education they received was given as a result of God's call and not as a preparation for His call. The inception of the idea of opening a school and the progress of the work until he had an excellent building well fitted to the needs of students engaged in the study of the Bible, all came naturally in one sense, and miraculously in another sense.

For Mr. Spurgeon simply "did the next thing" and trusted in the Lord that when one thing was well done he would be led to another. He was so led; and the vast good which the graduates of his school are now doing all over the civilized world is one of the wonders of this time. America has almost equal reason with England to send up her thanksgiving to God for the great man who had the courage and the divine wisdom to begin an enterprise of such great importance.

Mr. Spurgeon has told in a most concise manner the history of the College, and his own words carry better authority and clearer ideas than anything which others could write. In 1870 he said:

"The College was the first important institution commenced by the pastor, and it still remains his first-born and best beloved. To train ministers of the Gospel is a most excellent work, and when the Holy Spirit blesses the effort, the result is of the utmost importance both to the Church and to the world."

"The Pastors' College, commenced in 1856, has now entered on its fourteenth year, and during this long period has unceasingly been remembered of the God of heaven, to whom all engaged in it offer reverent thanksgiving. When it was commenced, I had not a remote idea of whereunto it would grow. There were springing up around me, as my own spiritual children, many earnest young men who felt an irresistible impulse to preach the Gospel, and yet

with half an eye it could be seen that their want of education would be a sad hindrance to them. It was not in my heart to bid them cease their preaching, and had I done so, they would in all probability have ignored my recommendation. As it seemed that preach they would, though their attainments were very slender, no other course was open but to give them an opportunity to educate themselves for the work."

"The Holy Spirit had very evidently set His seal upon the work of one of them, Mr. T. W. Medhurst, now of Landport, by conversions wrought under his open-air addresses; it seemed therefore to be a plain matter of duty to instruct this youthful Apollos still further that he might be fitted for wider usefulness. No college at that time appeared to me to be suitable for the class of men that the providence and grace of God drew around me. They were mostly poor, and most of the colleges involved necessarily a considerable outlay to the student; for even where the education was free, books, clothes, and other incidental expenses required a considerable sum per annum. Moreover, it must be frankly admitted that my views of the Gospel and of the mode of training preachers were and are somewhat peculiar. I may have been uncharitable in my judgment, but I thought the Calvinism of the theology usually taught to be very doubtful, and the fervor of the generality of the students to be far behind their literary attainments. It seemed to me that preachers of the grand old truths of the Gospel, ministers suitable for the masses, were most likely to be found in an institution where preaching and divinity would be the main objects, and not degrees and other insignia of human learning."

"I felt that, without interfering with the laudable objects of other colleges, I could do good in my own way. These and other considerations led me to take a few tried young men, and to put them under some able minister, that he might train them in the Scriptures, and in other knowledge helpful to the understanding and proclamation of the truth. This step appeared plain ; but how the work was to be conducted and supported was the question—a question, be it added, solved almost before it occurred."

"Two friends, Mr. Winsor and Mr. W. Olney, both deacons of the Church, promised aid, which, with what I could give myself, enabled me to take one student, and I set about to find a tutor. In Mr. George Rogers, then the pastor of the Independent Church, Albany Road, Camberwell, God sent us the very best man. He had been preparing for such work, and was anxiously waiting for it. This gentleman who has remained during all this period our principal tutor, is a man of Puritanic stamp, deeply learned, orthodox in doctrine, judicious, witty, devout, earnest, liberal in spirit, and withal juvenile in heart to an extent most remarkable in one of his years. My connection with him has been one of uninterrupted comfort and delight. The most sin-

cere affection exists between us; we are of one
mind and one heart; and, what is equally important,
he has in every case secured not merely the respect,
but the filial love of every student. Into this beloved
minister's house the first students were introduced,
and for a considerable period they were domiciled
as members of his family."

"Encouraged by the readiness with which the
young men found spheres of labor, and by their
singular success in soul-winning, I enlarged the
number; but the whole means of sustaining them
came from my own purse. The large sale of my
sermons in America, together with my dear wife's
economy, enabled me to spend from £600 (about
$3,000) to £800 (about $4,000) in a year in my
own favorite work; but on a sudden, owing to my
denunciations of the then existing slavery in the
States, my entire resources from that 'brook
Cherith' were dried up."

"I paid as large sums as I could from my own
income, and resolved to spend all I had, and then
take the cessation of my means as a voice from the
Lord to stay the effort, as I am firmly persuaded
that we ought under no pretense to go into debt.
On one occasion I proposed the sale of my horse
and carriage, although these were almost absolute
necessaries to me on account of continual journeys
in preaching the Word. This my friend Mr. Rogers
would not hear of, and actually offered to be the
loser rather than this should be done. Then it was

that I told my difficulties to my people, and the Weekly Offering commenced; but the incomings from that source were so meagre as to be hardly worth calculating upon. I was brought to the last pound, when a letter came from a banker in the city, informing me that a lady, whose name I have never been able to discover, had deposited a sum of £200 (about $1,000) to be used for the education of young men for the ministry. How did my heart leap for joy! I threw myself then and henceforth upon the bounteous care of the Lord, whom I desired with my whole heart to glorify by this effort."

"Some weeks after, another £100 (about $500) came in, from the same bank, as I was informed from another hand. Soon after Mr. Phillips, a beloved deacon of the Church at the Tabernacle, began to provide an annual supper for the friends of the College, at which considerable sums have from year to year been given. A dinner was also given by my liberal publishers, Messrs. Passmore and Alabaster, to celebrate the publishing of my five-hundredth weekly sermon, at which £500 (about $2,500) were raised and presented to the funds. The College grew every month and the number of students rapidly advanced from one to forty. Friends known and unknown, from far and near, were moved to give little or much to my work, and so the funds increased as the need enlarged. Then another earnest deacon of the Church, Mr. Murrell, espoused as his especial work the weekly offering, and by the unanimous voice of the Church under my care, the College was adopted as its own child. Since that hour the weekly offering has been a steady sourse of income, till in the year 1869 the amount reached exactly £1,869 (about $9,345)."

"There have been during this period times of great trial of my faith; but after a season of straitness, never amounting to absolute want, the Lord has always interposed and sent me large sums (on one occasion £1,000 (about $5,000), from unknown donors. When the Orphanage was thrust upon me, it did appear likely that this second work would drain the resources of the first, and it is very apparent that it does attract to itself some of the visible sources of supply; but my faith is firm that the Lord can as readily keep both works in action as one. My own present inability to do so much, by way of preaching abroad, occasions naturally the failure of another great source of income; and as my increasing labors at home will in all probability diminish that stream in perpetuity, there is another trial of faith. Yet, if the Lord wills the work to be continued, He will send His servant a due portion of the gold and silver which are all His own; and therefore as I wait upon Him in prayer, the all-sufficient Provider will supply all my needs. Nearly £5,000 (about $25,000) is annually required for the College, and the same sum is needed for the Orphanage; but God will move His people to liberality, and we shall see greater things than these."

"While speaking of pecuniary matters, it may be well to add that, as many of the young men trained in the College have raised new congregations and gathered fresh churches, another need has arisen— namely, money for building chapels. It is ever so in Christ's work; one link draws on another, one effort makes another needed. For chapel-building, the College funds could do but little, though they have freely been used to support men while they are collecting congregations; but the Lord found for me one of His stewards, who, on the condition that his name remains unknown, has hitherto, as the Lord has prospered him, supplied very princely amounts for the erection of places of worship, of which more than forty have been built, or so greatly renovated and enlarged as to be virtually new structures. Truly may it be said, 'What hath God wrought!'"

"Pecuniary needs, however, have made up but a small part of our cares. Many have been my personal exercises in selecting the men. Candidates have always been plentiful, and the choice has been wide; but it is a serious responsibility to reject any, and yet more to accept them for training. When mistakes have been made, a second burden has been laid upon me in the dismissal of those who appeared to be unfit. Even with the most careful management, and all the assistance of tutors and friends, no human foresight can secure that in every case a man shall be what we believed and hoped. A brother may be exceedingly useful as an occasional preacher;

he may distinguish himself as a diligent student; he may succeed at first in the ministry; and yet, when trials of temper and character occur in the pastorate, he may be found wanting."

"We have had comparatively few causes for regret of this sort, but there have been some such, and these pierce us with many sorrows. I devoutly bless God that He has sent to the College some of the holiest, soundest, and most self-denying preachers I know, and I pray that He may continue to do so; but it would be more than a miracle if all should excel. While thus speaking of trials connected with the men themselves, it is due to our gracious God to bear testimony that these have been comparatively light, and are not worthy to be compared with the great joy which we experience in seeing no less than two hundred and seven brethren still serving the Lord according to their measure of gift, and all, it is believed, earnestly contending for the faith once delivered unto the saints; nor is the joy less in remembering that eleven have sweetly fallen asleep after having fought a good fight. At this hour some of our most flourishing Baptist Churches are presided over by pastors trained in our College, and as years shall add ripeness of experience and stability of character, others will be found to stand in the front rank of the Lord's host."

"The young brethren are boarded generally in twos and threes, in the houses of our friends around the Tabernacle, for which the College pays a moderate weekly amount. The plan of separate lodging we believe to be far preferable to having all under one roof; for, by the latter mode, men are isolated from general family habits, and are too apt to fall into superabundant levity. The circumstances of the families who entertain our young friends are generally such that they are not elevated above the social position which in all probability they will have to occupy in future years, but are kept in connection with the struggles and conditions of every-day life."

" Devotional habits are cultivated to the utmost, and the students are urged to do as much evangelistic work as they can. The severe pressure put upon them to make the short term as useful as possible, leaves small leisure for such efforts, but this is in most instances faithfully economized. Although our usual period is two years, whenever it is thought right the term of study is lengthened to three or four years; indeed, there is no fixed rule, all arrangements being ordered by the circumstances and attainments of each individual.

"As before hinted, our numbers have greatly grown, and now range from eighty to one hundred. Very promising men, who are suddenly thrown in our way, are received at any time, and others who are selected from the main body of applicants come in at the commencement of terms. The church at the Tabernacle continues to furnish a large quota of men, and as these have usually been educated for two or more years in our Evening Classes, they are more advanced and better able to profit by our two years of study. We have no difficulty in finding spheres for men who are ready and fitted for them. There is no reason to believe that the supply of trained ministers is in advance of the demand. Even on the lowest ground of consideration, there is yet very much land to be possessed; and when men break up fresh soil, as ours are encouraged to do, the field is the world, and the prayer for more laborers is daily more urgent. If the Lord would but send us funds commensurate, there are hundreds of neighborhoods needing the pure Gospel, which we could by His grace change from deserts into gardens. How far this is a call upon the reader let him judge as in the sight of God. Shall there be the gifts and graces of the Spirit given to the Church, and shall there not also be sufficient bestowed of the earthly treasure? How much owest thou unto my Lord?

"The College was for some little time aided by the zealous services of Mr. W. Cubitt, of Thrapstone, who died among us, enjoying our highest esteem. Mr. Gracey, the classical tutor, a most able brother, is one of ourselves, and was in former years a student, though from possessing a solid education, he needed little instruction from us except in theology. In him we have one of the most efficient tutors living, a man fitted for any post requiring thorough scholarship and aptness in communicating knowledge. Mr. Fergusson, in the English elementary

25

classes, does the first work upon the rough stones of the quarry, and we have heard from the men whom he has taught in the Evening Classes, speeches and addresses which would have adorned any assembly, proving to demonstration his ability to cope with the difficulties of uncultured and ignorant minds. Mr. Johnson, who zealously aids in the evening, is also a brother precisely suited to the post which he occupies."

"These Evening Classes afford an opportunity to Christian men engaged during the day to obtain an education for nothing during their leisure time, and very many avail themselves of the privilege. Nor must I forget to mention Mr. Selway, who takes the department of physical science, and by his interesting experiments and lucid descriptions, gives to his listeners an introduction of those departments of knowledge which most abound with illustrations. Last, but far from least, I adore the goodness of God which sent me so dear and efficient a fellow-helper as my brother in the flesh and in the Lord, J. A. Spurgeon. His work has greatly relieved me of anxiety, and his superior educational qualifications have tended to raise the tone of the instruction given."

"As to the quality of the preachers whom we have been enabled to send forth, we need no more impartial witness than the good Earl of Shaftesbury, who was kind enough to express himself publicly in Finsbury Chapel, April 4th, 1870, in the following generous terms:"

"'It was an utter fallacy to suppose that the people of England would ever be brought to a sense of order and discipline by the repetition of miserable services, by bits of wax candle, by rags of Popery, and by gymnastics in the chancel: nothing was adapted to meet the wants of the people but the Gospel message brought home to their hearts, and he knew of none who had done better service in this evangelistic work than the pupils trained in Mr. Spurgeon's College. They had a singular faculty for addressing the population, and going to the very heart of the people.'"

"Those who measure effort by result will be gratified to learn that during the last five years our statistics show that the Churches under the care of our young pastors have received a clear increase of ten thousand members. How much of Divine power and grace this reveals, eternity alone can disclose. Had we reckoned in earlier years, we should have seen equal proportionate success; and it is no small matter for congratulation that the stricter examination of results which we have carried out of late manifests such a satisfactory total.

"Each year the brethren educated at the Pastors' College are invited to meet in the conference in the Tabernacle, and they are generously entertained by our friends. The week is spent in holy fellowship, prayer, and intercourse. By this means men in remote villages, laboring under discouraging circumstances and ready to sink from loneliness of spirit, are encouraged and strengthened: indeed, all the men confess that a stimulus is thus given which no other means could confer." The conference of 1870 was regarded by all as a visitation of the Holy Spirit, and the brethren returned to their labor full of zeal and hope.

"All things considered, gratitude and hope are supreme in connection with the Pastors' College; and with praise of God and thanks to a thousand friends, the president and his helpers gird up the loins of their minds for yet more abundant labors in the future. To every land we hope yet to send forth the Gospel in its fullness and purity. We pray the Lord to raise up missionaries among our students, and make every one a winner of souls. Brethren, remember this work in your prayers, and in your allotment of the Lord's portion of your substance."

In his report for 1881, Mr. Spurgeon gave an excellent résumé of the work, and it is still of great interest. He said:

"On inquiring the other day for the secretary of one of our largest societies, I was informed that he had gone to the seaside for a month, in order that he might have quiet to prepare the report. I do not wonder at this if he has aforetime written many descriptions of the same work, for every year increases the difficulty unless a man is prepared to say the same thing over and over again. Very few can, like Paganini, perform so admirably on one string that everybody is charmed with the melody. The task grows still harder when the year has been peaceful and successful. It has been truly said, ' Happy is the nation which has no history,' because it has been free from changes, wars, convulsions, and revolutions; but I may remark, on the other hand, unhappy is the historian who has to produce a record of a certain length concerning a period which has been innocent of striking events—making bricks without straw is nothing to it."

" The Pastors' College has of late maintained the even tenor of its way, knowing little of external attack and nothing of internal strife. Regular in its work and fixed in its purpose, its movement has been calm and strong. Hence there are no thrilling incidents, painful circumstances, or striking occurrences with which to fill my page and thrill my reader's soul. *Gratitude writ large* is about the only material at hand out of which to fashion my report. ' Bless the Lord, O my soul!' is my one song, and I feel as if I could repeat it a thousand times."

" The College started with a definite doctrinal basis. I never affected to leave great questions as moot points to be discussed in the hall, and believed or not believed, as might be the fashion of the hour. The creed of the College is well known, and we invite none to enter who do not accept it. The doctrines of grace, coupled with a firm belief in human responsibility, are held with intense conviction, and those who do not receive them would not find themselves at home within our walls The Lord has sent us tutors who are lovers of sound doctrine, and zealous for the truth. No uncertain sound has been given forth at any time, and we would sooner close the house than have it so."

" Heresy in colleges means false doctrine throughout the churches; to defile the fountain is to pollute the streams. Hesitancy which might be tolerated in an ordinary minister would utterly disqualify a teacher of teachers. The experiment of Doddridge ought to satisfy all godly men that colleges without dogmatic evangelical teaching are more likely to be seminaries of Socinianism than schools of the prophets. Old Puritanic theology has been heartily accepted by those received into our College, and on leaving it, they have almost with one consent remained faithful to that which they have received. The men are before the public in every part of the country and their testimony well known."

" This institution has now reached its twenty-fifth year, and its object, spirit, and manner of work remain the same. It was intended from the first to receive young men who had been preaching for a sufficient time to test their abilities and their call to the work of the ministry, and such young men have been forthcoming every year in growing numbers. Some bodies of Christians have to lament that their ministry is not adequately supplied: I know of one portion of the Church which is sending up to Heaven bitter lamentations because as the fathers depart to their rest, there is scanty hope that their places will be filled ; but among the Baptists the candidates for the ministry are, if possible, too plentiful. This is a new state of things, and is to be interpreted as indicating growth and zeal. Certainly the applicants are not tempted by rich livings, or even by the prospect of competent support ; or, if they are, I take abundant pains to set before them the assured truth that they will find our ministry to be a warfare abounding in long marches and stern battles ; but equally noted for meagre rations. Still they come, and it needs a very hard heart to repel them, and to refuse to eager brethren the drill and equipment which they covet so earnestly. If it were wise to increase the number of students, another hundred of suitable men could at once be added to those who are already under tuition."

"From the commencement our main object was to help men who from lack of funds could not obtain an education for themselves. These have been supplied not only with tuition and books, gratis, but with board and lodging, and in some cases with clothes and pocket money. Some very successful brethren needed everything, and if they had been required to pay, they must have remained illiterate preachers to this day. Still, year by year, the number of men who are ready to support themselves in whole or in part has increased, and I believe that it is increasing and will increase. As a college we have had to struggle with a repute based upon falsehood and created by jealousy; but this has not injured us to any great extent; for men come to us from America, Australia, and the Cape, and applications have frequently been made from foreign countries. German students have attended our classes during their own vacations, and members of other colleges are usually to be seen at our lectures. The institution never deserved to be charged with giving a mere apology for an education; and if ever that reproach could have been justly cast upon us, it is utterly undeserved now that the time of study has become more extended, and a fuller course of training has thus become possible."

"Scholarship for its own sake was never sought and never will be within the Pastors' College; but to help men to become efficient preachers has been and ever will be the sole aim of all those concerned in its management. I shall not, in order to increase our prestige, refuse poor men, or zealous young Christians whose early education has been neglected. Pride would suggest that we take 'a better class of men;' but experience shows that they are not better, that eminently useful men spring from all ranks, that diamonds may be found in the rough, and that some who need most pains in the polishing, reward our labor a thousand-fold. My friends will still stand by me in my desire to aid the needy but pious brother, and we shall rejoice together as we continually see the ploughman, the fisherman, and the mechanic taught the way of God more perfectly, and enabled through divine grace to proclaim in the language of the people the salvation of our God."

"During the past year about one hundred and twenty men have been with us; but as some have come and others have gone, the average number in actual residence has averaged one hundred. Of these a few have been with us three years, and more have entered upon the third year. The rule is that a man's usual period terminates at the end of two years, and his remaining longer depends upon the judgment formed of him. Certain men will never get beyond an English education, and to detain them from their work is to repress their ardor without bestowing a compensatory advantage. In other cases, the longer the period of study the better. Probably the third year is to many a student more useful than the other two, and he goes forth to his life-work more thoroughly prepared. I could not lengthen the course in former days, when churches tempted the brethren away before the proper time, as they too often did. They told these raw youths that it was a pity to delay, that if they left their studies souls might be saved, and I know not what besides; and some were induced to run away, as Rowland Hill would have said, before they had pulled their boots on. If I constrained them to remain, the good deacons of the eager churches thought me a sort of harsh jailor, who locked up his prisoners and would not give them up at the entreaty of their friends. One wrote and bade me loose the brother, for the Lord had need of him, and I would have let the young man go if I had thought that he was one of the donkeys to whom the passage referred. That a number of brethren may have entered upon their ministry prematurely was no fault of mine, but of those who tempted them to quit their classes too soon. However, there have been periods in which there is a lull in the demand of the churches for ministers, and then we have been able to retain the men for a longer season. Such a time is passing over us just now, and I do not regret it, for I am persuaded it is good to give the brethren a longer space for preparatory study."

"I have been very ill through the greater part of the past year, and have therefore been unable to give so much personal service to the College as I have usually done."

"This has been a sore trial to me, but it has been much alleviated by my beloved brother, J. A. Spurgeon, the vice-president, who has looked after everything with great care; and I have also been greatly comforted by the knowledge that the tutors are as deeply concerned about the holy service as ever I can be. It has been my joy to learn that the College was never in a better state in all respects than now, and that the men under training give promise of becoming useful preachers. I have had very little weeding work to do on my coming back to my place, and those whom I have removed were not chargeable with any fault, but their capacity was questioned by the tutors. All through the year this painful operation has to be carried on, and it always causes me much grief; but it is a necessary part of my official duty as president."

"Young men who come to us loaded with testimonials are occasionally found after a while to be lacking in application or in spiritual power; and after due admonishment and trial they have to be sent back to the place from whence they came. Others are as good as gold, but their heads ache, and their health fails under hard study, or from lack of mental capacity they cannot master the subjects placed before them. These must be kindly but firmly set aside; but I always dread the task. This thinning-out process is done with conscientiousness, under the guidance of the tutors; but this year there has been little need of it, and I have rejoiced in the fact, since frequent depression of spirit has made it undesirable to have much trying work to do. I am glad to say that very rarely have I had to deal with a case of moral failure. Bad young men have crept in among us, and no men are perfect; but I have great comfort in seeing the earnest and prayerful spirit which has prevailed among the brotherhood."

"Foremost among our aims is the promotion of a vigorous spiritual life among those who are preparing to be under-shepherds of Christ's flock. By frequent meetings for prayer, and by other means, we labor to maintain a high tone of spirituality. I have endeavored in my lectures and addresses to stir up the holy fire; for well I know that if the heavenly flame burns low, nothing else will avail. The earnest action of the College Missionary Society has been a source of great joy to me; for above all things I desire to see many students devoting themselves to foreign work. The Temperance Society also does a good work, and tends to keep alive among the men a burning hatred of England's direst curse."

"We need the daily prayer of God's people that much grace may be with all concerned in this important business; for what can we do without the Holy Spirit? How few ever pray for students! If ministers do not come up to the desired standard, may not the members of the churches rebuke themselves for having restrained prayer on their account? When does a Christian worker more need prayer than in his early days, when his character is forming and his heart is tenderly susceptible both of good and evil influences? I would beseech all who have power with God to remember our colleges in their intercessions. The solemn interests involved in the condition of these schools of the prophets compel me to entreat, even unto tears, that the hopeful youth of our ministry may not be forgotten in the supplications of the saints. For us also, who have the responsible duty of guiding the minds of these young men, much prayer is requested, that we may have wisdom, love, gentleness, firmness, and abounding spiritual power. It is not every man who can usefully influence students, nor can the same men have equal power at all times. The Divine Spirit is needed, and He is given to them that ask for His sacred teaching."

"In Great Britain three hundred and fifty-five former students are preaching the Word, some in the more prominent pulpits of the denomination, and others in positions where their patience and self-denial are severely tested by the present depression in trade, and the consequent inability of rural congregations to furnish them with adequate support. The College has reason to rejoice not only in the success of her most honored sons, but in the faithfulness and perseverance of the rank and file, whose services, although they are little noticed on earth, will receive the 'well done' of the Lord."

"This institution is not alone a College, but a Home and Foreign Missionary Society. Our three evangelists have traversed the land with great diligence, and the Lord has set His seal to their work."

"It is my greatest pleasure to aid in commencing new churches. The oftener brethren can create their own spheres the more glad shall I be. It is not needful to repeat the details of former reports; but many churches have been founded through the College, and there are more to follow. I announced at the beginning of this enterprise that it was not alone for the education of ministers, but for the general spread of the Gospel ; and this has been adhered to, a part of the income being always expended in that direction."

The buildings now known as the Pastors' College were begun in 1873 ; the foundation corner-stone being laid in October of that year. Mr. Spurgeon was led to the enterprise for the construction of a special building for the accommodation of students by a gift of five thousand dollars which was presented to him in the previous May. During the construction of the building he received a gift of five thousand more with fifteen hundred dollars from the students. Afterward a gentleman died, leaving him a bequest of twenty-five thousand dollars in his will. The students themselves entered with zeal into the work of raising money for the building, and although they were themselves universally poor they did have influence enough with others to raise twelve thousand five hundred dollars.

The completed buildings cost seventy-five thousand dollars, the debt for which was entirely paid within a few months after its completion. Fifteen thousand dollars toward the payment was given by a lady as a memorial to her husband, and ten thousand dollars was left to the College by the will of a stranger who had regularly read Mr. Spurgeon's sermons.

The statistics of the College as late as 1889, show that the students who had graduated had established over eighty churches in and about London, and in all over two hundred churches in the world. Some in the most distant countries and a few on the islands of the sea. They had baptized over forty thousand people, and the increase of their church membership had been over thirty-nine thousand. In America they have instituted fourteen different churches and proved themselves most efficient evangelists among all classes of people. They are men who not only preach and teach, but positively work, imitating very closely the example of Mr. Spurgeon. He was always engaged in some profitable labor, excepting only the hours positively necessary to physical and mental rest.

The following is a list of students from the Pastors' College up to 1891, giving first those who are at present preaching in America:

Former students now in the United States and Canada, members of Pastor's College Evangelical Association:

Auvache, F. W.
Avery, J. F.
Ball, G. W.
Biss, W. A.
Blaikie, P. H.
Brown, A. F.
Carnes, W.
Childs, H. W.
Clark, John
Clatworthy, W.
Cocks, H.
Coker, J.
Cook, C. A.
Cooper, A.
Cother, W. J.
Dann, Frank

Dunn, H.
Fairbrother, A.
Forth, Joseph
Foster, James F.
Gibb, Austin
Gilkes, W.
Gregory, C. W.
Harrison, R. M., D. D.
Holmes, R.
Hughes, R.
Irving, J. J.
Johnson, T. I
Kemp, G. H.
McArthur, A.
McKinney, W.
Mayo, W. L.

Noble, Mark
Ostler, W.
Perrins, W.
Prichard, W. E.
Read, Albert
Richardson, C. H.
Shadick, R. A.
Silke, W. G.
Smith, C. Wilson

Smith, Napoleon
Stote, Amos H.
Trapp, G. H.
Ward, P. J.
Willis, W. W.
Witham, A. A.
Wotton, W. T.
Yeatman, R.

Former students now in England and the Colonies, or in Missionary Stations:

Adams, H. F.
Adams, W.
Adamson, T.
Almy, J. T.
Anderson, J. G.
Archer, H. D.
Ashton, E.
Askew, J.
Aubrey, J.
Aust, F. J.
Ayers, R. W.
Bailey, G. T.
Baily, R.
Baker, S. J.
Banfield, J. H.
Barrell, H. E.
Barton, J.
Baster, W.
Bateman, F. R.
Bateman, John
Batts, H. J.
Batts, H. J.
Bax, A.
Beecliff, R. J.
Bennett, J. L.
Berry, E. W.
Billington, A.
Bird, A.
Blackaby, F. E.
Blackie, H. G.
Blaikie, J
Blake, J.
Blamire, T.
Blewett, E.
Blocksidge, W. W
Bloom, W. K.
Bloy, C.

Bonser, W.
Bool, H.
Boulsher, G.
Bowler, G. B.
Boyall, C.
Bradford, H.
Bradford, J.
Breewood, T.
Brett, J. E.
Bridge, A.
Bridge, I.
Brigg, B.
Briggs, J.
Broad, W. H.
Brown, A. G.
Brown, H. Rylands
Brown, J. A., M. R. U. S.
Bruce, D.
Bruce, J. S.
Bryan, W. C.
Budgen, A.
Bunning, W. C.
Burnham, J.
Burt, H. M.
Cameron, T. D.
Campbell, J. O'Neill
Campbell, J. W.
Carlile, J. C.
Carr, G. H.
Carter, E. A.
Carter, F. C.
Carver, T. A.
Case, H. B.
Chadwick, J.
Chambers, A. C.
Chambers, Clarence
Channer, H.

Chapman, C.
Chapman, D. C.
Chettleborough, R. E.
Chinnery, D.
Churcher, T. G., M. D., M. R. C. S.
Clark, C. J.
Clark, Henry
Clark, James A.
Clark, Joseph
Clark, W.
Clarke, A. J.
Clow, W. G.
Cockerton, F. M.
Cole, C.
Cole, E. S.
Cotley, J. W.
Collins, John
Compton, E.
Coombs, W.
Cooper, J. R.
Corbet, A. F
Cottam, J.
Cotton, A. F.
Cox, G. D.
Cox, J. M.
Crabb, S.
Crouch, C. D.
Crouch, J.
Cuff, W.
Cumming, M.
Curry, T. B.
Curtis, A.
Curtis, G.
Curwood, A. W.
Dallaston, C.
Dalton, J. J.
Dann, C. A.
Dann, G. J.
Davidson, A. K.
Davidson, G. W.
Davies, G.
Davies, James W.
Davis, H.
Davis, J.
Davis, W. A.
Day, A.
Deal, C.
Deane, J. J.
Dewdney, A.
Doubleday, J.
Dowen, Z. T., F. R. G. S.
Downing, J.

Driver, H. H.
Duncan, G., D. D.
Dunington, H.
Dunster, F. W.
Dupee, J.
Durbin, F.
Dyer, E.
Dyer, H. J.
Dyke, S. A.
Easter, J.
Edgerton, W. F.
Edgley, G. T.
Edwards, E. H.
Edwards, E. J.
Edwards, T. L.
Ellis, E. H.
Ellis, J. J.
Emerson, C. E.
Ennals, G. T.
Ensoll, R.
Evans, George D.
Everett, A. G.
Ewens, W.
Ewing, J. W., B. A.
Fairey, S.
Fellowes, C. A.
Feltham, F. J.
Field, H. C.
Field, John
Field, J. B.
Field, T. B.
Finch, R. R.
Fisk, E. E.
Flatt, F. J.
Fletcher, H. A.
Forth, Jacob C.
Foskett, L. R.
Foster, W. R.
Fowler, C. J.
Freeman, G.
Fullerton, W. Y.
Gathercole, T. G.
Genders, J. W.
George, E.
Gibson, Jesse
Gibson, J. G.
Gillard, W.
Gilmore, J. D.
Glendening, R. E.
Glover, J.
Goacher, W.
Good, C. E. L.

26

Goodchild, G.
Gooding, C. D.
Gordon, C. L.
Gordon, S. C.
Gower, H. F.
Gracey, D.
Graham, Arthur
Graham, R. H. C.
Grant, James
Grant, J. H.
Green, John
Greenwood, T.
Greer, A.
Hackney, W., M. A.
Hadler, E. S.
Hadler, John R.
Hagen, T.
Hailstone, W. G.
Haines, W. W.
Hall, A.
Hamilton, E. L.
Hancocks, T.
Harmer, A. A.
Harrald, J. W.
Harrington
Harris, G. H.
Harris, W. J.
Harrison, J. S.
Hart, Josiah
Harvey, F.
Haste, A. G.
Hay, D. H.
Hayman, J. J.
Hearson, G.
Heath, N.
Harries, R.
Hewitt, C.
Hewlett, A.
Hewson, J. C.
Hibberd, F.
Higgins, W.
Higlett, W.
Hiley, D. J.
Hillman, J.
Hobbs, W.
Hobby, E. A.
Hockey, J. S.
Hogbin, F. A.
Hollinshead. J.
Honour, D.
Hook, G. H.
Hopper, A. W.

Horne, J.
Hudgell, P. A.
Huntly, A. H.
Huntley, G. A. J.
Hyde, A.
Ince, E. G.
Ingram, C. A.
Ingrem, C.
Isaac, E.
Jackmann, G. H. F.
Jackson, F. A.
Jackson, John
James, F.
Jasper, J. E.
Jeffrey, R. F.
Johns, A. E.
Johnson, A.
Johnson, A. E.
Johnson, T.
Jones, Samuel
Jones, Sydney J.
Jones, W. Corden
Jones-Miller, N. T
Joseph, C.
Judd, T. A.
Julyan, W.
Juniper, W. J.
Kemp, F. G.
Kemp, J.
Kendon, J. J.
Keys, J. L.
Kidner, H.
Kilby, H.
King, A. H.
Kitchener, J.
Knee, H.
Knell, A.
Knight, G. J.
Knight, J. J.
Knight, W. H.
Laing, D. W.
Lambourne, W. T.
Lang, W. L., F. R. G. S.
Lardner, T.
Last, E.
Latham, A. W.
Latimer, R. S.
Lauderdale, E.
Layzell, R.
Lennie, R.
Lester, A.
Levinsohn, I.

Lewis, R. T.
Linnecar, G. W.
Llewellyn, W. S.
Loinaz, D.
Longhurst, T. J.
Lyne, S.
Lynn, W. E.
M'Allister, S.
McAuslane, J.
McCaig, A., B. A.
McCullough, R.
McDougall, A
Mackenzie, W. I.
Macmillan, D.
M'Nab, J.
Mace, D.
Mackey, H. O.
Macoun, T.
Malins, G. H.
Mann, W.
Maplesden, R.
Marchant, F. G
Markham, J.
Marshall, B.
Marshall, G.
Marshall, R.
Martin, H. J.
Martin, J. E.
Martin, W. A
Mason, E.
Mateer, J. T.
Maycock, T.
Mayers, W. J.
Maynard, W.
Medhurst, T. W.
Mesquitta, R.
Middleton, R. J.
Milledge, H.
Miller, G. A.
Mills, A.
Minifie, W. C.
Mitchell, W. S
Monk, G.
Moore, H.
Morgan, A. K.
Morley, E.
Morris, J. S.
Morris, M.
Morrison, R. B.
Moyle, J. E.
Murphy, J. M.
Myles, W. G.

Neale, E. S.
Near, I.
Needham, S.
Ney, J.
Nichols, W. B.
Oldring, G. W.
Osborne, E.
Osborne, W.
Padley, C. J. A. N.
Page, W.
Page, W. H. J.
Palmer, J.
Palmer, L.
Papengouth, C. A. V.
Papengouth, N.
Parker, A
Parker, A. J.
Parker, E. J.
Passmore, H. R.
Patrick, N. H.
Payne, A. J.
Peach, H. T.
Pearce, C.
Pearson E. B.
Peden R. J.
Perry, T.
Pettman, W.
Phillips, A.
Phillips, H. A.
Phillips, H. R.
Philpot, T.
Pidgeon, A.
Piggot, A.
Pilling, S.
Plumbridge, J. H.
Pope, G. W.
Porter, J.
Potter, F.
Potter, J. G.
Poulton, J. S.
Preece, H. J.
Price, W. F.
Pring, G.
Priter, A.
Prosser, W. H.
Pullen, E. R.
Pullen, H. H.
Pursey, R.
Rankine, J.
Rawlings, T. E.
Raymond, J.
Reid, Andrew J.

Rice, W. E.
Richards, E.
Richards, W.
Richardson, G. B.
Robert, G. W.
Roberts, E.
Robinson, W. W.
Roger, J. L.
Rootham, J. N.
Rudge, C.
Rumsey, G. H.
Russell, D.
Russell, F.
Ruthven, W.
Samuel, G.
Santos, J. M. G. dos
Saville, A. S.
Sawday, C. B.
Scamell, T. W
Scilley, J.
Scott, R.
Seaman, W.
Sexton, W.
Sharp, D.
Shearer, J. F.
Short, A. G.
Simmonds, H. W
Simmonds, G.
Skelly, W.
Skingle, S.
Slack, C. A.
Slater, W.
Smale, J.
Smathers, R.
Smith, Alber
Smith, B.
Smith, Frank M.
Smith, G. K.
Smith, Henry
Smith, H. Samue
Smith, James
Smith, James
Smith, James
Smith, J. Manton
Smith, T. H.
Smith, W.
Smith, W. H.
Sole, R. T.
Soper, J. A.
Soper, W. T.
Spanswick, J.
Spanton, E.

Speed, R.
Spufford, H. T.
Spurgeon, C.
Spurgeon, R.
Spurgeon, T.
Stalberg, I. O
Stanley, C.
Stanley, G.
Stanley, J.
Starling, C.
Stead, W. F.
Steedman, L. S.
Steward, F. J.
Stockley, T. I.
Stone, C. E.
Stone, H. E.
Stubbs, J.
Styles, W. J.
Sullivan, W.
Sumner, W.
Swift, J. T.
Tait, D.
Tansley, J.
Taylor, H. W.
Taylor, W. J.
Tessier, A.
Testro, C.
Thomas, J. W.
Thomason, T. W
Thompson, F.
Thompson, J. L.
Thorn, W.
Tomkins, W. J.
Townsend, C. W.
Tranter, F. D.
Tredray, W. H.
Trotman, H.
Trueman, H.
Tuck, F.
Turner, G.
Turner, Joshua J.
Tydeman, E. A
Usher, W., M. D.
Vanstone, W. J. N.
Vaughan, C. W.
Vaughan, E.
Waddell, T. F.
Wainwright, G.
Walker, G.
Walker, W.
Walker, W.
Wallace, R.

Walter, E. E.
Walton, J. E.
Ward, I. A.
Warren, J. B.
Warren, J. F. M.
Watson, I.
Webb, G. A.
Weeks, J. H.
Welch, A. W.
Welch, E. J.
Wells, W. E.
Welton, C.
West, F. G.
Westlake, F. T. B.
Whale, W.
Wheatley, T.
Whetnall, M. H.
White, E.
White, Frank H.
White, G. W.
White, W.
White, W. J.
Whiteside, T.

Whittet, G.
Whittle, T.
Wicks, W. A.
Wiggins, W.
Wigstone, J. P.
Wilkins, Joseph
Wilkinson, John
Williams, G. C.
Williams, J. G.
Williams, S. T.
Williams, W.
Williamson, R.
Williamson, R. J.
Wills, R. E.
Wilson, John
Wilson, J. A.
Winsor, H.
Wintle, W. J.
Wood, A. W.
Wood, Harry
Wright, G.
Young, James
Young, Joseph

CHAPTER XIV.

THE ORPHANAGE.

The Orphanage connected with the work of the Metropolitan Tabernacle is one of those institutions which presents most beautifully the tenderest and loveliest side of Mr. Spurgeon's character. His love for children was only exceeded by their love for him. It was one of the prominent features of his character which won for him so much of the success in his early ministry. The children admired him greatly. The hearts of the mothers and fathers always followed the love of their children, and, in fact, the man who can make himself attractive to the pure, sweet minds of childhood will also be necessarily interesting and helpful to those of older minds. Men are truly " but children of a larger growth." Mr. Spurgeon's childish simplicity, which was a wonderful feature of his noble life, convinced every person who knew him or heard of him that he was positively sincere. And this aided him in reaching their hearts and shielded him from the attacks of those who would malign him.

"Innocent as a child," said Mr. Gladstone, concerning him, and indeed few children of middle growth could be said to be as innocent as he. Evil thoughts found no place in his disposition and deceit had no part in his magnificent make-up.

Yet he mingled continually with the lower classes in their poverty and in their home life, being called to visit them in all conditions of want and distress. He saw the children bare-headed and bare-footed, often crying with cold, more often besmeared with dirt, sometimes crippled as a result of lack of parental care, and his heart went forth in prayer to God for some method of relief. He had a great admiration for George Müller, whose magnificent work of faith has greatly surprised the unbelieving world, and often said all that he could to encourage people to assist Mr. Müller in his special work for the orphans of London.

Mr. Spurgeon always entertained the idea that there might be arranged some grand institution which would not only provide for the parentless children but also for those little ones whose parents were unable or unwilling to provide for them the necessities of life; yet he never saw the way in which to engage personally in such an undertaking until it was thrust upon him unexpectedly.

While writing an article for his magazine, *The Sword and The Trowel*, in 1866, he incidentally mentioned the great need there was of some institution or work for the care of neglected orphans. The result of that little article has been surprisingly romantic. A lady who had been the wife of a clergyman of the Church of England and was left a widow with considerable means, had been but a few months before received into the Baptist Church, on the profession of her faith in its principles. She read Mr. Spurgeon's reference to the needs of the children, and, being especially impressed at the time with a strong desire to be of some special use in the Master's work, she thought at once of establishing the Orphanage herself. For a few days she prayed over the matter, and the impression deepening upon her, she at last decided to write to Mr. Spurgeon and offer him a sum of money for an Orphanage if he would establish it and superintend it himself. Consequently a letter was received by him from her containing the astounding offer of $100,000 for an Orphanage, and to be paid at once.

Mr. Spurgeon was so very busy in other matters connected with his religious work that he felt he could not give the proper attention to such a work, but Mrs. Hillyard, who gave the money, insisted that he should take charge of the matter, until he reluctantly consented. In fact, he regarded her persevering insistence as the direct call of God. After consultation with his friends, a small meeting was called and a board of trustees elected to take charge of the money and provide for the building of an Orphanage. Very soon after they purchased the ground at Stockwell on which the different homes for the orphans have since been constructed. It is especially interesting in this connection to know what

BOYS' HOME, STOCKWELL ORPHANAGE.

Mr. Spurgeon said himself in his diary with reference to the Orphanage.

In the following June after he had received the gift of $100,000, he said :

"The Lord is beginning to appear to us in the matter of the Orphanage; but as yet He has not opened the windows of heaven as we desire and expect. We wait in prayer and faith. We need no less than £10,000 to erect the buildings, and it will come; for the Lord will answer the prayer of faith."

And in July, 1867, he wrote.—"We have been waiting upon the Lord in faith and prayer concerning our Orphanage; but He is pleased at present to try us. As we have no object in view but the glory of God by the instruction of fatherless boys in the ways of the Lord, having a special view to their soul's salvation, we had hoped that many of the Lord's people would at once have seen the usefulness and practical character of the enterprise, and have sent us substantial aid immediately. The Lord's way, however, is the best, and we rejoice in it, let it be what it may. If the work is to be one of time and long effort, so let it be, if thereby God's name is magnified.

"We have engaged a sister to receive the first four orphans into her own hired house until the orphanages are ready. Our beloved friend, the original donor, has given her plate to be sold for this object, and in so doing, has set an example to all the believers who have surplus silver which ought to be put to better use than lying wrapped up in a box."

And in August, 1867, he wrote.—"Let the facts which with deep gratitude we record this month, strengthen the faith of believers. In answer to many fervent prayers, the Lord has moved His people to send in during last month, in different amounts, toward the general fund of the Orphanage, the sum of £1,075 (about $5,375) for which we give thanks unto the name of the Lord. More especially do we see the gracious hand of God in the following incidents:—A lady (Mrs. Tyson), who has often aided us in the work of the College, having been spared to see the twenty-fifth anniversary of her marriage-day, her beloved husband presented her with £500 (about $2,500) as a token of his ever-growing love for her. Our sister has called upon us and dedicated the £500 to the building of one of the houses, to be called The Silver Wedding House. The Lord had, however, another substantial gift in store to encourage us in our work: for a day or two ago, a brother believer in the Lord called upon us on certain business, and when he retired, he left in a sealed envelope the sum of £600 (about $3,000), which is to be expended in erecting another house. This donation was as little expected as the first, except that our faith expects that all our needs will be supplied in the Lord's own way. The next, day when preaching in the open air, an unknown sister put an envelope into my hand enclosing £200 (about $1,000) for the College and another £20 for the Orphanage. What has God wrought!"

A number of workmen who had been employed during the construction of the Metropolitan Tabernacle combined together and agreed to give their labor for the building of one of the Orphanage houses.

Mr. Spurgeon had the good sense to see that it was not desirable to crowd a great number of children of all classes and attainments into one large building. He saw that children of that age required most of all a home training and home care, hence he insisted upon the erection, if possible, of a large number of small houses so that only a few children would be received in each.

The corner-stones for three of the houses, which were named "The Silver Wedding House," "The Merchants' House," and "The Workingmen's House," were all laid on the 9th of August, 1867. They celebrated the occasion by a large gathering and public addresses, at which $25,000 was contributed. Eleven thousand dollars was soon afterward sent in directly in consequence of the public meeting at the laying of the corner-stones. The trustees then determined to erect as soon as possible eight different houses, but they were somewhat discouraged when they came to estimate the annual cost of maintaining them, finding it to be at least $15,000. Yet Mr. Spurgeon would only answer every question concerning it with the very simple remark, "it will come." The ways in which the money was contributed for building the other houses brings prominent again to the foreground the most miraculous powers which accompanied him in his charitable and philanthropic undertakings.

In the month of January, 1868, a gentleman handed him unostentatiously a package of $5,000 toward the Orphanage, giving no name or address with it. In March, of the same year, another, or the same unknown person, sent him a munificient gift of $10,000, and ever remained concealed. Many persons connected with the Tabernacle and the College had opposed the institution of the Orphanage upon the plea that it would be likely to impoverish the other great interests which the Church had at stake; but with nearly every one of these great gifts toward the Orphanage came either a check for the other work of the Tabernacle or a letter saying that the gifts toward the Orphanage should in no wise interfere with the regular offerings toward the Tabernacle or the College.

One friend, writing to Mr. Spurgeon mentioned this very thought and said: "I have this day dropped in your letter-box an envelope containing $2,000; $1,000 for the College and $1,000 to build the Orphanage. The institution of the Orphanage inclined me to contribute toward the College. I am a stranger to you but not to your printed sermons."

Two houses for the Orphanage were constructed by a general collection taken among the Baptist Churches of London, and are named "The Testimonial Houses." On Mr. Spurgeon's birthday, the 19th of June, 1868, the Sunday-School of the Metropolitan Tabernacle laid the foundation stones for two houses of the Orphanage and soon after completed the entire payment for them.

The young men who had graduated from the College combined to raise the capital for another house. It is curious to note how similarly Providence deals with such enterprises, and how often Mr. Spurgeon found the Orphanage with its bills all paid, but little or no money in the treasury.

In the conduct of Geo. Müller's great work of faith for the orphans, as has been found in a thousand other Christian enterprises, the Lord never left him in disgraceful debt, nor did he ever leave him with sufficient funds on hand to relieve him of a needed sense of dependence on Divine power.

In December, 1873, Mr. Spurgeon wrote concerning the Orphanage, saying, "To our surprise, the report of the secretary was, 'All bills paid, but only £3 ($15) in hand.' Prayer went to work at once, and results follow. Will the reader, however, picture himself with more than two hundred and twenty boys to feed, and only ($15) in hand. He may say, 'The Lord will provide,' but would he feel the force of this if he were in our straits."

But Mr. Spurgeon was continually being asked

why he did not institute a girls' Orphanage, as there were just as many of these poor creatures without a home as there were of the boys; but it was not until 1879 that he saw his way clear to establish such an institution. Many a poor mother's heart throbbed with increasing joy when she heard that it had been decided by Mr. Spurgeon to care for the orphan girls as well as for the boys.

Of the institution of this Orphanage Mrs. Spurgeon most sweetly wrote, in 1880:

" June 22.—My dear little book, you must faithfully bear the record of the Lord's great mercy to me and mine this day! With the loving shouts of the people still ringing in my ears—the warm grip of many fingers yet pressing on my hands—and my heart still throbbing with the unwonted excitement of appearing in the midst of a crowded gathering —I turn to you now in the quietude and rest of home to intrust to your pages a grateful memorial of a happy day!

"The 'Girls' Orphanage' has been inaugurated amidst great rejoicing, the Lord inclining His people's hearts to give liberally to the work, so that its 'stones were laid in fair colors' of faith and hope, and my beloved sees this new 'labor of love' abundantly prospering in his hands. Blessed be the Lord who thus giveth to His servant the 'desire of his heart,' fulfilling 'all his petitions.' The people gathered round with glad hearts and beaming faces, and many a prayer ascended from loving lips that the dear children, who should be housed, and taught, and cared for in the new homes, might all grow up there in the fear and love of God, and be a blessing in their day and generation.

"The band of thirty little girls marching along in front of the boys ('place aux dames!') attracted much attention, and touched all hearts; some of them are such wee mites, and they look very pretty and tender, when compared with the hosts of sturdy boys, who come tramping by in such overwhelming numbers that one wonders if there be any end to them! Few can look unmoved on such masses of orphan children; for in spite of their merry faces, their bright ways, and their happy laughter, the painful fact will force itself upon the mind of the observer that every one of these little ones is taken from a desolate home, where the saddest of all earth's bereavements has been suffered; for the children are 'fatherless,' and the wife is a 'widow.' There was 'April weather' on many a face to-day; I saw the tears stealing down cheeks on which approving smiles were struggling for the mastery; but the sunshine gained the victory, and the pitying drops were quickly wiped away, for the happy condition and appearance of the children led all to forget the sorrow which brought them there, in intense thankfulness for their present joy and future prospects.

"If ever the strange title of 'Godfather' were permissible, I think it would be in the case of Mr. Spurgeon toward his boys and girls at Stockwell;

for God has made him, as it were, in His stead, a 'father of the fatherless, and a judge of the widow !' The Lord bless him on his birthday, and on every other day, and give him many more years in which to be a blessing to the Church, the College, the Orphanage, and the world !"

Mr. Spurgeon's birthdays were especially observed by the congregation at the Tabernacle and by all his friends as a day on which to make special offerings for the philanthropic works which were under his oversight. The Orphanage was especially remembered each year.

Mr. Spurgeon was always fortunate in securing competent persons of excellent judgment to superintend his enterprises, and Rev. Vernon J. Charlesworth, who was formerly associate pastor with Newman Hall, accepted the superintendency of the Orphanage, and conducted it with wonderful skill and Christian affection. The Orphanage has required large sums for its buildings, its improvement and maintenance which would have appeared impossible to secure when the enterprise was begun. Yet it may be safely said that the institution of that charity has brought to the other enterprises of the Tabernacle more than double of the amounts which it otherwise would have received.

"There is that which withholdeth, which tendeth to poverty" said a wiser than any modern writer ; and how strikingly true this has been proven to be in the undertakings of the Churches to-day in the

noble work of the Lord. There are many philan
thropic people in every land who desire very much
to invest their money where it will perpetually do
good, but their business training has taught them
that they cannot safely entrust their funds to the
management of timid people, or to irresponsible
organizations.

Hence as soon as it was made clear to the practical business men of England that Mr. Spurgeon
possessed the necessary qualifications of making the
best possible use of funds entrusted to his care, he
did not lack for generous coutributions, and the
charities he prayed for were always fully supplied.

No question of creed or race was asked of an orphan, neither was it necessary for the single parent
or friend to canvass any board of trustees, in order
to secure a vote for the admission of the children
to Mr. Spurgeon's care. The whole matter was
conducted as a friendly kindness, and although
thousands of applications had been rejected for lack
of room, yet those who were received were not
compelled to pass through any ordeal of a "circum-
locution office" to reach the hearing or kindness of
the Orphanage trustees.

The cost per annum for maintaining the Orphanage has been about $25,000, including food and
clothing.

Mr. Spurgeon himself has stated that "No widow
ever goes away lamenting over time, labor, and
money spent in vain. The worst that can happen

is to be refused because there is no room, or her case is not so bad as that of others; not a shilling will have been spent in purchasing votes, no time lost in canvassing, no cringing to obtain patronage. Her case is judged on its merits, and the most necessitious wins the day. We have now so many applications and so few vacancies that women with two or three children are advised not to apply, for while there are others with five, six, or seven children depending on them they cannot hope to help themselves."

The orphans themselves after leaving the institution have often contributed directly or through their friends considerable sums toward its maintenance. Several of them are already most acceptably teaching the Gospel and one is a superintendent of another Orphanage.

Twice there has been held a bazaar for the purpose of raising money for the Orphanage which was successful both in securing funds and in carrying on personal religious work as was done in the case of the first bazaar held for the construction of the Tabernacle.

Mr. Spurgeon's own ideas concerning the work of the Orphanages will be more interesting to the reader than anything else we might give, and we quote what he said about them at a time when they were not placed on the stable basis where they now so securely rest.

Ten years ago he said :

"When we remember how this gracious work began by the consecrated thought of a holy woman, and then grew into an actual gift from her hand, and further developed, by the large help of others, into houses and schools, infirmary and dining-hall, and all manner of provision for destitute children, we feel bound to cry, 'What hath God wrought!' Our God has supplied all our need according to His riches in glory by Christ Jesus. The story of the Stockwell Orphanage will be worth telling in heaven when the angels shall learn from the Church the manifold wisdom and goodness of the Lord. Incidents which could not be published on earth will be made known in the heavenly city, where every secret thing shall be revealed. How every need has been supplied before it has become a want; how guidance has been given before questions have become anxieties; how friends have been raised up in unbroken succession, and how the One Great Friend has been ever present, no single pen can ever record.

"To care for the fatherless has been a work of joyful faith all along, and in waiting upon God for supplies we have experienced great delight. The way of faith in God is the best possible. We could not have carried on the work by a method more pleasant, more certain, more enduring. If we had depended upon annual subscribers we should have had to hunt them up and pay heavy poundage, or perhaps fail to keep up the roll; if we had advertised continually for funds our outlay might have brought in a scanty return; but dependence upon God has been attended with no such hazards. We have done our best as men of business to keep the Orphanage before the public, but we have desired in all things to exercise faith as servants of God. Whatever weakness we have personally to confess and deplore, there is no weakness in the plan of faith in God. Our experience compels us to declare that He is the living God; the God that heareth prayer; the God who will never permit those who trust in Him to be confounded. The business world has passed through trying times during the last few years, but the Orphanage has not been tried; men of great enterprise have failed, but the home of the fatherless has not failed; for this enterprise is in the divine hand, and an eye watches over it which neither slumbers nor sleeps.

"Let the people of God be encouraged by the fact of the existence and prosperity of the Stockwell Orphanage. Miracles have come to an end, but God goes on to work great wonders: the rod of Moses is laid aside, but the rod and staff of the Great Shepherd still compass us.

"The operations of the institution reveal to the managers the wide-spread necessity which exists. The cry of the orphan comes from every part of our beloved land, and the plea of the widow for Christian sympathy and help is restricted to no one class of the community. Faces once radiant with

SCHOOL-ROOM, STOCKWELL ORPHANAGE.

smiles are saddened with grief, for the dark shadow which death casts falls everywhere. How true are the lines of the poet :—

> " ' There is no fireside, howsoe'er defended,
> But has one vacant chair.'

"It is a constant joy to the president and the committee that they are able to mitigate to such a large extent the misery and need which are brought under their notice ; and it must be an equal joy to the subscribers to know that their loving contributions furnish the sinews for this holy war.

"As our Sunday-school is affiliated to the Sunday school Union, we allow the boys who desire to do so to sit for examination. Of the candidates who were successful at the last examination, three gained prizes, twelve first-class certificates, and thirty-eight second-class certificates.

"During the year the boys took part in the Crystal Palace Musical Festivals, arranged by the Band of Hope Union and the Tonic Sol-fa Association.

"In order to make the character and claims of the institution more widely known, the head master and the secretary have held meetings in London and the provinces, and the success which has crowned their efforts is of a very gratifying character. The boys who accompany them to sing and to recite furnish a powerful appeal by their appearance and conduct, and commend the institution to which they owe so much. The local papers speak in terms of the highest praise of their services, and thus a most effective advertisement is secured without any cost to the institution. So far as the boys are concerned, these trips have an educational value, for they get to know a great deal of the products and industries of different parts of the country, besides securing the advantage of being brought into contact with Christian families where they reside during their visit.

"The amount realized during the year, after defraying all expenses, is $3,320, and our thanks are hereby tendered to all who assisted in any way to secure such a splendid result.

"The committee record with thankfulness that there has been no lack of funds contributed for the efficient maintenance of the institution. Friends prefer to give donations rather than pledge themselves to send annual subscriptions, and the benevolence thus manifested is purely spontaneous. The admirable custom of making shirts for the boys is still continued by the young ladies of an educational establishment, who send in a supply of two hundred shirts every year. Their efforts are supplemented by several working associations, but the supply is not yet equal to the demand, and we cordially invite the co-operation of others, to whom we shall be glad to send samples and patterns.

"The work of caring for the widow and the fatherless is specially mentioned by the Holy Spirit as one of the most acceptable modes of giving outward expression to pure religion and undefiled before God and the Father, and therefore the Lord's people will not question that they should help in carrying it out. Will it need much pleading? If so, we cannot use it, as we shrink from marring the willinghood which is the charm of such a service. The work is carried on in dependence upon God, and as His blessing evidently rests upon it, we are confident the means will be forthcoming as the need arises. While commending the work to our Heavenly Father in prayer, we deem it right to lay before the stewards of His bounty the necessities and claims of the institution.

"The year 1880 will be a memorable one in the history of the institution, and we record with gratitude the fact that the foundation-stones of the first four houses for the Girls' Orphanage were laid on the twenty-second of June, when the president's birthday was celebrated. It was a joy to all present that Mrs. Spurgeon was able to lay the memorial stone of 'The Sermon House, the gift of C. H. Spurgeon and his esteemed publishers, Messrs. Passmore and Alabaster.' The memorial stone of another house, the gift of Mr. W. R. Rickett, and called 'The Limes, in tender memory of five beloved children,' was laid by C. H. Spurgeon, who made a touching allusion to the sad event thus commemorated. Mrs. Samuel Barrow laid the memorial stone of the house called 'The Olives,' the amount for its erection having been given and collected by her beloved husband. The trustees of the institution having subscribed the funds for the erection of a house, the treasurer, Mr. William Higgs, laid, in their name, the memorial stone which bears the inscription, ' Erected by the Trustees of the Orphanage to express their joy in this service of love.'

"At the present moment the buildings of the Orphanage form a great square, enclosing a fine space for air and exercise. Visitors generally express great surprise at the beauty and openness of the whole establishment. Much remains to be done before the institution is completely accommodated; there is needed an infirmary for the girls, and till that is built one of the houses will have to be used for that purpose, thus occupying the space which would otherwise be filled by thirty or forty children : this should be attended to at an early date. Baths and wash-houses will be urgently required for the girls, and we propose to make them sufficiently commodious for the girls to do the washing for the entire community of five hundred children, thus instructing them in household duties and saving a considerable expense. We would not spend a sixpence needlessly. No money has been wasted in lavish ornament or in hideous ugliness. The buildings are not a workhouse or a county jail, but a pleasant residence for those children of whom God declares himself to be the Father. The additional buildings which we contemplate are not for luxury, but for necessary uses ; and as we endeavor to lay out money with judicious economy, we feel sure that we shall be trusted in the future as in the past.

"Are there not friends waiting to take a share in the Stockwell Orphanage Building? They cannot better commemorate personal blessings, nor can they find a more suitable memorial for departed friends. No storied urn or animated bust can half so well record the memory of beloved ones as a stone in an Orphan House. Most of the buildings are already appropriated as memorials in some form or other, and only a few more will be needed. Very soon all building operations will be complete, and those who have lost the opportunity of becoming shareholders in the Home of Mercy may regret their delay. At any rate, none who place a stone in the walls of the Stockwell Orphanage will ever lament that they did this deed of love to the little ones for whom Jesus cares. Honored names are with us already engraven upon the stones of this great Hostelry of the All-merciful; and many others are co-workers whose record is on high, though unknown among men. Who will be the next to join us in this happy labor?

"When the whole of the buildings are complete, the institution will afford accommodation for five hundred children, and prove a memorial of Christian generosity and of the loving-kindness of the Lord.

"In our address at the presentation of the late testimonial, we disclaimed all personal credit for the existence of any one of the enterprises over which we preside, because each one of them has been forced upon us. 'I could not help undertaking them,' was our honest and just confession. This is literally true, and another illustration of this fact is now to come before the Christian public. Several of us have long cherished the idea that the time would come in which we should have an Orphanage for girls as well as for boys. It would be hard to conceive why this should not be. It seems ungallant, not to say unrighteous, to provide for children of one sex only, for are not all needy little ones dear to Christ, with whom there is neither male nor female? We do not like to do such things by halves, and it is but half doing the thing to leave the girls out in the cold. We have all along wished to launch out in the new direction, but we had quite enough on hand for the time being, and were obliged to wait. The matter has been thought of, and talked about, and more than half promised, but nothing has come of it till this present, and now, as we believe at the exact moment, the hour has struck, and the voice of God in providence says, 'Go forward.'

"The fund for the Girls' Orphanage has commenced, and there are about a dozen names upon the roll at the moment of our writing. The work will be carreid on with vigor as the Lord shall be pleased to send the means, but it will not be unduly pushed upon any one so as to be regarded as a new burden, for we want none but cheerful helpers, who will count it a privilege to have a share in the good work. We shall employ no collector to make a percentage by dunning the unwilling, and shall make no private appeals to individuals. There is the case: if it be a good one and you are able to help it, please do so; but if you have no wish in that direction, our Lord's work does not require us to go a-begging like a pauper, and we do not intend to do so.

"We have never been in debt yet, nor have we even borrowed money for a time, but we have always been able to pay as we have gone on. Our prayer is that we may never have to come down to a lower platform and commence borrowing.

"It has often happened that we have been unable to assist widows in necessitous circumstances with large families, because there did not happen to be a boy of the special age required by the rules of our Boys' Orphanage. There were several girls, but then we could not take girls, and however deserving the case, we have been unable to render any assistance to very deserving widows, simply because their children were not boys. This is one reason why we need a Girls' Orphanage.

"Everywhere also there is an outcry about the scarcity of good servants, honest servants, industrious servants, well-trained servants. We know where to find the sisters who will try to produce such workers out of the little ones who will come under their care.

"We have succeeded, by God's grace and the diligent care of our masters and matrons in training the lads so that they have become valuable to business men : why should not the same divine help direct us with the lasses, so that domestics and governesses should go forth from us, as well as clerks and artisans? We believe that there are many friends who will take a special interest in the girls, and that there are some whose trades would more readily enable them to give articles suitable for girls than those which are useful to boys.

"Here is a grand opportunity for Christian people with means to take their places among the first founders of this new institution, and if they judge that such a work will be good and useful, we hope that they will without fail, and without delay, come to our assistance in this fresh branch of service. We cannot afford to lose a single penny from the funds for the boys, but this work for the girls must be something extra and above. You helped Willie and Tommy; will you not help Mary and Maggie?

"It is very needful to add that foolish persons often say, Mr. Spurgeon can get plenty of money, and needs no help. If all were to talk in this fashion, where would our many works drift to? Mr. Spurgeon does get large sums, but not a penny more than the various works require, and he gets it because God moves His people to give it, as he hopes, good reader, He may move you. We have no personal end to serve, we do not, directly or indirectly, gain a single penny by the Orphanage, College, or any other society over which we preside;

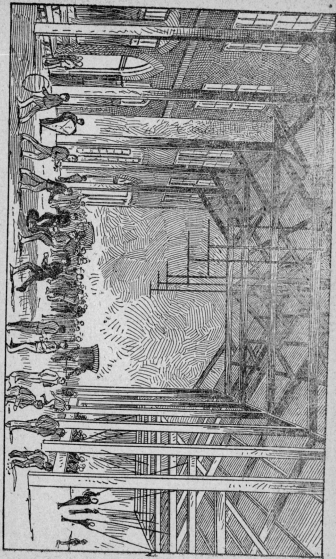

PLAY-GROUND, STOCKWELL ORPHANAGE.

neither have we any wealthy persons around us who are at a loss to dispose of their property; but our hard-working church keeps continually consecrating its offerings, and our friends far and near think upon us. Our treasury is the bounty of God, our motto is: THE LORD WILL PROVIDE. Past mercy forbids a doubt as to the future, and so in the name of God we set up our banners.

"The girls' part is not yet fully complete, but it soon will be so, and then we must take in the girls. Now it occurs to me to let my friends know the increased need which has arisen, and will arise from the doubling of the number of children. The income must by some means be doubled. My trust is in the Lord alone, for whose sake I bear this burden. I believe that He has led me all along in the erection and carrying on of this enterprise, and I am also well assured that His own hand pointed to the present extension, and supplied the means for making it. I therefore rest in the providence of God alone. But the food for the children will not drop as manna from heaven, it will be sent in a way which is more beneficial, for the graces of His children will be displayed in the liberality which will supply the needs of the orphans. God will neither feed the children by angels nor by ravens, but by the loving gifts of His people. It is needful, therefore, that I tell my friends of our need, and I do hereby tell them. The institution will need, in rough figures, about one thousand dollars a week.

28

"This is a large sum, and when I think of it I am appalled if Satan suggests the question: 'What if the money does not come in?' But it is nothing to the Lord of the whole earth to feed five hundred little ones. He has kept two hundred and fifty boys for these years, and He can do the like for the same number of girls. Only let not His stewards say that there is no need at Stockwell, for there is great and crying need that all my friends should inquire whether they may not wisely render me much more aid than they have done. The buildings are not all finished yet, nor the roads made, but this will soon be accomplished, and then the institution will be in full operation, and its requirements will be great. I have written these lines with a measure of reluctance; and I hope it is not in unbelief, but as a reasonable service, that I have thus stated the case."

CHAPTER XV.

THE OLD LADIES' HOME.

The institution of that excellent charity in connection with the new Park street church and the Metropolitan Tabernacle, which provides for the care of the Christian women of the church, when they were too old to care for themselves, may be placed almost wholly to the credit of Dr. Rippon, a previous pastor of the church. It is of that sort of charity which would naturally appeal to the tenderest side of human nature, and is one which many large churches would do well to copy. It provides all the comforts of a Christian home without expense to the inmates, and at present has a very commodious house constructed near to the Tabernacle and within sight of the Elephant and Castle Railroad Station.

Mr. Spurgeon gives a very interesting account of the beginning of this enterprise in his history of the Metropolitan Tabernacle and as he appealed for assistance, to which there was a liberal response, Mr. Spurgeon said:

"Dr. Rippon once said he had some of the best people in His Majesty's dominion in his church, and

he used to add with a nod, '*and some of the worst.*'
Some of the latter class seem to have got into office
at one time, for they were evidently a hindrance
rather than a help to the good man, though from his
independent way of doing things the hindrance did
not much affect him.

"As well as we can remember, the story of his
founding the almshouses and schools in 1803, it runs
as follows: The doctor urged upon the deacons the
necessity of such institutions; they do not see the
urgency thereof; he pleads again, but like the deaf
adder, they are not to be charmed, charm he ever so
wisely. 'The expense will be enormous, and the
money cannot be raised,' this was the unnecessary
croak of the prudent officers. At length the pastor
says, 'The money can be raised, and shall be. Why,
if I don't go out next Monday, and collect £500
($2,500) before the evening meeting, I'll drop the
proposal; but while I am sure the people will take
up the matter heartily, I will not be held back by
you.' Disputes in this case were urged in very
plain language, but with no degree of bitterness, for
the parties knew each other, and had too much
mutual respect to make their relationship in the
church depend upon a point of difference. All were
agreed to put the Doctor to a test, and challenged
him to produce the £500 ($2,500) next Monday, or
cease to importune about almshouses. The worthy
slow-coaches were up to time on the appointed evening, and the Doctor soon arrived. 'Well, brethren,'

said he, 'I have succeeded in collecting £300 ($1,500,) that is most encouraging, is it not?' 'But,' said two or three of them at once, in a hurry, 'You said you would get £500 ($2,500) or drop the matter, and we mean for you to keep your word.' 'By all means,' said he, 'and I mean to keep my word, too, there is £800 ($4,000) which the friends gave me almost without asking, and the rest is nearly all promised.' The prudent officials were taken aback, but recovering themselves, they expressed their great pleasure, and would be ready to meet the pastor at any time and arrange for the expending of funds. 'No, no, my brethren,' said the Doctor, 'I shall not need your services. You have opposed me all along, and now I have done the work without you, you want to have your say in it to hinder me still, but neither you nor any other deacons shall plague a minister about this business. So, brethren, you can attend to something else.' Accordingly, the old trust deed of the almshouses had a clause to the effect that the pastor shall elect the pensioners, *'no deacon interfering,'* The present pastor had great pleasure in inducing the Charity Commissioners to expunge this clause, and give the pastor and deacons, unitedly, the power to select the objects of charity.

'' The original endowments, after payment of repairs, do not suffice wholly to provide for six inmates, and there are now seventeen; the support of the remaining eleven involves a heavy draught upon the communion fund of our church, which is already fully weighed down with poor members. We greatly need at least £5000 ($25,000) to endow the alms-houses, and place the institution upon a proper footing. Already C. H. Spurgeon, Thomas Olney and Thomas Greenwood have contributed £200 ($1,000) each towards the fund, and we earnestly trust that either by donations or legacies, the rest of the £5,000 ($25,000) will be forthcoming. This would only provide five shillings ($1.25) per week for each poor woman, which is little enough. If more could be raised it would be so much the better for the pensioners. The pastors are anxious to see this matter put into proper order; they confess that the responsibility of having increased the number of rooms and alms-women rests mainly on them, and therefore they feel that their work is not done till at least five shillings per week shall have been provided for their poor sisters; if it could be double that amount they would be glad. We wish to leave the Tabernacle in good working order when our work is done; but the present burden might prove far too heavy for our successors; indeed, they ought not to be saddled with it. In future years the church may find itself barely able to support its own expenses, and we do not think that we are justified in leaving it the legacy of so heavy a charge. Our present anxiety is to get the ship tight and trim, and this is one of the matters which is not in a satisfactory condition. Brethren, let us set it straight. Our aged sisters are worthy of all that we can do for them, and their grateful faces often make our hearts glad. We should like to see more alms-rooms, and we hope some one will build and endow a row for aged men. We have had a hint that this project is taking shape in the mind of a generous friend; we hope he will carry it out in his own lifetime, rather than wait and have it done by a legacy."

Mr. Spurgeon took a personal interest in the affairs of the Home and frequently contributed largely for its support. He was the power behind the throne in the management and supplies, as he was in almost every other enterprise taken by the church. No one ever knew how many bills Mr. Spurgeon paid in connection with the Home for he was continually settling small accounts for gas, heating, groceries, clothing, errands, and small comforts. Although he has enjoyed the inestimable privilege of giving at times quite large sums such as that at his silver wedding when, being presented with $25,000, he gave the whole of it over as an endowment to the Home, yet what he gave in large sums did not approach the aggregate of what he contributed in a continuous stream of small gifts which he was ever granting to a great variety of charities.

There was a wisdom in this matter of expenditure which accomplished a double purpose; it not only provided for the sustenance of the noble charities but it also prevented any quarrels arising among the officials concerning the payment of disputed bills and relieved the object of charity from the unpleasantness of any public discussion.

Some newspapers accused him of hoarding large sums of money and he frequently was compelled to deny the assertion which was made that he was a very rich man. There was some reason behind the surmises in reference to his wealth, from the fact that it was well known that he had a very large income, and it was not equally well known to what purpose he applied his funds.

Yet, he conscientiously regarded his salary and the gifts which he personally received as a sacred trust given him of the Lord, all of which was to be devoted to Christ's cause and only a reasonable portion of it used economically in the support of his family and the payment for his home. Hence if the occupants of the Old Ladies' Home were seen to be in need of anything he did not wait for any vote of the board or action of the church, but simply went himself and purchased what he saw in his frequent visits was really needed. He paid almost innumerable bills in various directions which no one knew he had settled, unless perchance his wife should find the bundle of receipted bills in his pocket or lying upon his desk. It thus sometimes happened that the same bill was paid twice, where the officers of the church did not know that Mr. Spurgeon had settled the account; and the fact of his generosity thus becoming unexpectedly known led in several important cases to quite large donations toward his work from friends, who otherwise would not have understood the necessities.

The Home includes two school rooms and a class room, which are occupied every week-day by about four hundred children under the tutelage of a head master. There are seventeen rooms occupied by the old ladies, but only those who are over sixty years of age and destitute, are received.

CHAPTER XVI.

POWERFUL REINFORCEMENTS.

Mr. Spurgeon was wise enough to set a high value upon printed matter. In the very earliest days of his ministry some of his sermons were placed in print with his consent and encouragement, and he often wrote small articles for periodicals during the first five years of his pastorate in London.

The assistance which he has received from periodicals of his own and those published by other people will account in an a great measure for the success of his many undertakings. Some excellent judges regard the printing press as Mr. Spurgeon's stronghold in the evangelization of the multitudes he has reached. Certainly through his printed sermons he has reached a larger audience by a hundred fold than those who sat under the sound of his voice. It appears reasonable to state that Mr. Squrgeon's influence would have been very little compared to that which it did reach if he had not availed himself of this very powerful reinforcement in the establishment of public opinion.

He issued a sufficient number of printed sermons before his death to fill forty volumes. Certainly

Blucher's reinforcements at Waterloo were not more necessary to Wellington than has been the *Sword and Trowel* to Mr. Spurgeon's religious campaign.

Colonol Grant, United States Consel at Manchester, England wrote in 1890 concerning Mr. Spurgeon as follows:—

"He has fought his way to a commander's place in the religious world, and holds it with no abatement of faithfulness, although the work of years is leaving weak spots in his body. There's life in the old guard yet, however and he stands squarely to his work on the outpost, no matter how the storms may gather about him. His energy, his heroism under bodily pain, his sweet toil, all combine to make him stand out in the clear light as an evangel of the Lord worthy of the cross and crown. What a great loving heart he has: How his sympathies encircle the whole world: As one of God's workers, he has no superior among men."

As the qualifications of a great General require that he shall be a diplomatist and a tactician, as well as a brave leader, so Mr. Spurgeon exhibited his great generalship as much in his power to mass the different religious forces under his control and oversee the entire campaign as in those personal charges upon the forces of evil, as the leader of his own great church.

Too much will not be stated when we say that in all probability every one of the great enterprises which the church has undertaken and every charity which Mr. Spurgeon has espoused, either had its origin in some article in the *Sword and Trowel* or was chiefly indebted to that publication for a continued support.

That magazine was begun on the first of January 1865 and up to the time of Mr. Spurgeon's death was edited by him, not only with the contribution of articles, but by a personal oversight of everything printed therein. There were periods during the publication when as Mr. Spurgeon was laid aside by sickness, when others were called in to do his work. But that magazine was the last to be laid aside when pain afflicted him. He seemed to understand that upon its regular appearance depended the success of all the christian work over which Providence had made him the superintendent.

The circulation of the magazine reached in 1892, fifteen thousand subscribers at the high price of about 6 cents per copy. It began of course in a modest and small way and appealed directly to the local spirit of the Metropolitan Tabernacle. It put forth no flaring advertisements and found its readers among personal friends of the editor or among the personal acquaintances of his hearers.

But, when Mrs. Spurgeon began to use the income of her Book Fund to supply the magazine to missionaries for free distribution in the homes and for the supply of all the light house keepers of England, Australia and India, of course, the circulation leaped at once into most respectable proportions. Yet within ten years of the time the first number was issued it had found its way into nearly all the religious reading rooms of the English speaking world, was purchased for the large libraries, and found a ready sale on all the prominent news-stands of the railroad companies.

The circumstances gave it a position of honor among the other magazines of the world, which added great force to Mr. Spurgeon's evangelistic powers. We have already seen that the Orphanage was due to an article which **Mrs.** Hillyard read in that Magazine. It is also stated that the first gift for the building of the Pastors' College and the first donation towards the Girls' Orphanage came directly in response to an editorial article in the *Sword and Trowel*.

It advertised itself in most legitimate ways and also presented in the most effective manner all the needs of the church and its various mission stations. It was each month a personal letter from Mr. Spurgeon; he had not been educated by Universities out of that peculiar personality which made nearly all his communications seem like familiar conversations with a personal friend. He was not afraid to speak directly of himself and hesitated not to give his own opinion upon any matter which came under his attention. He seemed to be so artlessly unconscious of egotism and so regardless of criticism that he freely spoke of himself, his circumstances, his wishes and his experiences without a trace of embarassment.

The publication of that magazine would in itself have been a great achievement for the cause of Christ had it stood entirely alone with no connection with the Metropolitan Tabernacle. But each of these great institutions were a necessity to the other.

The Tabernacle could not have been what it became had it not been for the "*Sword and Trowel*" and the Magazine could not have reached the dignified position it held had it not been for the large congregations in the Tabernacle. His audience of fifty-five hundred in the Tabernacle was only one tenth the size of the audience he reached through the Magazine, for the best estimates which have been given concerning its circulation show that it is largely taken in families where a single copy furnished a whole household with reading matter.

Like the volumes of his sermons it went into the humblest homes and the finest palaces; into the office and the workshop, into the hospital and the sick room; into the poor-house and the great libraries; into the hands of the school children and the aged professors; under the eye of vigorous manhood, and before the spectacles of ripe old age.

The Magazine had an immense advantage over his spoken words in preserving in a permanent form the exhortations and advice which Mr. Spurgeon so freely gave. If a person was touched by any article they could take up the Magazine again and re-read it scrutinizingly or prayerfully, as often as they chose. That many of his articles were frequently re-read most effectively is shown by the continued testimony coming incessantly through all the years from generous givers toward his work, and from persons testifying concerning their conversion of their renewed power in Christian undertakings.

The Magazine made the Metropolitan Tabernacle known all over the English speaking countries and answered a better purpose in making each reader feel personally acquainted with Mr. Spurgeon himself. It had a marvelous reflex influence upon the attendance at the Tabernacle in London and upon every department of its local work. Persons in America would read some interesting item in the *Sword and Trowel* connected with the missionary work or the church service of the Tabernacle and would, under the inspiration of the article, write to their acquaintances in London and urge them to attend Mr. Spurgeon's preaching services. In the great metropolis there were thousands of people who for years had lived near the Tabernacle and had not heard mention made of its preacher or its work until some friend in America, Australia or India wrote them concerning it. "A prophet is not without honor save in his own country and among his own kin."

It is safe to state that one-third of the present membership of the Tabernacle consists of persons

29

who were advised to attend Mr. Spurgeon's service by their acquaintances living outside of London. The potent influence which the Magazine exerted upon all the local interests of his church could be partially measured by the continual statement of visitors at the Tabernacle, saying, "I have come to-day to bring friends from out of the city, who desired very much to hear Mr. Spurgeon." The deacons and ushers in the church were constantly appealed to by persons crowding the doors who reiterated the same request as though thousands had learned it together by heart. "I do not care so much for a seat for myself as I do for friends who are here from a great distance."

The exalted opinion which strangers entertained of Mr. Spurgeon who had made his acquaintance through his Magazine and sermons, increased the respect for him among his neighbors. He exhibited a striking instance of the necessity that a Bishop should be in good report "among those that are without."

The amount of gifts received in small offerings by mail from distant places presented to Mr. Spurgeon for his Christian work has been estimated by a personal friend of the writer, who was also an honored acquaintance of Mr. Spurgeon, at the annual average of sixteen thousand dollars.

The hold which Mr. Spurgeon secured upon his hearers could scarcely have been so permanent and so effective had it not been reinforced and persistently sustained by the publication of this periodical. There are lessons to be learned from this in the conduct of church work and in arousing spiritual life which are not fully appreciated yet by the churches of England or those of other lands.

The difficulty in applying the excellent teachings of Mr. Spurgeon's useful example will be found in the natural tendency of persons and churches to imitate him under widely different circumstances from those which surrounded his life. Hence they must fail. No imitator of Mr. Spurgeon can ever reasonably hope to succeed. His circumstances, his physique, his education, his training, will never be repeated in the entire history of the rolling years ; yet a general application can be made of the lessons which his example furnishes which must be very useful to the individual churches and very inspiring to the cause of christianity. It is not enough to preach the gospel by word of mouth. Christ indeed wrote nothing which remains for our instruction, but the Apostles trained in His own school and following out implicitly His divine direc-tion, not only disputed in the schools and officiated in the Synagogues, but wrote down in order that we might have the books of the New Testament without which our preaching would be vain. The Gospel may be preached to the eye as fully as to the ear and he who uses but one method is like he who sculls in competition with a fully accoutred oarsman. True orators and great editors are brothers, giants both, together they can save the world. In fractricidal combat they can ruin it.

Mr. Spurgeon brought both forces into a most compatible alliance. In one of Mr. Spurgeon's notices appearing in the *Sword and Trowel* as an introduction to another volume for a new year he gives a most excellent insight into the purpose and management of the Magazine.

"KIND READERS.—Throughout another year you have sustained the magazine; and as very many of you have expressed your satisfaction, and few, if any, have favored me with a complaint, I feel encouraged to believe that you have been pleased with my monthly numbers. It was once observed in my hearing by a friend who wished to account for my fulfilment of numerous duties, that as for the magazine, it was a merely nominal thing to be the editor, for few editors ever saw their magazines till they were in print. However this may be as a rule, it does not contain a spark of truth in my case, for I have personally superintended every page, and I do not think a single line of the magazine has passed through the press without having been read by me. Whether I succeed or not, I certainly do not delegate my task to others. If I had more leisure I am sure I could do better, and it is with unfeigned satisfaction that I find my subscribers contented with what I can procure for them."

"The *Sword and Trowel* has been the happy

means of uniting in gracious service a band of gracious givers and workers, who now for these seventeen years have joined to aid the institutions which, though they locally surround the Tabernacle, are really the off-spring of a congregation which is found scattered throughout all lands. By means of this warm-hearted brotherhood the Pastors' College has been sustained from year to year, until some six hundred ministers have been educated in it, the most of whom are still faithfully preaching the old-fashioned gospel in which they have been trained. In connection with this enterprise three brethren have been supported as evangelists and their itinerant labors bave been signally successful. Testimonies that churches have been aroused and sinners converted by their means, have been plenti-fully sent in, and these pages have been increased in interest thereby. Hundreds of thousands have heard the gospel through this instrumentality."

"The Stockwell Orphanage originated through an article in this magazine, and from time to time its support has been mainly supplied by its readers. During the past year the houses for the girl's side have been completed and partly furnished; and at the present time the first detachment of little ones has entered into occupation. More remains to be done by way of furniture for other houses, and the further contracts for the infirmary, baths, and out-buildings have to be met; but it is a great comfort to have seen the project so far in progress, and to

feel assured that all that is yet required will be forthcoming in its season. The bazaar which is so soon
to be held will, we hope, secure the amount needed
to bring the enterprise up to the next stage, and
then we may lay our plan for the final outlay on the
chapel of the Orphanage, and a few other necessaries. All that has been done has been accomplished without personal solicitation, or the allotment of votes, or the dissemination of heart-rend-
ing appeals: it has sufficed to lay the case before
the Lord in prayer, and then to mention it to His
people in plain and earnest terms, and the funds
have come in with marvellous regularity, the larger
amounts having been timed to meet the hour of need
as exactly as if the whole went by clock work. The
hand of the Lord is in this thing, and to Him be
glory. That this institution has brought honor to
God is plain enough, for many a time those who
would have abused our ministry have admitted that
a good work has been wrought, and have had no
heart to revile. There is something about orphan
work which wins the sympathy of the most careless,
and none can tell till the last great day how many
have been by this means led to think well of the gospel, and next to hear it and experience its power."

"The Colportage Association has held on its most
useful course. It has been sustained with difficulty,
for somehow it does not chime in with the tastes and
views of large donors, but its influence for good is
second to no existing agency. Where there are

not enough dissenters to support a minister, or where ministers are unable to cover large and scattered districts, the colporteur makes his way with his pack, and speaks a word for Jesus at every door, either by personal conversation or by leaving a tract. Besides this, he preaches by the roadside or in village chapels, gets up temperance meetings, visits the sick, and above all sells good books. This society, and several other useful works, report themselves in these pages, and enlist good friends thereby."

" Mrs. Spurgeon's Book Fund quietly pursues its beneficent course. It is putting sound theology just now upon the shelves of many a poor curate and ill-paid minister, and this it does so largely that it would be a miracle of a strange sort if it did not greatly affect the ministry of the day. That the sermons distributed and the " Treasury of David " furnish material for preachers is saying very little: that they have evangelized the tone of many has been confessed in numerous instances, and is true of far more.

" Brethren and sisters, you have aided me so far in a benevolent enterprise of no small dimensions, and I hope I have in no degree lost your loving confidence. Continue, then, to bear me up in your prayers, and to sustain me by your contributions. More can be done, and more should be done. Every living work is capable of growth; every work which has God's blessing upon it is under necessity to advance. Our watchword still is *forward*. Possibly we cry forward more often than pleases those who lag behind. Some time ago I asked for men and means to send evangelists to India; one man only offered, and that one man was sent. Up till now I have had sufficient money, and I believe that when more men offer I shall have larger funds; but here is room for prayerful uplooking to the Lord. Brethren, pray for us. I would fain live to the utmost of my own life, and I would draw out from all my brethren more and more for God's glory by the propagation of the gospel, the alleviation of suffering, and the arousing of the Church. Thanks to all helpers, and a thousand blessings."

CHAPTER XVII.

IN COMBAT.

It may be important as a matter of history although it is less agreeable to the general reader, to give some account of the controversies into which Mr. Spurgeon at times was drawn. We have before stated that he had strong friends and bitter enemies. No man could have been more deeply and sincerely loved by promiscuous congregations of people than was Mr. Spurgeon. Some of them even asserted that their affection for him was stronger than their affection for their own families. He was a tower of defence to his friends and no persecuted person went to him for protection who did not at once secure all that his genius and generosity could give. The admiration of his acquaintances which amounted almost to worship naturally awoke in the jealous bosoms of ordinary human beings a counterpart spirit of envy and criticism.

The people well knew that it would please Mr. Spurgeon far more than any personal gift if they would remember the poor, the sick, the lame, the blind and the aged, as an indication of their respect for him.   It is a magnificent thing to contemplate in the life of any person when the love of his friends for him manifests itself in deeds of Christian charity and the promotion of salvation.

A very excellent idea of the esteem in which he was held by those who had been acquainted with him through his ministry is shown in an address which was presented to him beautifully embossed on the occasion of his fiftieth birthday.

The twenty-five thousand dollars which was presented to him on that Fiftieth Anniversary with the assurance that he could do with it as he chose. He refused to accept it for himself and appropriated it to the various charities of the church.   The accumlated power of ten thousand deeds of kindness necessarily exalted him in the minds of his friends and lifted him to such an eminence that he was a most prominent mark for the arrows of the infidel, the atheist and the unsuccessful.   Even that Fiftieth Anniversary, while it multiplied his friends, also brought upon him severe contests with the enimies of the good and the true.   The address which was presented to him on that occasion we give in full that it may be preserved as an important matter of history.

"To the Rev. C. H. Spurgeon, *Pastor of the Metropolitan Tabernacle:—*

"With an united voice of thanksgiving to our ever-blessed God on your behalf; with a cordial acknowledgment of the good services you have rend-

ered to the universal Church of our Lord Jesus
Christ and with a profound sense of the high character and wide reputation you have established
among your fellow-Christians, we beg to offer you
our sincere congratulations on this the fiftieth anni
versary of your birthday.

"Accept our assurance that no language but the
language of personal affection could fitly express the
esteem in which you are held by ourselves and by
the numerous constituency we represent. Were it
possible for the lips of all those who love you as a
brother, and those who revere you as a father in
Christ, to sound in your ears the sentiments of their
hearts, the music of their chorus at this glad hour
would be like the noise of many waters.

"Gathered together, as we now are, in this
sacred edifice—sacred not by reason of any superstitious ceremony at the opening, but by the soul-
saving miracles of grace subsequently wrought beneath its roof—it becomes us to greet you first as
Pastor of this Ancient Church. More than thirty
of those fifty years you chronicle to-day have been
spent in our midst. As our Minister you are known
to the utmost ends of the earth. Richly endowed
by the Spirit of God with wisdom and discretion,
your conduct as our Ruling Elder has silenced con-
tention and promoted harmony. The three hundred souls you found in fellowship at New Park
Street Chapel have multiplied to a fellowship of
nearly six thousand in this Tabernacle. And under

your watchful oversight the family group has increased without any breach of order.

"You came among us in the freshness of your youth. At that flowering age when boys of good promise are wont to change their curriculum from school to college, you had already developed into manliness, and there was ripe fruit as well as pleasant foliage on your branches. The groundwork of your education appeared to be so solid, and the maturity of your character so thoroughly reliable, that you were unanimously elected by venerable members of the Church of Christ to preside over their councils. The fair prospect of your spring-time has not suffered from any blight. Your natural abilities never betrayed you into indolent habits. The talents you possessed gave stimulus to your diligence. A little prosperity did not elate you, or a measure of success prompt the desire to settle down in some quiet resting-place. You spread your sails to catch the breeze. The ascendency you began to acquire over the popular mind, instead of making you vain-glorious, filled you with awe, and increased the rigour of that discipline you have always exercised over yourself. These were happy auguries of your good speed. Not that the utmost vigilance on your part could have sufficed to uphold you amidst the vast and accumulating responsibilities that have devolved on you as the sphere of your ministry widened. He who ruleth in the heavens has screened you in times of peril, and piloted you through shoals and quicksands, through straits and rapids. His grace and His goodness, His promises and His providence have never failed you. From the hour when you first committed your soul, your circumstances, and destinies to the keeping of our Lord Jesus Christ, you have never feared such a disaster.

"To your unwavering faith in His guardian care we venture to attribute the coolness of your head and the courage of your heart in all the great adventures of your life. Some of us have been with you from the beginning of your charge. According to a law as legibly written as any law of nature, the Scripture has said, "Instead of the fathers, shall be the children." Hence, in not a few instances, you must miss the sires while you meet the sons. The retrospect of your career, to those who have followed it throughout, appears like one unbroken series of successes; but as our memory retraces the steps you have taken, we can testify to the exhaustive labours in which you have blithely engaged, the constant self-denial you have cheerfully exercised, and the restless anxieties that have kept you and your comrades incessantly calling on the name of the Lord. By such an experience you have enlarged the field of evangelical enterprise in the various institutions of the Church. And it has been your happiness not only to see the growth of those institutions beyond the most sanguine hopes you cherished when planting them, but

to have received the grateful thanks of those who
derived unspeakable benefit in partaking of their
fruits.

"Such gratitude demands our notice, though
only in the lowest degree. Your skilful generalship has laid ten thousand happy donors to your
charities under lasting obligations to you for provid-
ing outlets for their benevolence. It has pleased
the Lord to make whatever you do to prosper.
You have been the faithful steward and the kindly
executor of hundreds and thousands of pious individuals, whose fond design has been to lay up
treasure for themselves in heaven by paying into
the exchequer on earth of their substance for the
widow and the fatherless in their distress, for the
poor, and those who have no helper. Let the
acknowledgments of subscribers to the various
purses you hold in your hands, as well as those
of recipients, cheer you as you enter on a fresh
decade of the days of the years of your earthly
pilgrimage.

"An occasion like this is so solemn, and an address like the present is so serious, that we may
well search the sacred volume for suitable words.
We feel sure that brethern in all parts of the earth
pray for you. And we are equally certain that the
churches which are in Christ throughout the world
glorify God in you. The Lord preserve and keep
you to the end. To this hour you have maintained
an unsullied reputation among men. Erring as we

all are before God, it is our sincere conviction that if such a thing were possible, a second edition of your life, revised by yourself, could hardly be an amendment.

"You braved much calumny on the outset of your career, and you have outlived it. The secularists, who once denounced, now salute you. Where your theology has failed to convert them your philanthropy has sufficed to enchant them. You are lifted in public esteem above suspicion, as a true man— no traitor or time-server. Your kindness to everybody has made everybody kind to you. You have illustrated the force and the fulness of a divine proverb which has puzzled many a philosopher: "When a man's ways please the Lord he maketh even his enemies to be at peace with him."

"If, dear sir, you give us full credit for the intense sympathy we have felt when sickness and sorrow have weakened your strength in the way, you will not deny us the gratification of alluding to the private and domestic joys that pour down like sunbeams on your face and gladden your Jubilee.

"Your beloved and estimable wife, whose life long trembled in the balance, has been restored to health. Had she been less heroic and more exacting in her protracted illness, you must have been more reserved and less generous in the consecration of your time and thought to the good works you were doing. In the stillness of enforced retirement her inventive genius discovered new channels of usefulness. Her 'Book Fund' is beyond all praise. Her delicate mission has been so appreciated, that throughout the British Isles, and in foreign lands, her name has become linked with your own at every station where an ambassador of Christ publishes the glad tidings of the Gospel.

"Your father and mother, walking before God in quiet unpretentious piety, have both been spared to see their first-born son in the meridian of a career that has made their once obscure patronymic famous throughout the world.

"Your worthy brother and trusty yoke-fellow in the pastorate is still by your side rendering good service, for which his fine business tact, and his manly but modest desire to second all your motions to go forward, eminently qualify him.

"Your two sons have both devoted themselves to the ministry; and each of them in his own sphere of labour has found proof that he was divinely anointed to his pastorate.

"To yourself, however, we turn as a central figure, recognised from afar by tens of thousands of people, to whom your name is an emblem of purity and power, and by whom you are accounted second to none among living Preachers, and your sermons are appreciated as a faithful exposition of the Gospel of God, instinct with the witness of the Holy Spirit, and therefore quickening in their influence on the conscience and the hearts of men.

"On your head we now devoutly invoke those blessings which we believe the Almighty is abundantly willing to bestow.

"May your steps in the future be ordered of the Lord as they have been in the past. May a generation yet unborn witness that your old age is luxuriant and fruitful as your youth. May your life on earth wind up like the holy Psalter that you so much love. Be it yours to anchor at last in David's Psalm of Praise, prolific as it was of other Psalms, into which no groan or sigh could intrude. So may you rest in the Lord with a vision of the everlasting Kingom dawning on your eyes, and Hallelujah after Hallelujah resounding in your ears."

Throughout all the years after his name had become so prominent it was not possible for him to espouse any cause without becoming its principal champion. He was so much better known than any other man and his example had so much more force that he was at once selected from among the entire ranks as the chief object in the battle. Mr. Spurgeon's disposition shows that balance of ability and judgment which is rare to find among persons even in his profession. His heart was large, his affections very strong and his sympathies most tender; and yet when aroused to conflict he could strike almost fiercely and hurled a free lance with a strong hand.

He spoke decidedly and bluntly, he called evils by their right names and was unsparing in his bit-

30

ter denunciation of deceit, hypocricy and sin. It made no difference to him to what class in society his opponents might belong nor how aristocratic may have been their familiy's coat of arms. If they were found in the ranks of the enemies of Christ they must surrender or give most valiant battle.

From the beginning of his pastorate in London he was called upon often to espouse some forlorn hope or to stand prominently forth as the defender of some cherished doctrine and while he made many enemies in these contests he also increased the number of his supporters. He held himself strenuously to the Baptist doctrines of the separation of Church and State and was necessarily set in opposition to the established Church of England.

During the early years of his pastorate the dignitaries of the established Church did not deign to notice the "Essex bumpkin," otherwise than to make slurring reference to him in private conversation. But when the common people heard him so gladly and thousands waited upon his ministrations until the public press was compelled as a matter of ordinary news to report the proceedings at his gatherings, these dignified occupants of a political office found that they must enter into the conflict for the defence of their cherished faith.

Some of them conducted most honorable warfare and the greater portion of them respected Mr. Spurgeon for his plain advocacy of his conscientious principles, but occasionally there were found men who used their clerical positions to say contemptibly false things concerning him and to sadly misrepresent his doctrines and his practices.

The replies he made to them contained some of the sharpest thrusts from his intellectual sword and some of the hottest shot from his doctrinal battery that are to be found in any literature. But he did not confine his assaults to the members or doctrines of other denominations. Whenever he found a traitor in the camp or a spy in the fortress, he pounced upon him with a vigor and alertness that often astonished his most intimate acquaintances. It is a surprising thing in his history that in all these assaults upon the different forms of evil and the persons who represented them, that he never had occasion to retrace his steps and seems never to have met with defeat. In some cases his companions felt for a time that he ought to apologize for the hot chain shot which he sent into the enemy's country, but the subsequent experience confirmed the wisdom of his utterances and often led his opponents to an apology. He stood forth for the doctrines of his denomination with a strength and perseverance which would be noble in the advocate of any denomination or creed, and could not overlook errors in Christian faith or principles even among his dearest friends. His sectarian feelings were always subordinate to his Christian charity, but he was, nevertheless, that which every disciple of Christ should be, an open defendant of the principles which as a Christian he had espoused.

He serves his denomination best who serves Christ most, and it may be stated with approximation to the truth that he serves Christ best who serves his denomination most.

He would not remain in voluntary association with any assembly of churches where the principles in which he believed were not closely and conscientiously adhered to. If preachers or churches advocated or practiced the principles which were at variance with the fundamental doctrines of Christianity as he understood them he insisted without fear or favor in withdrawing from their fellowship unless they changed their teaching and conduct. A most excellent idea of this feature of his character may be gained from one of the later controversies in which he engaged which became known to the religious world as the "Down-Grade" controversy. In the articles which he wrote upon it before his withdrawal from the Baptist Union, and before uniting with the Surrey and Middlesex Baptist Association we see this side of his character most strongly exhibited. One of the articles will give the reader a more accurate and comprehensive view of this side of Mr. Spurgeon's life than anything that could otherwise be written concerning him.

The Baptist Union was composed of Baptists and Congregationalists and was a very free and liberal organization which did not attempt to hold any person very strictly to doctrine or creed. Yet many of the strongest preachers in the Baptist denomination in and about London were members of that Association. In the membership there were also a number of pastors who taught in their pulpits some of the modern ideas of science—so called — and who advocated the theories of the higher criticism and a more liberal and loose construction of the old Testament records. Upon this subject Mr. Spurgeon wrote:—

" No lover of the gospel can conceal from himself the fact that the days are evil. We are willing to make a large discount from our apprehensions on the score of natural timidity, the caution of age, and the weakness produced by pain; but yet our solemn conviction is that things are much worse in many churches than they seem to be, and are rapidly tending downward. Read those newspapers which represent the Broad School of Dissent, and ask yourself. How much further could they go? What doctrine remains to be abandoned? What other truth to be the object of contempt? A new religion has been initiated, which is no more Christianity than chalk is cheese, and this religion, being destitute of moral honesty, palms itself off as the old faith with slight improvements, and on this plea usurps pulpits which were erected for gospel preaching. The Atonement is scouted, the inspiration of Scripture is derided, the Holy Ghost is degraded into an influence, the punishment of sin is turned into fiction, and the Resurrection into a myth, and yet these enemies of our faith expect us to call them brethern, and maintain a confederacy with them!

"At the back of doctrinal falsehood comes a natural decline of spiritual life, evidenced by a taste for questionable amusements, and a weariness of devotional meetings. At a certain meeting of ministers and church-officers, one after another doubted the value of prayer-meetings; all confessed that they had a very small attendance, and several acknowledged without the slightest compunction that they had quite given them up. What means this? Are churches in a right condition when they have only one meeting for prayer in a week, and that a mere skeleton? Churches here are which have prayer-meetings several times on the Lord's day, and very frequently during the week, yet feel their need of more prayer; but what can be said of those who very seldom practice united supplication? Are there few conversions? Do the congregations dwindle? Who wonders that this is the case when the spirit of prayer has departed?

"As for questionable amusements, time was when a Non-comformist minister who was known to attend the play-house would soon have found himself without a church. And justly so; for no man can long possess the confidence, even of the most worldly, who is known to be a haunter of theatres. Yet, at the present time, it is a matter of notoriety that preachers of no mean repute defend the play-house, and do so because they have been seen there. Is it any wonder that church members forget their vows of consecration, and run with the unholy in the ways of frivolity, when they hear that persons are tolerated in the pastorate who do the same? We doubt not that, for writing these lines, we shall incur the charge of prudery and bigotry, and this will but prove how low are the tone and spirit of the churches in many places. The fact is, that many would like to unite church and stage, cards and prayer, dancing and sacraments. If we are powerless to stem this torrent, we can at least warn men of its existence, and entreat them to keep out of it. When the old faith is gone, and enthusiasm for the gospel is extinct, it is no wonder that people seek something else in the way of delight. Lacking bread, they feed on ashes; rejecting the way of the Lord, they run greedily in the path of folly.

An eminent minister, who is well versed in the records of Nonconformity, remarked to us the other day that he feared history was about to repeat itself among Dissenters. In days gone by, they aimed at being thought respectable, judicious, moderate, and learned, and, in consequence, they abandoned the Puritanic teaching with which they started, and toned down their doctrines. The spiritual life which had been the impelling cause of their dissent declined almost to death's door, and the very existence of evangelical Nonconformity was threatened. Then came the outburst of living godliness under White- field and Wesley, and with it new life for Dissent, and increased influence in every direction.

Alas! many are returning to the poisoned cups which drugged that declining generation, when it surrendered itself to Unitarian lethargy. Too many ministers are toying with the deadly cobra of " another gospel," in the form of "modern thought." As a consequence, their congregations are thinning, the more spiritual of their members join the "Brethren," or some other company of "believers unattached;" while the more wealthy, and show-lov- ing, with some of the unquestionable devoutness, go off to the Church of England.

Let us not hide from ourselves the fact that the Episcopal Church is awake, and is full of zeal and force. Dissenting as we do most intensely from her ritualism, and especially abhorring her establish- ment by the State, we cannot but perceive that she grows, and grows, among other reasons, because spiritual life is waning among certain dissenters. Where the gospel is fully and powerfully preached, with the Holy Ghost sent down from heaven, our churches not only hold their own, but win converts; but when that which constitutes their strength is gone—we mean when the gospel is concealed, and the life of prayer is slighted—the whole thing be- comes a mere form and fiction. For this thing our heart is sore grieved. Dissent for mere dissent's sake would be the bitter fruit of a wilful mind. Dissent as mere political partisanship is a degradation and travesty of religion. Dissent for truth's sake, carried out by force of the life within, is noble, praiseworthy, and fraught with the highest benefits to the race Are we to have the genuine living thing, or are we to have that corruption of the best, from which the worst is produced? Conformity, or nonconformity, *per se*, is nothing; but a new creature is everything, and the truth upon which alone that new creature can live is worth dying a thousand deaths to conserve. It is not the shell that is so precious, but the kernel which it contains; when the kernel is gone, what is there left that is worth a thought? Our nonconformity is beyond measure precious as a vital spiritual force, but only while it remains such will it justify its own existence.

"The case is mournful. Certain ministers are making infidels. Avowed atheists are not a tenth as dangerous as those preachers who scatter doubt and stab at faith. A plain man told us the other day that two ministers had derided him because he thought we should pray for rain. A gracious woman bemoaned in my presence that a precious promise in Isaiah, which had comforted her, had been declared by her minister to be uninspired. It is a common thing to hear working-men excuse their wickedness by the statement that there is no hell, the parson says so. But we need not prolong our mention of painful facts. Germany was made

unbelieving by her preachers, and England is following in her track. Attendance at places of worship is declining, and reverence for holy things is
vanishing; and we solemnly believe this to be largely attributable to the scepticism which has flashed
from the pulpit and spread among the people. Possibly the men who uttered the doubt never intended
it to go so far; but none the less they have done the
ill, and cannot undo it. Their own observation
ought to teach them better. Have these advanced
thinkers filled their own chapels? Have they, after
all, prospered through discarding the old methods?
Possibly, in a few cases genius and tact have carried these gentry over the destructive results of
their ministry; but in many cases their pretty new
theology has scattered their congregations. In
meeting-houses holding a thousand, or twelve hundred, or fifteen hundred, places once packed to the
ceiling with ardent hearers, how small are the numbers now! We could mention instances, but we
forbear. The places which the gospel filled the new
nonsense has emptied, and will keep empty.

"This fact will have little influence with "the cultured;" for, as a rule, they have cultivated a fine
development of conceit. 'Yes,' said one, whose
pews held only here and there a worshiper, 'it will
always be found that in proportion as the preacher's
mind enlarges, his congregation diminishes.'
These destroyers of our church appear to be as content with their work as monkeys with their mischief.

That which their fathers would have lamented they rejoice in ; the alienation of the poor and simple-minded from their ministry they accept as a compliment, and the grief of the spiritually-minded they regard as an evidence of their power. Truly, unless the Lord had kept his own, we would long before this have seen our Zion ploughed as a field.

"The other day we were asked to mention the name of some person who might be a suitable pastor for a vacant church, and the deacon who wrote said: 'Let him be a converted man, and let him be one who believes what he preaches; for there are those around us who give us the idea that they have neither part nor lot in the matter.' This remark is more commonly made than we like to remember, and there is, alas ! too much need for it. A student from a certain college preached to a congregation we sometimes visit such a sermon that the deacon said to him in the vestry; 'Sir, do you believe in the Holy Ghost ?' The youth replied: 'I suppose I do.' To which the deacon answered: 'I suppose you do *not*, or you would not have insulted us with such false doctrine. A little plain speaking would do a world of good just now. These gentlemen desire to be let alone. They want no noise raised. Of course thieves hate watch-dogs, and love darkness. It is time that somebody should spring his rattle, and call attention to the way in which God is being robbed of his glory, and man of his hope.

"It now becomes a serious question how far those who abide by the faith once delivered to the saints should fraternize with those who have turned aside to another gospel. Christian love has its claims, and divisions are to be shunned as grievous evns; but how far are we justified in being in confederacy with those who are departing from the truth? It is a difficult question to answer so as to keep the balance of the duties. For the present it behoves believers to be cautious, lest they lend their support and countenance to the betrayers of the Lord. It is one thing to overleap all boundaries of denominational restriction for the truth's sake; this we hope all godly men will do more. It is quite another policy which would urge us to subordinate the maintenance of truth to denominational prosperity and unity. Numbers of easy-minded people wink at error so long as it is committed by a clever man and a good-natured brother, who has so many fine points about him. Let each believer judge for himself; but, for our part, we have put on a few fresh bolts to our door, and we have given orders to keep the chain up; for, under color of begging the friendship of the servant, there are those about who aim at robbing THE MASTER.

We fear it is hopeless ever to form a society which can keep out men base enough to profess one thing and believe another; but it might be possible to make an informal alliance among all who hold the Christianity of their fathers. Little as they might be able to do, they could at least protest, and as far as possible free themselves of that complicity which will be involved in a conspiracy of silence. If for a while the evangelicals are doomed to go down, let them die fighting, and in the full assurance that their gospel will have a resurrection when the inventions of "modern thought" shall be burned up with fire unquenchable."

The characteristics exhibited in that controversy, the history of which the world will soon care little about, displays his fearlessness and shows how delighted the oppressed, the injured, or the fearful would be to secure such a champion for themselves for their cause.

CHPATER XVIII.

THE POET.

Mr. Spurgeon was a man, as we have seen, who most sincerely believed in the use of printers' ink, and he used it in many different forms, where it would catch the eye or strike the heart.

He organized the Colportage Association, for the express purpose of distributing books, tracts and sermons ; and these missionaries going from house to house in prescribed districts of London, selling books if they could and giving them away if they could not make a sale; added greatly to the influence of Mr. Spurgeon's church.

A book or a leaflet would reach into homes or shops where the spoken word could not go and touch the hearts of persons who never attended church.

In one of his sermons referring to the annual report upon the work of the Colportage Association, he gave his opinion of the value of printed matter in the furtherance of the gospel.

Mr. Spurgeon most pertinently said :—"The printing-press is the mightiest agency on earth for good or evil. The position of a minister of religion standing in his pulpit is a responsible position, but it does not appear so responsible a position as that of the editor and the publisher. Men die, but the literary influences they project, go on for ever. I believe that God has made the printing-press to be a great agent in the world's correction and evangelization, and that the great final battle of the world will be fought, not with guns and swords, but with types and presses, a gospellized and purified literature triumphing over and tramping under foot and crushing out a corrupt literature. God speed the cylinders of an honest, intelligent, aggressive, Christian printing-press."

Many of the leaflets used by the Colportage Association contained the gospel message in verse, written by Mr. Spurgeon. Often in his sermons, but more frequently in his writings he introduced original poetry, some of which is positively beautiful, but the greater portion of which was intended directly to teach the most practical thought.

If Mr. Spurgeon had given his attention to the composition of poetry, he might not have reached a position of one of the standard poets, but he would have produced poems that would have lived on in the pages of standard literature; but he was too intensely in earnest and in too much of a hurry to save souls to stop long enough to permit his muse to lead him into the fairy realms of poetic imagination. Yet he fully appreciated the value of figures,

pictures, simlies and poetic illumination and expressed his admiration of them in the following most remarkable manner, "The worlds of nature and of
providence are full of parallels to things moral and
spiritual, and serve as pictures to make the written
book of inspiration more clear to the children of
God. The Bible itself abounds in metaphors, types
and symbols; it is a great picture-book; there is
scarcely a poetical figure which may not be found
in the law and the prophets, or in the words of
Jesus and His apostles. The preacher is bidden to
speak the oracles of God, and consequently he
should imitate their illustrative method, and abound
in emblems and parables. A sermon which is full
of "likes" is full of windows to enlighten the mind
and hands to hold it captive. Discourses decked
with simlies will not only give pleasure to the
children, but persons of riper years will be charmed
and instructed thereby."

His arrangements of the Psalms in rhyme
and his composition of the hymns which were published in the hymn book used in the Metropolitan
Tabernacle, showed too clearly a direct and earnest
purpose to admit of much poetical ornament.

He used the poetical forms of expression
simply because his knowledge of human nature
convinced him that it was the best form to attract
the eye, yet it is clear to every reader of his literary productions that he had a natural genius for the
expression of his ideas in the truest poetry. He

loved the standard English poems and in his quotations generally selected the most sublime or the
most touching portions of other productions yet his
own compositions were like iron spears adorned
with ribbons intended more for use than for aesthe-
tic purposes, and his poetry was of great use in the
salvation of many thousand people. Verses from
his hymns and songs found their way into all classes
of society, and many of them in the form of proverbs have become a part of the common language
of the working people of London. When he was
but eighteen years of age he exhibited no little
poetic taste which seemed afterwards to be consid-
erably marred by the fierce conflicts in which he was
compelled, as a popular preacher, to engage.

Probably nothing has appeared in print out of his
many hymns and poems, which was more sweetly
devout than his composition written at eighteen,
entitled "Immanuel." We will give the poem entire.

IMMAMUEL.

When once I mourned a load of sin ;
When conscience felt a wound within ,
When all my works were thrown away ;
When on my knees I knelt to pray,
　　Then, blissful hour, remembered well,
　　I learned Thy love, Immanuel.

When storms of sorrow toss my soul ;
When waves of care around me roll ;
When comforts sink, when joys shall flee ;
When hopeless griefs shall gape for me,
　　One word the tempest's rage shall quell—
　　That word, Thy name, Immanuel.

31

When for the truth I suffer shame ;
When foes pour scandal on my name ;
When cruel taunts and jeers abound ;
When "Bulls of Bashan" gird me round,
   Secure within Thy tower I'll dwell—
   That tower, thy grace, Immanuel.

When hell enraged lifts up her roar ;
When Satan stops my path before ;
When fiends rejoice and wait my end ;
When legioned hosts their arrows send,
   Fear not my soul, but hurl at hell,
   Thy battle cry, Immanuel.

When down the hill of life I go ;
When o'er my feet death's waters flow ;
When in the deep'ning flood I sink ;
When friends stand weeping on the brink,
   I'll mingle with my last farewell
   Thy lovely name, Immanuel.

When tears are banished from mine eye ;
When fairer worlds than these are nigh ;
When heaven shall fill my ravished sight ;
When I shall bathe in sweet delight,
   One joy all joys shall far excel,
   To see Thy face, Immanuel.

The hymn which has been most extensively used in the hymn books published by other churches and other denominations, was hastily written on one Saturday afternoon and used the next day at the celebration of the Lord's supper. It was entitled "Jesus' Presence Delightful," and although familiar to many of our readers, yet it does not always appear complete in the hymn books and hence we will print it here.

JESUS' PRESENCE DELIGHTFUL.

Amidst us our Beloved stands,
And bids us view His pierced hands;
Points to His wounded feet and side,—
Blest emblems of the Crucified!

What food luxurious loads the board
When at His table sits the Lord!
The wine how rich, the bread how sweet,
When Jesus deigns the guests to meet!

If now, with eyes defiled and dim,
We see the signs, but see not Him,
Oh may His love the scales displace,
And bid us see Him face to face!

Our former transports we recount
When with Him in the holy mount;
These cause our souls to thirst anew,
His marred but lovely face to view.

Thou glorious Bridegroom of our hearts,
Thy present smile a heaven imparts;
Oh lift the veil, if veil there be,
Let every saint Thy beauties see.

In his own hymn book appears a composition from his pen, which was so strikingly appropriate for the services of his church after he had been taken up into the "Shining," that we can not forbear to quote it.

Lord, Thy church, without a pastor,
Cries to Thee in her distress,
Hear us, gracious Lord and Master,
And with heavenly guidiance bless.

Walking midst Thy lamps all golden,
Thou preservest still the light;
Stars in thy right hand are holden,
Stars to cheer Thy church's night.

Find us Lord the man appointed
　　Pastor of this flock to be,
One with holy oil anointed,
　　Meet for us and dear to Thee.

Send a man, O King of Zion,
　　Made according to Thine heart,
Meek as lamb, and bold as lion,
　　Wise to act a shepherd's part.

Grant us now thy heavenly leading,
　　Over every heart preside,
Now in answer to our pleading,
　　All our consultations guide.

CHAPTER XIX.

THE DEATH OF THE RIGHTEOUS.

Mr. Spurgeon died at Mentone in Southern France on the 31st day of January, 1892; but he had been grieviously afflicted with a serious disease for several years and was especially an invalid for a number of months before his demise. He inherited the tendency to the gout which, with a complication of other diseases seemingly not clearly understood by the physicians, carried him steadily down and finally took him away from his labors. Most of the time for a year preceding his death he was absent from his pulpit. It had often been prophesied that when he died the many enterprises for which he furnished the motive power would cease to shed their blessings over mankind. Thirty-five years before his death some of his congregation were troubled lest if they should enter into any of his proposed plans he might suddenly die and leave the work unfinished. "What if Mr. Spurgeon should die?" was the continual question and hidden insinuation on the part of many faithless ones who tried to discourage the church in its noble work. He himself was led by these frequent warnings to carefully arrange for the sustentation of the church charities in case of his death. A few friends combined together at one time for the purpose of relieving him of any anxiety and collected twenty-five thousand dollars, the income of which was to be used in supporting the College and Orphanage and Home and the principal to be paid in should Mr. Spurgeon die.

He had the good sense to recognize the fact that he was an important factor in the spread of the gospel, and endeavored as far as possible to provide against any cessation of the Christian work in case the Lord should call him hence. He believed very thoroughly in the doctrines that the Lord would care for his own, and often said that "there is none so important to the Lord's work that the Lord could not replace him by another more efficient." It seems to us as though he presented a very unique character and possessed a genius which is rare to find, and while the work may still progress it must necessarily assume a different phase, unless the Lord perform another miracle by creating another man his counterpart.

At the time of his death there were in circulation thirty-seven volumes of sermons, some printed in every civilized language, which he had delivered in the thirty eight years of his ministry. His large Commentary upon the Psalms entitled "The Treasury of David" became a standard work of theology long before his death, and found its way into the homes and studies of nearly all preachers in England

and America. These are published in seven volumes and contain the cream of twenty years of his work. He published a number of books upon religious subjects, three of which were entitled "The Interpreter," "Morning by Morning" and "Evening by Evening;" but a great number of smaller works and uncounted pamphlets. His Orphanage then contained five hundred boys and girls and was conducted at a cost of fifty-five thousand dollars a year.

The Pastors' College had reached its highest degree of usefulness and was crowded with an able body of young and enterprising ministers. There were at that time connected with the church twenty-seven Sunday-schools, twenty-two missions where the Gospel was preached, and there were a great number of societies in the church organized to send the Gospel to the heathen, support teachers among the poor of London, maintain Gospel wagons for the distribution of tracts and the preaching of the Word, flower missions, and several aid societies.

His brother the Rev. James A. Spurgeon, was the associate pastor, having held the office continuously from 1868, to the great satisfaction of his brother and the great edification of the church.

His two sons, Charles and Thomas, were remarkably successful preachers of the gospel and he had the satisfaction of knowing in his last days that he would leave behind him worthy sons, capable of doing a work nearly if not quite equal to his, only in different directions.

The membership of his church at that time was 5,334, being the largest independent church in the world. The membership was composed of very active Christians each of whom had been trained by Mr. Spurgeon himself personally to engage conscientiously in some practical enterprise for the furtherance of the gospel. The world has never seen assembled under one roof such a great number of vigorous workers or a people so deeply interested in the welfare of their fellow men. Their great grief at his death, which was as sincere as it could have been had each of them lost an own father, naturally led the world to feel that they depended largely upon him for direction and inspiration. But biographers are apt to forget while they sing the praises of the subject of their sketches, that the honors which were given to him are very frequently in a strong measure due to others who assisted him. Not Mr. Spurgeon himself could have succeeded with some churches. There was a providential oversight in bringing the man and the people together. In his marvellous success and distinguished commendations there is mingled the biography of a great many humbler individuals who stood by him with a heroism that was wonderful, and with a devoutness that was touchingly sacred. His words were accepted with authority, many of his mistakes overlooked, many of the most munificent gifts presented, because of the beautiful and loving character of the congregation over which he presided. Who shall say that in that great day when the books shall be opened there will not be found in the throng many an humble, unnoticed person receiving from Christ an equal commendation with the blessing which descends upon Mr. Spurgeon. He stood forth as a representative of a noble people, and all honors done to him are directly or indirectly a tribute of praise to them.

They gave in their poverty freely. They economized valuable time to visit the sick; they were regular attendants upon the church services, they continuously prayed for the welfare of their pastor. One of the deacons expressed the sentiment of the church most clearly when he said to a visitor, "We would any of us die for Mr. Spurgeon." Children vied with each other in earnest competition to help him; and aged women worked far into the night for the good of some poor souls, thinking all the while it would please Christ and Mr. Spurgeon.

His College was composed in a large measure of young men who at great sacrifice of earthly ambitions and hopes had laid themselves on the altar, and who had endured privation Mr. Spurgeon never saw. There were missionary ladies connected with the church who worked among the ignorant poor and the vicious with a self abnegation and painful persistency which he often felt he could not have endured.

The meetings of the church were characterized by that depth of feeling and holy conscrecration which threw a powerful influence upon the heart of every person who visited them whether Mr. Spurgeon was present or not. Certainly great changes must be expected to follow the death of such a giant; and for a time after his departure from this world many felt paralyzed and a few became hopeless; but the great cause of Christianity moved rapidly on. It will not stay. The converted Sunday-school children grow up into active Christian men and women scattering over the world and sowing the seeds of a true faith, while the ministers and orphans disperse into various countries preaching the same gospel and leading thousands to love the same Christ.

When his dear old mother died in 1883, he startled a number of his friends shortly after the funeral by saying "I feel that I will follow her soon, I will set my house in order." From that time on the disease crept closer and closer to the springs of life and pressed upon him more and more convincingly the thought that soon "he should go hence." When he went to Mentone for the last time he dictated two letters and one of them directed to a friend in America says, "I am laid aside, perhaps forever, this world may have no more use for me."

It was a sad but a sweet privilege to Mrs. Spurgeon that she was sufficiently strong to be at his bedside during his last sickness, and to lean over him at the time when he breathed his last. One of the last messages which he sent out from his "home in the sun-shine" at Mentone was a tender greeting to his much-loved church. The funeral services at Mentone were held in the Scotch church, being simple and informal, yet made historical by the receipt of so many messages from the noted men of many countries. The Prince of Wales and Mr. Gladstone being among their number.

But his death was one of the saddest events in this century. It was felt to the furthermost ends of the earth. Rulers, statesmen and those whose names are great in literature, expressed their feelings most decidedly in prompt and sincere communications sent to the church and to Mrs. Spurgeon. The news was telegraphed all over the world that "Spurgeon is dead." It sent a shadow into ten thousand homes; it caused many hard working ministers to pause and wonder at the providence of God that he should not have lived beyond fifty-seven years. It furnished themes for great preachers, and subjects for noble poets. It was used as an illustration in various ways of Christian heroism in thousands of Sunday-schools. Many men and women wrote books and pamphlets concerning his life, while all over the earth wherever the English and American flag were recognized, tears fell and impassioned prayers were offered up for the comfort of his noble wife the encouragement of his sons, and the consolation of his deeply afflicted church.

The funeral services at the Tabernacle in London

were attended by an assembly of the most afflicted people probably ever gathered under a single roof; the services were plain as would become the friends and the wishes of Mr. Spurgeon, but there was a spirit of prayer and a degree of solemn hope which made the occasion startlingly impressive. They carried him to the grave while whole communities and even nations mourned the loss of a friend.

This humble country boy taken up by the providence of God and carried on by strange providences, without title, money or political position, reached the very pinnacle of earthly fame. He ascended to that position by means of good deeds and grand thoughts. It is not necessary for a poor boy even in a land of aristocratic titles to resort to dishonesty to become great even in the eyes of men. Surely the steps of a good man are ordered by the Lord.